The Theater of Augustin Daly

AN ACCOUNT OF THE
LATE NINETEENTH CENTURY
AMERICAN STAGE

Marvin Felheim

GREENWOOD PRESS, PUBLISHERS
NEW YORK

For my Mother and Father

Preface

The nineteenth-century theater has been curiously handled by most historians, for it has generally been treated with either indifference or contempt. Although we may justify the sneer, we cannot heartily cheer the neglect. Fortunately for the American theater, one figure, that of Augustin Daly, epitomizes the period; his life and career have been scrutinized here.

This study provides an insight into the theatrical phenomena of the years from the Civil War to the turn of the century. It is not, in the usual sense, a biography; for that, one can still turn, as I did, to Joseph Daly's life of his brother, published in 1917. One will find there that the only dates of importance in Augustin Daly's life which were not directly connected with the theater were his birth in 1838 and the death of his two sons in 1885; he even married, in 1869, the daughter of a business associate, a successful theatrical manager. As a consequence of this singular identity of private life and public career, Daly provides a focus for the whole theatrical period. For twenty years, from 1879 to 1899, he was the director of America's foremost theater as well as an outstanding theatrical figure in England and on the continent.

Newspapers, playbills, letters, and journals have given me their evidence, and I have studied the plays themselves as they were written and as they were played. What has emerged has ordered itself naturally into a chapter of the history of the American drama: first in the consideration of Daly's original plays and his dramatizations of novels; then his adaptations of German and French plays; and finally, his revivals of Shakespeare and of old English comedies, and his productions of contemporary English and American plays. In this way, his career is presented in terms of the theater—in terms, that is to say, in which it has its greatest meaning and significance.

One of the pleasures of such a study as this one is the reading and research one does in preparation for writing, and many puzzles must be solved in order to write. The major problem is to account for all the information one finds. The best theater libraries for study of the American drama are certainly the Harvard Library, the New York Public Library, and the Library of Congress, and they provide a great wealth of material. But much of the best material is in unlabeled scrapbooks, in undated clipping files, in unsigned letters, undoubtedly authentic, relevant, and of great interest. These materials are most enlightening; unfortunately they are not always identifiable. A writer must ask his readers' indulgence in quoting so many of these really significant but baffling items.

There may be some persons who will wish to examine various bits of evidence more closely than this book allows, persons who will regret the lack of such scholarly apparatus as footnotes and bibliography. For them, my original thesis, entitled *The Career of Augustin Daly*, which was the precursor of this book, is available for consultation or loan from the Harvard Library. Joseph Daly's biography, *The Life of Augustin Daly*, is also full of information which has not been included here. And literally volumes of facts are incorporated in Odell's monumental *Annals of the New York Stage*. In both the Daly and Odell works, one can follow in chronological order the career of Augustin Daly and the parade of his plays season by season.

To be able publicly to acknowledge the help of many

persons in these investigations is, at long last, my great pleasure. My initial inquiries into the American theater were prompted by graduate study under the careful tutelage of Professor Howard Mumford Jones. Professor Perry Miller later guided the completion of the research. To these two, and to Mr. Thomas J. Wilson of the Harvard University Press, for their encouragement and help, I owe a world of gratitude.

The major part of my researches was accomplished in the extensive files of the Harvard Theatre Collection, where the help of the director, Dr. William van Lennep, and his staff was invaluable. The assistance of Dr. Giles Dawson and the staff of the Folger Shakespeare Library, the courtesy of Miss Mary Isabel Fry and the staff of the Huntington Library, and the resources of the theater collection of the New York Public Library all were drawn upon in the course of my work. I should like to express my appreciation to these individuals and institutions here. The final revision of my manuscript was accomplished in the summer of 1952 while I enjoyed a Faculty Research Fellowship, the award of the Horace H. Rackham School of Graduate Studies at the University of Michigan.

Finally I should like to put on record the material assistance of Jane Lawson and Marion L. Hawkes as editors, Rosannah C. Steinhoff as indexer, and the less tangible, but no less meaningful, assistance and interest of my friends Tom Cranfill, Irwin Swerdlow, Richard Ludwig, and William McBurney.

M.F.

Ann Arbor, Michigan
1956

Contents

71578

Illustrations

Augustin Daly (about 1875). *Photo by W. Kurtz. Courtesy of the Theatre Collection in the Harvard College Library*

A scene from *The Railroad of Love* (1887). Photo by Sarony. *Courtesy of the Theatre Collection in the Harvard College Library*

Ada Rehan as Katherine (about 1887). *Courtesy of the Theatre Collection in the Harvard College Library*

Augustin Daly (about 1898). *Courtesy of the Theatre Collection in the Harvard College Library*

Fifth Avenue Theatre (reconstructed). *Courtesy of the Theatre Collection in the Harvard College Library*

The Theater of Augustin Daly

CHAPTER 1

From Drama Critic
to Theater Manager

Hamlet. *Suit the action to the word, the word to the action;
with this special observance, that you o'erstep not the mod-
esty of nature.*

Shakespeare, *Hamlet*
Act III, Scene 2.

The American theater, like many other
social institutions, survived the period of the Civil War
superficially unchanged. Theaters kept open even in besieged
border towns. New as well as old plays were presented, and
actors went about their business of interpreting roles for the
amusement or instruction of their audiences.

Not so evident as this vigorous, normal activity, changes
of many kinds were being effected; repertories, personnel,
staging and acting techniques—all were undergoing a continual
sifting and shifting. And by the time the spotlights of the
twentieth century were ready to be trained on it, the American stage was indeed a far different world from that candle-
lighted one which had been so familiar to Civil War audiences.

When Augustin Daly was born—on July 20, 1838, at
Plymouth, North Carolina—romanticism, as applied both to
the technique of acting and to the dramatic vehicles employed,
was firmly entrenched on the stage. Edwin Forrest and James
H. Hackett had begun their impressive careers in the previous

decade. Their interpretations of the great tragic roles were setting the tone of the highly exaggerated, declamatory style of the times. The dominance of Shakespearean character parts on the American stage was in full swing, to remain so till the 1900's. The new plays being offered by Bird and Willis and Boker were, by and large, imitations of the old: the language was poetic, the central characters either were tragic figures or were thought to be so, and the plots were a series of melodramatic incidents loosely strung together in the conventional five-act pattern. Just such a play, the "thrilling" *Rookwood*, enacted by the popular James Murdoch, was the first theatrical performance that Daly attended as a schoolboy in Norfolk, Virginia. When the family moved to New York a few years later he joined one of several amateur acting groups flourishing there, an organization called, appropriately enough, "The Murdoch Association."

These connections with the theater are almost all that is known of the early life of Augustin Daly. He first attended school in Norfolk under a pedagogue named Primrose Scott, and in New York this schooling was briefly resumed at the public school on Broome Street. This educational activity evidently had to compete with the theater for Augustin's attention, for his brother records that ho sooner did the two boys and their mother get settled in the metropolis than Augustin set up a little theater in the confined back yard of their house in Ridge Street. This first venture disclosed Augustin's capacity for management. "He never acted in these boyish plays," reported his brother, "but would often rush in among them all and show them how to do things." Even then, his temper frequently flared up and he would discharge the lot of his young associates.

At sixteen he quit school to become apprenticed to a firm of house furnishers in Maiden Lane; thereafter, he became clerk in "one concern after another." But he never lost sight of theatricals. Two years later, on April 6, 1856, he "perpetrated his first scheme of management." Hiring the old Brooklyn Museum, he introduced to a small reluctant public "The Melville Troupe of Juvenile Comedians." The evening's entertainment consisted of a farce, *Poor Pillicoddy*, followed by the second act of *Macbeth*, and concluded with the "celebrated" drama, *Toodles*, starring Master William Melville. The young manager was to have played the Porter in *Macbeth* but was too busy with creditors and financing to appear on stage when his cue came. Receipts totaled $11.25 and expenses were $76.

Through the generosity of an aunt and uncle, Augustin and his brother Joseph were enthusiastic frequenters of the professional theater, and in mid-century America what they encountered there was vigorous and flourishing. There was a variety of dramatic fare available to the lover of the theater, and one could find entertainment to suit every appetite and every pocketbook. Adah Isaacs Menken was the hit of the season of 1859–1860 at the National Theatre playing *The French Spy* and having herself occasionally billed as Mrs. John Heenan. That was the year the New Bowery Theatre, "the most ample" in the country, seating over 4000, was opened. Full of bustle and gaiety, it offered to the working boy a glimpse of Elysium, according to Odell, where "for a shilling he got four hours of knights, heroes, distressed maidens, funny servants, a terrible plot, etc." There was also Niblo's, Burton's, and Wallack's, and, of course, there was Barnum's; a total of six legitimate theaters in New York. Finally, one must not forget the French and German theaters and, above all, the Opera.

Augustin preferred Burton's and Wallack's. Both houses maintained fine repertory companies and presented classical as well as new dramas. Certainly the brothers must have seen the accomplished Fanny Morant there in 1860 when her current vehicle, *The Romance of a Poor Young Man*, achieved the splendid record of sixty-four performances. The great theatrical event of the war year 1861–1862 was the opening of

Wallack's new theater at Broadway and Thirteenth Street, a location considered at the time far uptown. The season commenced on September 25, 1861, with Tom Taylor's comedy, *The New President*. After the presentation of four new plays, no one of which was more than fairly successful, a series of old comedies, for which the theater was famous, was offered. Included in this group were such favorites as *She Stoops to Conquer, The Rivals, Love for Love, The Road to Ruin, The Belle's Stratagem*, and others. From January to June the bill changed almost nightly.

The most glamorous aspect of the Civil War theater was its parade of stars. This was the period of Booth and Brougham, of E. L. Davenport, J. S. Clarke, and of many charming talented ladies, Mathilda Heron, Kate Bateman, Lucille Western, and Maggie Mitchell whose rendition of Fanchon was known from coast to coast.

For these theaters and particularly for the stars who controlled the repertories, Augustin Daly exerted his first efforts at playwriting. These handwritten scripts were submitted and circulated without success. His friend and the historian of his theater, the dramatic critic E. A. Dithmar, has preserved the only list of these unsuccessful dramas in *Memories of Daly's Theatres*. For W. E. Burton, "who did not want it," Daly concocted *A Bachelor's Wardrobe*. The prominent Joseph Jefferson, not yet famous as Rip Van Winkle, "declined with thanks" *Joe's Wife*. *Master and Man* was returned by Mrs. John Wood as "out of her line." But the most unhappy turn in this series of events came when Laura Keene not only rejected but actually "mislaid the manuscript" of *Napoleon III*. This last play was designed to capitalize upon the sensational attempt of Orsini and his confederates to murder the Emperor, and the manuscript was completed within a week after the receipt of the news.

These early plays occupied Daly's attentions during the years from 1856, the date of composition of *A Bachelor's*

Wardrobe, to 1862, the date of production of his first success, *Leah the Forsaken.* Then in 1863, Laura Keene turned down another play. This time she was more careful of the manuscript, however, for she wrote Daly from Louisville asking him to acknowledge receipt of the play, *The Red Ribbon.*

Daly's was the common experience of many young playwrights and the list of rejections is mainly interesting because of the rejectors. The "star system" was then paramount on the American stage. These figures ruled the managers, determined the vehicles, and moved about the country with amazing ease when one considers the difficulties of travel in those times. Stock companies were well organized and actors knew their business; the stars' advance agents went ahead, rehearsed the companies, arranged publicity, and squeezed a living from many a hard-boiled theatrical manager. Success as a playwright, as young Daly quickly recognized, frequently depended upon getting the interest of one of these stars. Energetically he continued to grind out plays, each with a particular actor in mind; he did not hesitate to offer his work to Booth and Davenport, to J. W. Wallack, Clarke, and others. These were the initial efforts of the young hopeful. His method was not in the least revolutionary and his ideas were based not on a desire for change, but on a wish for success.

He had some good fortune. In a letter to his brother dated October 2, 1864, he related that he had sold *Andree* to Maggie Mitchell, an old "Murdoch Association" acquaintance, for her use in Cincinnati. For the rights to the piece, he was to receive $400 at $10 a night plus a "benefit" on the seventy-fifth night. All the income from such a performance went to the person whose benefit it was, since actors all performed for nothing and no rental charges for theater were deducted. For an author this was particularly meaningful as his fees, by present-day standards, were small, so much a performance, $10 perhaps— and when one considers that a play's run was at best twenty performances in the 1860's, and frequently only five or six, the financial rewards to a playwright were slim indeed. Other stars were finding his tailor-made melodramas, including adaptations of French and German plays, adequate and useful vehicles. Kate Bateman achieved fame for herself and for Daly with *Leah the Forsaken;* then Mrs. John Wood produced a comedy called *Taming a Butterfly;* and *Lorlie's Wedding* helped introduce the German actress, Methua-Scheller, to American audiences, while another German star, Madame Janauschek, used Daly's one-act adaptation, *Come Here!,* for her own debut in English. For Avonia Jones, daughter of the fraudulent Count Johannes, Daly scraped up *Judith, The Sorceress,* and *Garcia.* And the Conways, who managed their own theater in Brooklyn, presented *Hazardous Ground.*

The "incomparable" Camille, Mathilda Heron, even requested a play from him in 1865. So did the "enchanting" Adah Isaacs Menken. And from Acushnet, Massachusetts, Laura Keene wrote him about an interesting unfulfilled project:

I want a comedy!! I have the plot—situations etc. etc.—all sketched. It would not be a task of any great length for you, and would certainly not diminish your rapidly growing reputation as an author.

Will you undertake it? And what terms pernight, for U.S. and England will you name?

I have given the subject a great deal of thought, and have been collecting matter for it, for the last three years. Boucicault and Tom Taylor are willing to do it, but I am not. I see it as an *American* comedy, *I* cannot see it as an *English* one, for it is of *us* most essentially, and will I am convinced go better in England for being American.

Daly's writing activities were not at first confined to playwriting. He applied to James Smith and Charles F. Briggs, editors of *The Sunday Courier,* who engaged him in 1859 as a "general writer" at a salary of $8 a week. He immediately set about doing a series of articles on the working classes, research for which stood him in good stead later when he produced *Under the Gaslight, A Flash of Lightning,* and other plays about city, and especially low-class, life. Daly had really begun a career as a reporter when, within a few weeks, the post of drama critic luckily falling vacant, he was promoted to the position at the age of twenty-one.

The next ten years were enormously important in shaping the career of Augustin Daly. He "authored" a number of successful plays, including *Leah the Forsaken, Griffith Gaunt,* and *Under the Gaslight,* began his functions as a manager with the Batemans and Avonia Jones, and engaged in a variety of journalistic enterprises as drama critic, press agent, adaptor. The extent of his activities connected with the theater was indeed tremendous. He learned many lessons and gained much practical information about the theater, actors, and the public.

In those days he used to squire the dashing Adah Isaacs Menken and the popular actress, Rose Eytinge, to various theatrical and musical performances, and he also acted as press agent both for Miss Menken and for Kate Bateman. Letters from Adah instructed him to publicize her as "the most versatile artiste in the world"; describing an accident which befell her while riding horseback in *Mazeppa,* she wrote "Nothing daunts this intrepid and fearless girl," obviously a sentence designed for publicity.

Rose Eytinge, who was a star in 1867, gives us a glimpse of Daly at that time. In her *Memories* she tells of going to his home on Horatio Street to have him read *Under the Gaslight* to her.

Even then, his artistic aspirations and longings were struggling for expression. The walls of his conventional little room, which was fitted up as a sort of "den" and writing-room, were colored a dark blue, and there were little plaster casts and small pictures scattered about; and everywhere there were evidences of his reaching out after a literary and artistic atmosphere.

Daly undertook his first professional experiences as a manager during these important years. In 1863, he accompanied Kate Bateman to Philadelphia, and perhaps to Baltimore and

Washington as well, managing the production and handling the publicity for *Leah the Forsaken*. Then in the autumn of 1864, he toured the battle areas—"those cities occupied by the Federal troops"—of Virginia, Tennessee, Kentucky, and Missouri with Avonia Jones. The expedition was hazardous. Even in peacetime, traveling in those regions was troublesome, and wartime added exhilaration to the ordinary difficulties and sharpened the resourcefulness of the young impresario. Perhaps the experiences of this time colored his later productions such as *Norwood* with a feeling for American subjects.

The best account of Daly at this period is contained in a letter from Joseph Daly to the critic, William Winter, on July 6, 1868. In the letter Joseph outlined Augustin's activities as follows:

1860   Augustin Daly first appeared as a regular attache of the New York Press as Dramatic Critic of the *Courier;* his columns were signed "Le Pelerin."

1862   *Leah the Forsaken*

1864   *Taming a Butterfly; Lorlie's Wedding; Judith; The Sorceress.* In this year he assumed the post of Dramatic Critic of the *Express* salary: $10 per week as well as of the *Courier* and held both positions.

1866   *Griffith Gaunt*
        In this year he was appointed dramatic critic of the *Sun* which position he held with the *Express* and *Courier.*

1867   *Under the Gaslight*
        In this year he was also appointed Dramatic Critic of the New York *Times* and held the position with those of the other three papers. He was also afterwards in this year appointed Dramatic Critic of the N. Y. *Citizen* and thus held the position on five papers at once.
        Norwood
        At the close of this year he resigned his position as dramatic critic on the *Sun, Express, Citizen,* and *Courier,* retraining only that on the *Times* which he now holds.

1868   *Pickwick Papers; A Flash of Lightning*

One would have to turn to the biographies of Edison or Astor or Ford to find equally successful bursts of energy.

The enormous journalistic achievements of these years proved valuable to Daly, for his position demanded constant theater-going and criticism, and constant exercise developed his standards of taste and gave him ideas about production. He acquired habits of tireless devotion to his chosen field, and so profited from the pressure of newspaper deadlines that in later life he found it no hardship to turn out quantities of writing even after exhausting hours of rehearsing and interviewing and of planning the many details of a production.

The collaboration between Augustin and his brother Joseph began in this early period, perhaps even originating in the letters they exchanged while "Gus" was on the road. Joseph had become a person of prominence in his own right. At the age of twelve he had been office boy and apprentice in the law firm of S. W. and R. B. Roosevelt, and when they retired in 1866 he succeeded to their practice. Four years later he was elected a Judge of the Court of Common Pleas of New York.

Joseph admits in *The Life of Augustin Daly* that during Augustin's absence on tour in 1864 "I substituted for him upon his various newspapers." But even in the biography he conceals all other evidence of collaboration, leaving this sole official acknowledgment of his services to Augustin. The letters are not so cautious; they reveal the method and the facts. One can, on the basis of their disclosures, discover that as long as Augustin lived, Joseph's part in their joint literary labors was great, and often more than halfway. Not only newspaper articles, but the adaptations of plays, writing of plays, composition of speeches, all went through Joseph's hands—without public acknowledgment. In only one instance did the brothers ever hint at Joseph's role in their playwriting procedure. On the playbill for the opening night of *Love's Young Dream* (1879), a one-act comedietta, the piece was announced as the work of "Joseph Francis, Esq., of this city," an obvious pseudonym for Joseph Francis Daly. The printed version, however, listed Augustin Daly as the author.

This period of Augustin's life was rounded out in a fittingly dramatic way in 1869. In that year, on January 9, he married Mary Duff and on August 16 he undertook the management of his first theater.

Daly's wife was the daughter of John Duff, a theatrical entrepreneur of some importance who was later associated with his son-in-law in several managerial ventures. Very little is known of Mary Duff Daly, since Augustin made it his practice to keep his public and private lives completely separated, and his wife accommodated herself to the task of providing him with the comforts of home. In contrast to the dozens of portraits of other contemporary figures in the theater world, her portrait is rarely, if ever, seen. She was never interviewed. Of the many books about the theater of the time, only one, Mrs. G. H. Gilbert's *Stage Reminiscences*, mentions her individually.

She was a Miss Duff, daughter of the famous manager, and she knew the stage and stage life thoroughly, from Mr. Daly's own point of view. She was a good wife to him and a great helper in every way. She knew her husband's business thoroughly, and never told a word of it, and that is saying a great deal, for curious people would often ask her questions about affairs when they would not dare ask her husband. And she was always pleasant and merry with him and with everybody else. They say he used to come home at night and fling himself down on the sofa, wholly worn out with the day's hard work, and say: "Tell me a funny story, May, and take my mind off all this." And she always had the story ready.

Following their marriage, the young couple moved in with the Dalys at 214 West 25th Street. There Daly's two sons were born, Leonard in 1870 and Francis in 1873. Little is known of these children. A photograph of them and their father, taken by Sarony, the famed theatrical photographer, shows them to have been attractive and intelligent looking. Mrs.

Gilbert has preserved an account of Daly and his sons. "I have seen him on his hands and knees, making a most obedient horse for his own boys. He was devoted to those two boys, planning their future with more care and thought even than he put into the plays on which all their fortunes depended." It was during these years, too, that Daly was building his collection of books on the theater. He was particularly fond of "extra-illustrated" books, cut up and rebound with many additional pictures.

Daly opened his first theater on August 16, 1869. He rented the building, known as the Fifth Avenue Theatre, from its proprietor, James Fisk, Jr., for the then staggering sum of $25,000 a year. His father-in-law gave him six weeks "to get into the poor house." Miss Eytinge records that some years afterwards Daly told her that "when he became the lessee of that theatre his entire capital did not reach the sum of $500." Yet with characteristic energy, he pushed through an amazing repertory of twenty-one plays in six months until he achieved his first success, *Frou-Frou*, in February 1870. He assembled a distinguished company of actors: George Holland (whose funeral gave "The Little Church around the Corner" its sobriquet), D. H. Harkins, George Clarke, Mrs. Jennings, Mrs. Gilbert, and Mrs. Chanfrau were already well-known stage personalities; among the unknowns were Fanny Davenport, Agnes Ethel, James Lewis, Amy Ames, and H. C. Ryner. In addition to a group of competent performers, he also provided his theater with an excellent orchestra under the direction of Robert Stoepel, and skilled designers, including James Roberts and Charles Duflocq.

For the next six years the theater and the young manager prospered, and even successfully endured the panic of 1873 which brought ruin to many theatrical, as well as other business, enterprises. His day at the theater often began as early as 7:30 in the morning—never later than 9—and he remained there until midnight or later almost every night. "After the play of the evening was over," reports Mary C. Crawford in *The Romance of the American Theater*," he would frequently begin a regular set-to rehearsal of the scenery for a new production and continue there, working with the scene painter and the stage artisans until seven o'clock in the morning. Then he would breakfast and begin on the business of another day." His energy was untiring; his devotion all-absorbing.

He found time for attention to everything, including the publicity and advertising. Perhaps his experience as la Menken's press agent had accustomed him to stretching the truth in her constant need for a favorable press; at any rate, duplicity marred his managerial record in one instance. He perpetrated a flagrant and reprehensible bit of false advertising in connection with his production of *Oliver Twist* in 1874. The fraud consisted of using extracts from newspaper criticisms to advertise the play, but the difficulty was that the quotations he used, purportedly from the *Evening Post, Mail, Sun, Graphic, Times,* and *Herald,* had never been printed in those papers. They were simply eulogies written either by himself or someone in his employ. The whole affair was brought to light by *The Dramatic News* in an editorial labeled "Theatrical Charlatanism"; the method of exposure was to print the ads and the actual reviews side by side. "Mr. Daly," commented *The News,* "has coolly attributed to the Herald, Times, Sun, Post and Graphic fulsome endorsement of his play which never, in whole or in part, appeared in those journals." Daly's attitude toward the press, conditioned by this experience, in later years was an extension of this method— he simply made sure that the material was actually published first.

He met real reverses with his usual whirlwind efficiency. The season of 1873–1874 was disastrous, but not in the theatrical or managerial sense; on January 1, 1873, his theater burned down with a great loss of property, all uninsured. This building, though it was on 24th Street, had nevertheless been

called the Fifth Avenue Theatre. Following the fire Daly
reëstablished his company within three weeks, through almost superhuman efforts, at a theater at 728 Broadway which
he completely renovated. This was now named the Fifth
Avenue Theatre (previously it had been called the New
York). The name Fifth Avenue Theatre was transferred again
when he opened a new theater built for him on 28th Street
in December of the same year. This time the christening, of
the third "Fifth Avenue Theatre" in a year, was celebrated
by a poem written for the occasion by Oliver Wendell
Holmes.

Far from suffering under these emergencies, Daly wound
up the year 1873 as manager of three theaters: the building at
728 Broadway, whose address was to be celebrated by his
play *7–20–8* and whose name was once again The Broadway;
the new Fifth Avenue; and the Grand Opera House. A cartoon
in the *Graphic* of November 11, 1873 showed Daly bending
beneath the burden of his theaters with the caption "An Atlas
of Theatres."

The years from 1869 to 1877 could be called the first period
of Daly's career as a manager. During this time, he established
those general patterns of management which eventually
brought him fame and fortune. First in importance, he set
the highest standards of "natural" acting by the whole company, and complementary to this, a strict discipline applicable alike to all members of his theatrical family. He established as a principle the presentation of a varied repertoire
including Shakespeare, Old English comedies, his "own"
plays—originals, dramatizations, adaptations—and the best of
contemporary English and American drama. And always, the
most careful attention to staging, including setting, costuming, and music.

When Daly assisted in the productions of *Griffith Gaunt*
and *Under the Gaslight* and later entered the managerial ranks
himself, the American theater, as far as "stage business" was

concerned, was largely following outmoded and conventional practices. John Drew, discussing his mother's Arch Street Theatre as it was in the sixties, has described the prevailing conditions accurately and succinctly.

Business in the theatre was all according to very definitely defined rules; thus there were leading men and leading juveniles and first comedians and second comedians, old men and second old men, first old women and second old women, chambermaids and leading women and juvenile women. The first old woman might be anything from the duchess to a rag picker, but there was no doubt in anyone's mind as to who would play the part. Stars travelled without support. . . . A stage manager . . . came on ahead and told the theatre exactly what was wanted and gave special instructions for the playing of certain scenes. This could easily be done, because the lines of business were so well established. . . .

Otis Skinner's reminiscences, *Footlights and Spotlights,* indicate that these conditions were still only slowly disappearing in 1878–1879, when he accepted an engagement at the Walnut Street Theatre in Philadelphia. He tells of his experiences in a local company which offered support to a series of visiting stars. "When a number of pieces were to be produced during the engagement, the star's stage director would precede him (or her) to conduct rehearsals in advance; the star and company coming together on Monday morning for the first time to run through the lines 'perfect,' and the bill presented that night." It was, then, into an essentially standardized and conventional theater that Daly made his way.

There has been a tendency on the part of critics to deprecate Daly's management and notions of stagecraft by insinuating that he got his ideas from Henry Irving. Daly was himself fully aware of these assertions and of their untruth, and attempted to establish his own position in a letter to Winter:

My style of management [he wrote] has not been an imitation of anyone's else's. That precision of detail, luxury, completeness of surroundings, and general unity of company and performance

—which was found so fascinating in Irving's performance, was inaugurated by me in 1869, ten years before Irving began his career as manager.

At his right hand, as always, was Joseph Daly. They usually met every afternoon in New York, as hasty notes between them show. The legal and theatrical districts were not so far apart that they could not meet for lunch, or Joseph drop into the theater conveniently, and as they ordinarily walked home together, much of the business of the theater must have been gone over thus. Letters when one or the other was out of town bear witness to the relationship. The letters are full of Joseph's suggestions about running the theater. Although he had little connection with the technical details of production, in the actual management of the theater he exerted great influence. His advice was sought by Augustin upon every occasion, and he gave help freely and graciously.

On September 10, 1874, he wrote advocating the reinstitution of "memorable Saturday nights," by which he meant Saturday night openings to attract "fashionable" audiences. In this early letter he also set forth a number of precepts for the theater. "Let us no longer try to get pieces for a run!" he suggested, and offered the following reasons for producing a new play every week:

1. It is harder work. If you play a new piece every week you need not elaborate it so much nor try to get in all the company, for whoever is left out one Saturday comes in the next.
2. If you make one big "run" you've got to make another or people will say you are not successful.
3. The actors don't get lazy nor saucy nor treacherous, if you keep them well at work.
4. You can do without stars.

Having given so much practical advice, Joseph continued with specific instructions. "No more Jewett [Sara Jewett made her debut in *Diamonds*] in pathetic roles. Let her do the *ingenue* cold but frisky—or the *haut ton* damsel. But her Elaine [in *What Should She Do?*] killed the piece."

The success of Daly's Theatre is inextricably bound up with Daly's players, and in turn, their performances were the result of a carefully considered theory of acting. From the beginning Daly insisted upon the perfection of the ensemble. He had an ideal: a company in which there should be no stars. Of course he had to make compromises in order to keep afloat financially and he inevitably got into quarrels with others who were as temperamental as himself, but until the 1894–1895 season he kept to his resolution. With few exceptions—short engagements of such stars as E. L. Davenport, Edwin Booth, E. A. Sothern, Mrs. Scott-Siddons, Adelaide Neilson—from 1869 on the history of Daly's is the history of America's foremost acting company.

As manager of his own theater, he immediately set about with reforms. E. L. Davenport, the "star" of *A New Way to Pay Old Debts*, complained of Daly's stage management, because Davenport's conception of Sir Giles was "too big" for Daly's stage. The old emphasis upon histrionics was gradually giving way.

A statement of Daly's establishes beyond doubt the consciousness behind his efforts to found a style of "natural" acting. As the result of difficulties in San Francisco, where his company suffered an unaccountable lack of success on their western trip in 1875, Augustin wrote Joseph on July 22, "The press here still growl & call our acting tame & colorless—The fact is acting out here is all 15 yrs. behind the age. The thunder & lightning & absurd farce acting of our boyhood era." Winter, in his *Life of Belasco*, has quoted one of these reviews, from the San Francisco *Evening Bulletin*.

The 5th Ave. Theatre Co. have a style of their own. It is emasculated of vigor, force in action, and anything like declamation in reading. It is *quiet, elegant, languid;* making its points with a French shrug of the shoulders, little graceful gestures, and rapid play of features. The voice is soft, the tone low, and the manner at once subdued and expressive. It pleases a certain set of fashionables, but to the general public it is acting with the act of acting left out.

Daly recognized that he was attempting something new, that, as he wrote to Joseph, he was "the first to introduce *natural acting* in its perfection here—& I have to suffer as all pioneers do." It was, indeed, a change from the "thunder & lightning" school of acting, but it was a change which later made possible the writing of plays like *Divorce* and *Saratoga;* they, in turn, would revolutionize the American drama.

While Daly was breaking up one method of acting and establishing another, he was also a pivotal figure in a second historical sense, in which his own role complemented his theory of acting. He was one of the first and most successful non-acting theatrical managers in America or anywhere. Previous to his time, theaters—Wallack's, Burton's, Booth's, Laura Keene's—and companies were generally under the control and direction of actor-managers, persons like Lewis Hallam, Lester Wallack, Mrs. John Drew, John Brougham. Their methods were the old methods. Daly changed all that. From the moment the play was read and the parts were given out until the final curtain when the piece was withdrawn from the boards, he, the manager, was in absolute control. Eric Scott, son of the English dramatic critic, Clement Scott, has described the "solemn" occasion of the distribution of parts. Also, "The governor is no respector of persons; all come in for their share of somewhat hasty correction from the leading man down to the super." For on Daly's stage, "It is no exaggeration to say that Mr. Daly made each play a monologue with himself as principal performer."

Daly's methods may have been autocratic, it is true, but one finds from records of other theaters that such famous managers as Forrest, Cushman, Booth, and Jefferson were also domineering. One of the strict contract rules of Daly's Theatre was that every member of the company should obey, under penalty, the directions of the manager as to the performance and "business"; if Daly was exacting, he was exacting in a profession which requires discipline for success. As John Drew has pointed out,

Daly was often impatient with the actors. He was tireless in the theater and he seldom went elsewhere. He was an excellent producer of plays, and he knew how to manage his stage. I think that his countless rehearsals had much to do with the smoothness of the plays, for by the time a play reached production it was cut and dried and there was no need for a try-out. . . .

Dora Ranous, who published her *Diary of a Daly Debutante*, has likewise praised Daly's capabilities. "He was a wonderful teacher of acting; I believe he could teach a broomstick to act; he shows everyone just how to move, to speak, to look; he seems to know instinctively just how everything should go to get the best effect."

Under such a policy Daly's was proclaimed the leading theater in America, perhaps in the world, at the height of its power. "There is not at this present time any company in the world speaking the Anglo-Saxon tongue, that can compare with Mr. Daly's company for harmony of action, unity of purpose, perfectness in discipline, excellence of artistic ability and general completeness," wrote one reviewer. Archer was forced to agree that "Mr. Daly has realised the ideal of what may be called absolute acting—acting unconditioned by either plot or character." And William Dean Howells added the praise that "Mr. Daly's Theatre has been the nearest approach to a national school of acting we have had in America. His work in elevating the American Stage can scarcely be overestimated."

Partly as a consequence of these rules and partly because of clashes of temperament, Daly had sporadic difficulties with his players. The famous actor, E. L. Davenport, had more than one run-in with Daly early in the young manager's career. Davenport, "an incorrigible guyer," tormented his fellow actor, Rose Eytinge, by repeating the exclamation, "The axe, the axe!" which she had to shriek out at the climax of *Under the Gaslight*. Miss Eytinge tells that Daly "threatened" Davenport with "immediate discharge" if he did not take his work "seriously," and the actor retaliated by appearing completely in black, even wearing black kid gloves. The audience laughed more and more at the actor's assumed solemnity, so that Daly was forced to relent, "a magnanimous action," concludes Miss Eytinge.

This incident with Davenport was one of Daly's few "magnanimous" actions, however. From that time on, his disputes with actors generally led to their withdrawal from his company. Agnes Ethel, who left in 1872, set the pattern; she was the first of Daly's leading ladies to leave him. Clara Morris, the sensation of *Man and Wife, Madelein Morel,* and *Article 47,* was the next. She "severed her connection with Mr. Daly's company" in 1873, and was shortly thereafter announced as a "star" at the Union Square Theatre. These continual desertions occasioned little surprise, according to comments in *Actors and Actresses.*

It was Joseph who had to reconcile Augustin on these occasions. Referring to Miss Morris, he wisely pointed out in a letter dated October 19, 1873, "If she will break her contract what can you do? Not sue her because she would only get immense popular sympathy as a 'victim.' In fact the only thing is to 'let her go' . . . . Her time will be short because she needs so much management." Clara Morris was not the only actress to desert Daly in 1873. His theater records show that Marianne Conway and Minnie Walton both "annulled" their contracts that year. According to a letter from Joseph, Linda Dietz also left the company in 1873.

Daly had difficulties with two outstanding actresses in the following year. The first was Fanny Morant. Her disaffection resulted in a legal action by Daly in which he was represented by A. Oakey Hall, and the suit was settled in Daly's favor. Miss Morant was restrained from playing in any theater in New York except under Daly's management; Daly had simply to continue paying her one-fourth her regular salary in order to keep her inactive. The second deserter in 1874 was Ada Dyas, a charming and capable Englishwoman who later became very popular at Wallack's. Miss Dyas' leaving was particularly involved. According to the letters, it is apparent that she was befriended and encouraged by a protector—ironically—A. Oakey Hall. In his letter to Joseph on September 12, 1874, Daly reveals that Hall offered to "buy" Miss Dyas for the $35,000 he had invested in the theater. Hall's letter, quoted by Augustin, argued that the actress was unhappy. "I think your idea of not making stars of any special person is a mistake," wrote Hall. "You can't help the public doing so." Miss Dyas, continued the ex-mayor, "doesn't like the *Republic* you have organized & *enforce* here!" Joseph pointed out to Augustin that he had only a verbal contract with Miss Dyas, and realizing this and accepting the fact that "considerable negotiation" had gone on behind his back, Daly made no official remonstration. Joseph assuaged his brother's anger with calm and irony, writing, "The public may ask: why do Daly's actresses all leave him? Ethel in 1872, Morris in 1873, Dietz in 1873, Morant & Dyas in 1874? The Answer: Because they are not Happy." Then he added the facetious advice: "The duty of a manager is to pay his actresses largely, furnish them dresses and make them Happy!"

Daly also had difficulty that year with one of his leading men, George Clarke, who

withdrew from the theatre on November 2 under the following circumstances: it is the custom in all first-class theatres that all artists engaged in old comedies shall, if so required wear no hair upon the face, so as to accord with the fashion of the period. On November 2, *The School for Scandal* was revived for two nights, and a notice intimating as above was posted in the greenroom of the theatre. George Clarke did not remove his mustache which had "embellished" *Moorcroft,* and on the evening in question some words passed between him and Mr. Daly in reference to his disobedience of the order. This occurred before the screen scene, and Mr. Clarke refused to appear in it, telling Mr. Daly that he might read the part himself.

Clarke added to the offense by allowing himself to be interviewed by reporters, and H. C. Bunner wrote a humorous poem, "The Rape of the Moustache," which appeared in *The Arcadian.* Clarke repented twelve years later, however, and was then taken back, and he ultimately became Daly's stage manager.

In 1877, D. H. Harkins, jealous of Charles Coghlan over the assignment of roles, broke his contract, was discharged, and he subsequently sued for damages. Henrietta Crosman also quit the company at this time. Daniel Frohman, in his *Memories of a Manager,* has thrown some light upon the situation.

Miss Crosman had been at Daly's and left his company to join mine. Mr. Daly . . . had sent me word not to encourage any members of his company to join mine. I replied that I never encroached upon another manager's company, but when applications were made to me I had no other recourse, if they were free, than to consider them. However, I said I would notify him when members of his company applied and would ask whether they were free. I had a number of such experiences. When Miss Crosman applied I notified Mr. Daly; and as I received no reply I engaged her.

None of these defections was responsible for bringing this period of Daly's management to a close. "Atlas" Daly was eventually overcome, not from within his theater, but by the sheer weight of his financially top-heavy establishment. The burden of a debt of $45,000 became too heavy. With tears in his eyes and a heavy heart, he sold his library, the loving accumulation of ten years. The books brought only $8300, which he turned over to his creditors in exchange for "peace and rest." On September 10, 1877, he posted the closing notice backstage for the members of his company. In his box-office book under the heading, *9th season, 7th week, 47th performance*, September 15, he wrote, "The end of the first book! Tonight A.D. retires from the theatre he built up."

A few weeks later he managed a brief season at Booth's Theatre, presenting Jefferson in *Rip Van Winkle* and Fanny Davenport in Shakespeare and Old English Comedy, and following that he took a group of players on an extended tour of the South. But he needed his own theater, in which he could express his own production ideas, and the following August he determined to try his fortune in England. It was his hope that he would be able there to establish a reputation and get capital which would enable him to come back to New York as a success. But his plans to sell or produce his plays there and his hopes for achieving fame abroad were unfulfilled. He found in London that English plays were much like American in type, and that English playwrights were drawing as heavily as their American counterparts on French adaptations for material. Money and popularity went to the producer of amusing musical pieces. With this wisdom he returned to New York.

Daly returned after a year's absence still possessed with an intense, almost fanatic devotion to the theater. "He not only loved the theater ardently," commented his friend Brander Matthews, "he lived for it alone." He found encouragement and help from his father-in-law. Mr. Duff was willing to produce a play Daly brought back in his luggage, which had been successful on the continent. It was *L'Assommoir*, and Mr. Duff's production at the Olympic Theatre was enough of a failure to underline for Daly the fact that musicals were what the public wanted.

Mr. Duff continued to offer Daly support, and enabled him to open his own theater once more, this time in a renovated theater called Wood's Museum at Broadway and 30th, which they renamed Daly's. The opening, on September 17, 1879, was a gala occasion. The success of the venture was soon apparent. Whatever the reasons—artistic, economic, or simply accidental—what was to be America's foremost theater for the next two decades had come into being, and with Daly's Theatre a new period in Daly's career had begun.

In his devotion to the theater he was constantly considering the stage and its possibilities and its needs. Devising plans for his own playhouse he actually instituted many innovations which contributed to the development of the American theater as a whole, with pioneering work in acting, directing, and in the use of such stage techniques as lighting and scenery. He made innovations in policy as well. On October 1, 1879, during the first season at his second Daly's Theatre, he began a "series of special Wednesday matinees." These performances were "devoted to the revival of the more emphatic successes of his earlier management," stated the playbill. For the 1888–1889 season, Daly changed from matinees to a series of subscription nights—"an innovation in theatrical practice in America," according to Judge Daly. The first series included ten revivals; seats were sold for the entire set.

Daly's use of one-act plays as curtain raisers had been advocated by Brander Matthews as "the best possible practical training-school for the coming American dramatist." Unfortunately, this high-minded purpose was not accomplished as only a few one-acts, and those mostly adapted from the French, were ever used. If he did not thereby offer a new scope for dramatic writing, Daly did, strangely enough, help with a new vogue in dramatic writing in another capacity. His process of "amalgamating" scenes of Shakespeare into one complete act and of combining acts themselves had a far-reaching effect. Forbes-Winslow has indicated that these "slashings" of Shakespeare and other classics exerted an extensive influence, not only on revivals but also on new plays which henceforth "inclined more and more to unbroken acts which unfolded the story in sustained action. Daly was,

therefore, in a sense the first of all 'continuity-writers.' "
Certainly, in this capacity, he was not the only practitioner.
But it is interesting to note that his earlier Shakespearean revivals and his own early original plays were generally in five
acts whereas his later revivals and his most successful adaptations were in versions streamlined to three or four acts. For
example, Boucicault's *London Assurance*, which Daly had produced in 1869 in five acts, was reduced to four in 1896. The
other innovation—presenting each act of a classic in a single
scene—had been a feature of Daly's first reconstruction of
The School for Scandal in 1874.

The clearest insight into the daily policies of the new
theater can be gained not so much by consulting the playbills
for the first season, when three German and three French
adaptations made up the offerings, as by reading the letters
Augustin and Joseph exchanged when the second season was
getting under way. On September 1, 1880, Joseph wrote to
congratulate Augustin upon his

wonderful first season . . . *considering*

I   Absence of a claque
II   Exclusion of deadheads
III Exclusion of professionals
IV   Hostility of the clan that *wouldn't* go to see what every-
     body praised because Daly hadn't any company so he
     couldn't do anything fit to be seen
V   A new house
VI   On the site of a decayed old one
VII New people behind the curtain.

The "new people behind the curtain" who had to adjust
themselves to the Daly discipline included Ada Rehan, John
Drew, Otis Skinner, Catherine Lewis, May Fielding, Hart
Conway, and the "Daly Debutantes."

Augustin wrote him a note of thanks the next day for his
"consoling" and "reassuring" letter. The trials of the manager
are clearly indicated.

Your letter of yesterday was more than consoling: it was reassuring. Sometimes—yes, very often, of late, I have doubted myself, & the wisdom of some of my moves. . . . So often my worst failures have been made when trying to follow someone else's theory that I only seem to grow more obstinate in my own ways after each such drawback. To go no further than this season: this early opening August 15 & this melodramatic programme [*Tiote*] were both urged by Mr. Duff. . . . Hindsight is on me again, & I blame myself for allowing anyone or anything to persuade me out of the bright & cheery musical programmes I originally planned for this theatre. . . . I shall be so glad when you get back to the city so we can talk over matters.

It was such disagreements about theater policy that led to strained relations with Mr. Duff. The situation had become none too pleasant by the beginning of the second year, and on September 4, 1880, Mr. Duff withdrew his support. Augustin turned immediately to his brother for assistance. Two days later Joseph sent a check for $1000, the first of dozens of such loans. In the same mail Joseph also dispatched a letter which Augustin signed and remailed to the Editor of the *Herald*, setting forth the aims of Daly's Theatre.

The real achievement of the first year seems to have been Daly's adherence without any compromise to a rigid policy of management. That he succeeded must be regarded as a triumph of purpose and devotion to his own ideals.

With the financial and moral assistance of his brother, Augustin continued to produce musical comedies during the 1880–1881 season. *Zanina* and *Cinderella at School*, both with the complete company of Debutantes, were lavishly presented. But the successful run of *Needles and Pins* from November 9, 1880 to January 15, 1881 and particularly the hit made in it by the "Big Four"—Ada Rehan, John Drew, Mrs. Gilbert, and James Lewis—convinced him that comedy alone would suffice. So the 1881–1882 season opened, as Judge Daly reports, with "a notable change of policy; the plan of a musical comedy in addition to a dramatic force was abandoned." The four-month success of *The Passing Regiment* in the winter of 1881–1882 justified the change and confirmed the new policy. Daly was now committed to a comedy theater; German farces, Shakespearean and Old English Comedies became his trademark. Discussing Daly's accomplishments in a review of the 1882–1883 season, Odell wrote in his *Annals of the New York Stage:*

> In journeying through the records of this period, one easily sees how and why Augustin Daly forged ahead as provider of the freshest and most interesting theatrical pleasures then to be found in America. Alert, always present at the performances in his theatre, incessantly searching repertoires, old and new, for any possible addition to the offerings of his company, eagerly finding and developing new players of talent, himself energetic, forceful, suggestive, he became the leading theatrical manager of his time in America, and stands today, a half-century later, as the finest force the theatre in this country has known.

And in 1884, Nym Crinkle (A. C. Wheeler), dramatic critic of the New York *Sun*, praised Daly for his adherence to these standards:

1. the pursuit of art for its own sake, not merely to make money
2. the encouragement of native talent
3. the creation of a new order of drama, e.g., *Frou-Frou, Divorce, Pique*
4. the introduction of elaborate stage settings
5. the creation of a thoroughly adequate stock comedy company

At the height of his professional success, personal tragedy struck Daly through his sons. One of the children promised to follow in his father's footsteps, for he had written a little play called *The Family Doctor* that was given at home, with his father and mother in the audience. Only a few days later, on January 5, 1885, both boys died of diphtheria. The notes which Augustin wrote Joseph are characteristically brief and poignantly simple.

> My little Austin has just died. He seemed to fall asleep—it was

only a little after quarter past ten here, but I am sure he has awakened in heaven.

And twelve hours later, he added,

Leonard has joined his saintly little brother.

His loneliness and sense of loss are clearly indicated in the note he wrote his brother on September 20, 1885. "I am so *by myself* now that probably my loneliness at times makes me incline to selfishness." After the death of his sons Daly turned once more to his lifelong interest in book collecting; outside the theater it became his chief interest in life. His magnificently enlarged Douay Bible, extra-illustrated and specially bound at an estimated cost of $25,000, was the memorial he dedicated to his sons. Throughout his sorrow, Daly kept his trouble to himself. Even in the tragic days following the sudden death of his boys, he kept his theater open and attended to the business connected with it. His heartache seems only to have driven him more deeply into theatrical activity. Mrs. Gilbert has observed that "Mr. Daly would have been a very different man if his boys had lived."

He was constantly at the theater and rarely missed a performance of any play. "He knew every line of the play," reported Deshler Welch. And when there was a lapse or a slip his wrath descended upon the offender. So, in 1884, he posted the following notice on the bulletin board to the cast of *A Wooden Spoon:* "Be distinct—be earnest—do not trifle." On July 13, 1885, he wrote this warning:

There is a growing evil to which I must call particular attention and insist upon its immediate amendment. . . .
I refer to the additions of "ifs" "ands" and "buts," of "ha-has"— or repetitions and interjections in their own speeches. . . .
The author's text *must be adhered to.* Permit him to rise or fall by his own lines—not by your additions.

On March 17, 1886:

The performances of Nancy & Co are drifting away from the

true spirit of the piece—& from the condition desirable in a perfect representation.

Some have grown listless—some slothful—some so by rote as to get their words & sentences tangled—gigglings and suppressed laughter are frequent & ill disguised—some have become *so easy* as to give no *force* to their voice & their words do not carry half the distance of the house—others have grown to make unnecessary pauses & breaks—others hurry & talk through laughs, altogether there is a lack of that freshness & alertness which I want to see at every performance.

The spirit which can permit such a condition of affairs is unworthy of members of my company. Out of it grows grumblings and mutiny—a spirit natural to the Rabble, and not to Ladies and Gentlemen who are treated with the extreme consideration with which I treat my company.

And on April 3, 1889:

I must positively protest against the spirit of carelessness and disposition to alter the business of lines in this play which is creeping upon the principals in the cast. I want my lines spoken, and I want the business I gave at rehearsals followed. Anything else is contrary to my directions and will be punished by an exemplary fine.

Daly's constant supervision of the acting and his desire to have his players perform naturally and as an ensemble were the basis of his theater's success. Thus, Melvin Schoberlin, author of *From Candles to Footlights,* could write that "to Daly is given the credit for being the first stage manager to bring order out of the Chaos of the Civil War Theatre by making acting an art in which a technique was learned. . . ."

Writing to Joseph in 1886 of the indifferent reception of his company on their first trip to Paris, he nevertheless found solace in the fact that "the most unprejudiced French critics gave us praise. Almost all praised the *ensemble,* which, as you know, is my pride." In truth, the theater of the eighties represented by Daly's had made remarkable progress, and Daly himself was in great measure responsible. "What pace and 'ensemble' he got from his company!" exclaimed Ellen Terry.

John Drew has indicated that these standards led to a happy and contented organization. "It would be difficult to imagine a company in which there was greater accord," he wrote. "Everything was so fine, and the associations were so pleasant." And George Clarke, who had frequent quarrels with Daly and who left the company twice, nevertheless remarked, "I could not keep away. I was able to make a great deal more money elsewhere; but I never found elsewhere the artistic atmosphere, the home of art, that remains unchanged here always."

Having established a new mode of acting, Daly tended to standardize it. Whereas the original impetus had been beneficial to the stage and to the drama, in the end Daly and his methods became passé and conventional. Some of the more specific complaints against Daly illustrate how his domination in time became stereotyped. Henry Miller has related the following experience which shows how Daly's methods were eventually rendered meaningless.

I had just left Augustin Daly's Company, and I was sure at that time that he was the greatest man of the theater the world has ever known. There was fresh in my mind one of his remedies for a lack of action created by unbroken dialogue. Whenever we had a particularly long speech to read, Daly taught us to interpolate a stroll from one side of the stage to the other, under the pretense that some object at the further end of the room had caught our attention. This was known as the "Daly cross."

I shall never forget what followed when I introduced that bit of business to Dion Boucicault.

I had a particularly long speech to read in my first role under his direction. Incidentally, the part was a character in a play of his own authorship. Just about the middle of this speech, I shifted tranquilly from stage right to stage left and pretended to examine with keen interest a work of art on a mantelpiece against which I leaned with graceful ennui. Down came Boucicault's fist on the arm of the orchestra chair in which he was seated.

"Just a minute," he shouted. . . . "Why did you make that cross, Mr. Miller? There is nothing in the stage directions to warrant your change of position."

Very confidently, indeed very glibly, I plunged into my defense. . . .

Boucicault studied my face for a moment in eloquent silence. "Mr. Miller," he observed, with biting contempt, "if I cannot hold my audience with my pen, I am sure you cannot with your feet. Go on with the rehearsal."

Even Winter was forced to admit that

A radical error in the stage management of the late Augustin Daly arose from his propensity to insist that every part should be acted in strict accordance with his personal view of it. "If my actors will only do exactly what I tell them to do," he once said to me, "I will never complain of them." It often happened that his views were correct, that his suggestions were excellent, and that his actors could not have taken a wiser course than the one he prescribed; but the ironclad application of his rule—or of any man's rule—would inevitably efface individuality in an actor and convert him into a machine.

Shaw was one of the few critics who saw this in perspective. In the old days of the 1880's, he pointed out, Daly's farces were "natural, frank, amusing, and positively lifelike in comparison with the plays then regarded as dramatic masterpieces." Then Ibsen "smashed up" the drama. But whereas the genius of Ibsen caused many of his plays to be carried over into the succeeding century as plausible and intelligent studies of human beings and human nature, Daly never created, either in his own plays or in his remarkable company, any such enduring masterpieces. His role was that of an emancipator, but the freedom he brought eventually became itself sterile and retrograde, so that Shaw could finally cry, "What is to be done with Mr. Daly? How shall we open his mind to the fact that he stands on the brink of the twentieth century?" How, Shaw might have added, can we convince Daly that techniques of acting and staging, and opulence and realism are merely externals which must guarantee intellectual freedom and development or else simply freeze into pictorial prettiness?

Not everyone in the company was willing to see it Daly's

way at first. May Irwin, who came to Daly's from Tony Pastor's, found it difficult to adjust to the discipline. Once Daly yelled at her. "I had never been spoken to like that in my life. And before all the company! . . . I broke down and blubbered," she reported to Amy Strang. Daly was "inexorable." Finally, he relented. "Come, come," he said, "you mustn't do this. I treat all my people alike. If you don't do well, you, as well as I, will be criticised. It is for your sake as much as for mine." Miss Irwin concluded, "It did not take me long to understand that Mr. Daly knew more than I did and to learn that to follow him was to make a hit." She did make "hits," many of them, so many in fact that she was finally able to leave Daly's for three times the salary he paid her.

Daly's strict regulations naturally resulted in many disciplinary problems which recall similar difficulties he had in his earlier period of management. Dissatisfaction with his methods and his rules occasionally led to rebellion, particularly by the more temperamental. Yorke Stephens and his wife, Helen Leyton, began a two-year engagement with Daly in 1882 that ended in ruffled feelings. Kate Claxton was the next to leave, followed shortly by Phoebe Russell and Edith Kingdon, who, said John Drew, "left the company on account of a misunderstanding."

Even Winter, in *The Life of Tyrone Power*, acknowledged that "Daly was not readily accessible and towards actors he was usually frigid." Wilton Lackay made his first appearance at Daly's in 1889 and scored a big hit, but he and the "martinet-manager," as Odell called him, could not agree, and in a short time, he left the fold. In 1893, Arthur Bourchier quarreled with the manager and refused to appear in *Twelfth Night*. Just the year before, John Drew, after thirteen years of association, had left the company, lured by the much larger salary and stardom offered by Frohman. Even Ada Rehan had a disagreement with Daly in the summer of 1894 and remained with her old manager only after he agreed to star her and to pay her a salary commensurate with her improved status. Finally, in 1899, Blanches Bates, who took the town by storm, left the company after playing the lead in *The Great Ruby* only twice. Norman Hapgood's comment, "naturally there was trouble between her and Mr. Daly," indicates that through the years people had grown accustomed to squabblings in the Daly company.

Daly's tight control over the stage techniques was matched by control over the lives of the company. He endeavored, as Deshler Welch relates, "to suppress all Bohemian tendencies on the part of his people. He tried to enforce some idea of personal dignity and insisted that the ladies and gentlemen of the company should not appear conspicuously in public places." This avoidance of "Bohemian tendencies" became a fetish with Daly. These rules elicited many unfavorable comments. Julia Marlowe called them "peculiar." Daly's actors, she recalled, "must not walk in Broadway day or night; they must not speak to him until he had spoken to them; they must not follow certain fashions in their attire; they must not do divers other things held to be the proud privileges of the sons of freedom. . . ."

Even as late in his career as March 1899, Daly was still posting rules on the bulletin board. On March 9, he specified: "It is not permitted for any member of this company to go out of the theatre after once entering and reporting for the performance. A fine of from $1 to $5 will be exacted for disobeying this rule."

Clara Morris complained of the "astounding list of rules" and "endless forfeits" which hedged about the members of the company, which included a penalty for wounding a companion's feelings. On this last matter, Daly posted a bulletin, dated October 20, 1890:

I have been much surprised to learn that a habit of mocking—imitating—and ridiculing the peculiarities of certain members of the company has become quite common—both in and out of the

theatre. Nothing can be more unkind, ungenerous, uncharitable—
or more reprehensible: and if my request that it would cease will
not be regarded outside of the theatre—I shall fine anyone a
night's salary whom I shall convict of this offense against good
breeding inside the theatre.

There were fines for being late, for making the stage wait,
for lack of courtesy. For addressing the manager on business
outside of his office there was a fine of $1 for the first offense;
considering that salaries started as low as $7 a week and
averaged about $35, this fine was actually rather stiff.

But the "mortal" offense, reports Miss Morris, "was . . .
that rule forbidding the giving to outsiders of any stage information whatsoever; touching the plays in rehearsal, their
names, scenes, length, or story." The London critic, H. G.
Hibbert, also remarked upon this regulation against commerce with the press. "Daly forbade, under penalty, any
traffic with newspaper representatives in the way of an 'interview' or any reclame by the individual. He treated his artists
as puppets in his scheme of *mise en scene*." On June 23, 1899,
The Sun ran an article which noted that "he was extremely
sensitive and resentful. . . . He kept a scrapbook containing
all the articles published concerning his theatre, and beside
each was written the name of the author." *The Sun* further
related that on another occasion Daly went to the editor of one
daily newspaper to have the drama critic discharged. Daly's
objection was that his publicity release, forwarded from his
theater, had been mangled, and, inexcusably, had been signed
by George Parsons Lathrop, whom Daly had quietly hired as
a press agent. The editor, needless to say, refused to accede to
Daly's demand.

Many contemporaries complained of Daly's undue influence on the press. Julia Marlowe's biographer has summed
up the situation from that actress' point of view.

A pleasant superstition was abroad in leading newspaper offices
that Mr. Daly partook of royal attributes, at least to this extent,

that in his productions he could make no error nor could anything be done better than by his company of talented and popular players. At times this amiable belief seemed to amount to a sacred writ. Mr. Daly was able, skillful, indomitably active, avid of success and at once an expert and an artist in the principles of applied publicity. His attitude toward the writers of newspaper criticism was both friendly and commanding; toward some it took on the intimate relation of employer and employed. Thus one dramatic critic was engaged to prepare the prompt-books for the Daly company; another to assist in the Daly theater's publicity work; anothers to paint the portrait of Miss Ada Rehan.

These accusations may not be sloughed off simply as the charges of a jealous rival, for the facts bear out the claim. William Winter was dramatic critic of *The Tribune* from 1864 to 1909; he wrote the introductions for almost all of Daly's Shakespearean and Old English Comedy revivals, and prepared versions of Shakespeare plays for production at Daly's Theatre. He was always allowed the privilege of reading new plays in advance of the performance, and he accompanied Daly on summer trips to Europe, frequently at the manager's expense; he borrowed money from Daly, the repayment of which was refused; he wrote, at Daly's request, "A Study of Ada Rehan," published as *A Daughter of Comedy;* and it is obvious from a letter written in 1884, and quoted by Winter in *Vagrant Memories,* that he was called upon to defend Daly, his methods, and his company in the press.

Beside the many-faceted Winter, there was Edward A. Dithmar, drama reviewer on *The Times* from 1884 to 1901, who prepared the souvenir volume, *Memories of Daly's Theatres,* a handsome and biased tribute to the theater and the members of the company. In 1888, Daly gathered a whole group of critics, H. C. Bunner of *Puck,* E. A. Dithmar, Laurence Hutton of the New York *Mail* and *Harper's Magazine,* Brander Matthews who was a regular contributor to *The Saturday Review* and other periodicals, and of course William

Winter, to compose *A Portfolio of Players,* a collection of eulogies to Ada Rehan, Mrs. Gilbert, James Lewis, John Drew, and Charles Fisher. George Parsons Lathrop was in the eighties the literary editor of the New York *Star;* and Leander P. Richardson, who became editor of *The New York Dramatic News,* acted as a scout for Daly in Europe in 1883, picking up English and French plays for the American manager. A number of these people were also engaged in hack work, largely translating, for Daly. In 1883, Richardson worked on a German play; H. C. Bunner and Julian Magnus, the managing editor of *The Arcadian,* did a number of French adaptations as did Joseph Hatton who from 1874 to 1905 was editor of *The Gentleman's Magazine.*

The climax of these journalistic activities came when Daly actually purchased the majority of the stock in *The Theatre* magazine. Deshler Welch, who was then the editor, later wrote that "Daly had another positive aspiration outside of his theatre and this was to found a magazine." But the venture never got beyond the purchase state.

Barton Baker and Norman Hapgood were among the critics who noted the consequences of Daly's devious control of the press. Daly's "was a competent troupe of well trained artistes," wrote Baker in his *History of the London Stage,* "but a section of the press gushed over them most fulsomely. . . ." And Hapgood, writing of the Theatrical Syndicate in *The International Monthly* in 1900, and complaining of the evil power of the Syndicate, pointed out that the baleful influence of this "trust" upon "any New York newspaper of the first class is probably not greater than Mr. Daly exercised on the *Tribune* and the *Times.*"

He was not always successful with the press; many incidents proved the critics as rebellious as some actors. Because of an unfavorable review of *The School for Scandal* by Meltzer of *The Herald,* Augustin wrote Joseph, "I won't allow that man to enter the theatre."

Tom Williams, editor of *The Evening Post*, had praised the "beauty and surprising historic quality" of Edith Kingdon in a San Francisco performance, calling her "the real star of the performance." Outraged at the inferred slight to Miss Rehan, Daly ordered Leavitt, the owner of the theater, not to admit Williams, and even tried to have him ejected by the police at the next performance. Other critics, George Barnes of *The Call* and Peter Robinson of *The Chronicle*, sided with Williams. Daly was "very savage" about the incident, reported Mr. Leavitt. While "there is no denying his extraordinary qualities as manager and author," concluded Leavitt, "his personal peculiarities were many and not always agreeable, as he was much of a martinet."

Daly seems to have been quite unconscious of the feelings he frequently aroused. He once said, "I am told that I am unmannerly because I do not lift my hat every time I meet one of my young ladies in the theatre or say 'good morning' to this or that member of the company. I have no time for those little pleasantries, and my mind is too seriously involved in my purposes for the day." As Jessie Millward has described him, Daly was a "curious individual. . . . He was an expert in the gentle art of making enemies, and was too much oppressed with a sense of the importance of being Augustin Daly to become really popular."

With success had come public recognition as a distinguished citizen. In 1884, the Penn Club had invited Daly to be its guest of honor. In 1886 and again in 1887, *The North American Review* asked for articles. He joined Booth, Barrett, Palmer, Mark Twain, and others in 1887 to found "The Players," of which he became the first vice-president, yet after the initial meetings, Joseph Jefferson commented, Daly had never attended a meeting within his memory. He was awarded the Laetare Medal by Notre Dame University in 1894.

He was honored abroad also. John Drew has described a

"most brilliant entertainment" given for the company by John Hare at the Garrick Club, London, on June 9, 1888. The guest list included Millais, Henry James, Du Maurier, and a number of distinguished noblemen. But "for some reason, known only to himself, Daly absented himself from this supper. It was believed that he was annoyed that Hare had not submitted to him the list of those members of the Daly Company who were to be asked. Irving was furious at Daly, and so was William Winter, who was one of Daly's closest friends." Daly evidently never participated in any activity in which he could not exercise control.

At the New York Shakespeare Society's annual dinner in 1896, Daly was the guest of honor, chosen "as the one who has done more than any other man that lives to give to the men and women and children of this generation a practical realization of what Shakespeare said and was." An insight into Daly's personality can be gained from a few paragraphs of the speech he made at this dinner—a speech written for him by Joseph.

A man who has a clear purpose in what he does is apt to be a man of a single purpose. To that single purpose, rightly or wrongly, all else is subordinated. . . . Hence, complaints of the man's methods of doing business, of his manners, and of his so-called "peculiar ways."
Perhaps it does not tend to make a man companionable or sociable or clubable to have engrossing ambitions and unsatisfied longings for still higher achievements, which apply a continual spur to exertion. It does not make a man more tolerant of easy going indifference, nor of critical raillery.

The remarkable thing about all these honors was not that Augustin should have been so singled out for distinction, but the strange role that Joseph played in each event.

On the occasion of the Penn Club dinner Joseph wrote to Augustin,

I send you back the Penn Club invitation. It is a great honor and I have jotted down a few sentences for you to say if you rise to speak—& of course you will. . . . I have put "cues" in the margin of the speech. Transfer them to a card & as you walk about try to see how much of the speech you can recall by glancing at each cue. Hold the card in your hand when you rise to speak.

There is no absolute proof that Joseph helped Augustin prepare his article, "The American Dramatist," for *The North American Review* in 1886, but the subject matter of the piece certainly suggests such an arrangement. In the essay, Daly makes a strong plea for "American authors of distinction to try their fortunes" at playwriting. But he adds that "what is most to be deplored is, that the few who are willing are not disposed to pursue *a plan of collaboration, which alone assures success to beginners.*" In order adequately to justify this position, he points out the advantages of a literary partnership.

By this plan or system the writer of clever dialogue assists the inventor of interesting plot and of striking incident and character; or writers of equal invention and wit assist each other in that fuller development of the possibilities of plot or situation which one mind alone is commonly unable to accomplish; or, and this is most important, if not indispensable, dramatists of unquestioned experience help to shape for the stage the productions of playwriters of little or no experience.

The striking aspect of this suggestion is that it is based, completely, upon his own practice. Certainly it must have been with his own successful formula in mind that he exclaimed, "How effectually [functions] the clear, common sense of a friendly collaborator, who has no weakness for your weakness." That Joseph helped to frame this article can be derived also from a note Augustin wrote him in the following year, on May 9, 1887, when he reported to Joseph that the editor of the magazine had asked for another article. "Will you think it over & let us talk it out again?" was Augustin's request. Their method of collaboration, so successful in practice, was also clearly enunciated now in theory.

Daly's views and beliefs, as well as some light on contemporary conditions in the theater, are contained in the conclusion of *The North American Review* essay.

To sum up, I should say the prospects of our national drama are bright, because: 1st, our theatres as places of resort are wholesome and are controlled by the best classes; 2nd, the development of dramatic capability and power in the art of acting is marked and increasing in Americans; 3rd, our native authors are numerous and industrious, wanting but the resolution and perseverance of American writers in other departments to systematically help the native drama and not leave its development too much to chance; 4th, the standard of the best management is high except where theatres are managed purely as commercial speculations.

Daly generalized from his own practices again in an article he wrote for *Harper's Weekly* of February 2, 1889. The conclusion of this article contains a further statement upon the wisdom of collaboration and a caution to the critics that "if the theatre is attacked, the critics are animadverting on the tastes of the best society." Here again Mr. Daly is the self-conscious defender of his own principles and position, dangerous and narrow-minded as they frequently were.

Besides these articles, Daly was occupied during this period with a more ambitious literary project. *Woffington, A Tribute to the Actress and the Woman* was published in 1888 in a limited edition of 150 copies for the author, Augustin Daly. The volume was magnificently bound and illustrated with eleven handsome portraits, including Hogarth's painting of Woffington as "Sir Harry Wildair," the original of which was "in the possession of Augustin Daly." Daly's own extra-illustrated copies sold for $2100 and $2850 in 1900.

The biography was praised for its richness of detail, and for its completeness and scholarly accuracy. A great deal of loving and careful research went into it and the book has been an artistic contribution of value to theatrical history. *The Saturday Review* gave the work a flattering notice, pointing out that "The usual good fortune of Peg Woffington has attended her in the matter of her biography. . . . For Mr. Daly writes sensibly and eloquently."

Joseph Daly had a hand even in the composition of this biography. On September 4, 1887, Joseph wrote Augustin that he was sending the *Woffington* "corrected—with a memorandum as to my alterations." Two years later, on the occasion of a second edition, Augustin wrote to Joseph for assistance as usual, on November 14, "I am getting out a second edition of the Peg Woff—for the Holidays: it wants a preface—will you give me a foolscap page or so for the purpose referring to the way it has been received—but lay the credit of all on the charming subject." Needless to add, the "Preface to the Second Edition," signed with a flourish by Augustin Daly, was prepared by the devoted Joseph.

More remarkable today than the literary achievement of *Woffington* is the undisguised parallel which Daly draws between the careers of Woffington and Ada Rehan. Discussing Peg's first appearance in one of her most famous roles, Sylvia in *The Recruiting Officer*, he writes that it is "the very part for an actress whose talents do not run in a single groove and who is blessed with something more than a mere monotone." Peg's one great defect as an actress was the "mere monotone" of her voice, which Daly elsewhere admits "was far from being enchanting"; on the other hand, Ada Rehan's voice was praised for its amazing range and "velvety" quality. It must surely have been of Ada's Sylvia that Daly was thinking when he wrote of Peg's. One suspects that Daly consciously modeled Miss Rehan's repertoire on Peg's; they both played Portia, Beatrice, Rosalind, Viola, Mistress Ford, Sylvia in *The Recruiting Officer*, Hypolita in *She Wou'd and She Wou'd Not*, Oriana in *The Inconstant*, Violante in *The Wonder*, and Woffington also acted Lady Percy in *Henry IV*, a part projected for Miss Rehan in 1898. This identification of the two actresses who played so many of the same roles was so prominent in Daly's mind that he seems constantly to have confused one with the other. When he praises Peg's "faithfulness" to the management of the theatres in which she was engaged, he admits that her loyalty actually transcends time to console him for his own "diappointments in the defection of some restless members of my company." The loyal Miss Rehan remained with him for twenty years. Further, he writes of Peg that "she was possessed of the tempting beauty of eye and mouth, the glowing health, the flashing wit, the sprightly humor and the quick intelligence of the native-born Irish girl," all qualities remarked time and again as being the peculiar possessions of Irish-born Ada Rehan. Finally, in his discussion of contemporary criticisms of Peg, Daly bursts out into an honest admission of his identification of the two women. He calls to the readers' attention the similarity between the two comediennes in their acting, saying that "Woffington was the first woman to assume a comedy character with ease and speak its lines with naturalness" and that Rehan's "ease and unconscious chattiness . . . match the simplicity of her manner and the naturalness of her diction."

Daly constantly dwells upon Woffington's "goodness of heart," "sense of honor," and "devotion to duty," and he correctly credits her with generosity in assisting at the benefits for other performers and commends her magnanimous lack of jealousy. These are the very qualities for which Ada Rehan was also commended. "I've heard the same foolish cry raised in my own time," he confides, "on behalf of the incompetent, and with as faint a show of reason. Why should the Lioness be jealous of the Cat?"

In the summer of 1894, Daly and Miss Rehan had their only disagreement. The resolution of their differences resulted in Daly's agreeing, against his principles, to "star" her. Then he sent her "a brief summary" of her first week's business as "A Star." He praises her in words that echo the lauding of Woffington for having "conscientiously [done] your duty with all your heart and soul proving yourself the most faithful, loyal and unselfish Helper that man or manager ever had." The wording is significant. "I assure you," he concludes, "I am more proud of your present success than of any event in my 25 years of Managerial life."

The relationship between Daly and Ada Rehan has always aroused speculation. Contemporaries evidently accepted the situation with such composure that actual accounts are scarce and generally noncommittal. Isadora Duncan has, after her fashion, made no secret of what she considered the true state of affairs. Ada Rehan "had long been the adoration of Augustin Daly," reported the dancer in *My Life*, "and perhaps she resented his subsequently picking out of the company some pretty girl who would be for two or three weeks—or two or three months—suddenly lifted into leading parts for no apparent reason whatsoever." But la Duncan's assertions must be regarded with skepticism because she felt her position in the Daly company was not equal to her abilities and because her autobiography was notoriously "doctored" to appeal to a wide and scandalized audience.

W. Graham Robertson, who in the eighties and nineties designed costumes for Daly, was a more cautious commentator. In his reminiscences, *Life Was Worth Living*, he refers to the unsolved "mystery of Ada Rehan, to which Augustin Daly alone held the key." Finding the actress a shy and rather unimaginative but charming person off-stage, and discovering the magnetism of Daly, Robertson evolved a sort of real-life Trilby-Svengali drama.

Daly must have been a great actor who could not act. He was rough and uncouth, with harsh utterance and uncultured accent; a singer without a voice, a musician without an instrument. But in Ada Rehan he found his means of self-expression; Ada Rehan with her quaint charm, her voice of music, her splendid presence and her gentle good nature which he could mould to his will.

Whether in real life Daly and Miss Rehan played the romance of Trilby and Svengali, it is certainly true that after Svengali's death his Trilby lost her voice. In *Footlights and*

Spotlights, Otis Skinner has pointed out that after Daly's death Miss Rehan was never able to act again and that "without him she was helpless." On tour with Skinner, she was frequently ill or moody and took "no interest in anything about her." Her own letters to William Winter bear this out. "I am very indifferent to the future," she writes a month after Daly's death. "If I ever go on again with my work I fear it will be more of the machine than the artiste. I shall do all in my power to help carry out his desires. . . . I am so indifferent I cannot think." And even more revealingly, she complains a month later

> I have been very miserable. I try to be strong . . . my strong affection & regard for him—the strongest thing in me. I was fully alive to all he ever did for me & he knew my devotion to him & his ambitions. It was all so well understood between us—that we had really grown into being one: we both worked heart & soul—for one end. My loss no one can understand.

It has remained for time and for Otis Skinner's daughter, Cornelia, to publish the truth. Miss Skinner has accepted Robertson's description of the affair as a Trilby-Svengali relationship, but her greater knowledge of the doings of the individuals has allowed her to be much more frank. In *Family Circle* she states as fact that

> Ada Rehan, besides being leading lady, enjoyed the off-stage rôle of *grande maîtresse*—although *enjoyed* is a debatable word. For she could not have derived much happiness from the relationship. Daly had a wife. He was a strict Catholic. But even if he had been free, it is doubtful if he would have considered marrying Rehan. To hold the whip handle by keeping a woman of her beauty and prominence in the compromising position an extra-marital liaison involved in those cautious times was a sop to his will to power. It gave him a feeling of prestige.

Daly's own explanation—or Joseph's—of the affair between Peg Woffington and David Garrick serves best as a final word.

Whatever of love there may have been between them at this time was prudently concealed, and both fared all the better for it in the estimation of a world which prefers to consider its idols as models of propriety, even if they be not so. In this way it offers a premium on prudence and regard for appearances—virtues in themselves, when the virtues they simulate are absent.

The puzzle of Joseph's anonymous part in his brother's successful career has not been solved, since his collaboration itself has been till now unknown. Presumably such friends as William Winter, and members of the company who saw him often engaged in conversation with his brother in the daily business of the theater, must have taken his share of the work for granted. On his part, Joseph enjoyed the life of the theater, perhaps in contrast to his own professional obligations. As a judge, he was required to keep up a certain position, and yet judges did not make salaries sufficient to keep up with the Tammany crowd so it may have been true that the money that came to him in this way was important. But this is speculation; only the public facts of Joseph's life are on view.

After *Woffington,* Joseph continued to be his brother's literary ghost. Augustin wrote him on December 31, 1897 that "The *Herald* wants about 15 or 20 words from me *today anent* New Years & Greater New York:—can you give me a sentence or two?" New Year's 1898 was the birthday of Greater New York, consequently the *Herald* had a special page for prominent citizens. After a lifetime of dependency upon Joseph's able mind and pen, "two sentences" seem an anticlimactic request, but they bring the pattern of collaboration to an appropriately calm close.

Joseph had combined his prolific clandestine writing activities with a successful public career. In 1890, he became the Chief Justice of the Court of Common Pleas, and when that court was merged with the New York Supreme Court he became a Justice and served until he was defeated for reëlection by Tammany forces in 1898. He then returned to private practice, emerging from private life to accept the chairmanship of a commission appointed by President McKinley to revise the laws of Puerto Rico, and once again to serve under Governor Roosevelt on the drafting of a new State Education Law. He received honorary degrees from both Fordham and Villanova and in 1916, the year of his death, Pope Benedict XI made him a Knight Commander of the Order of Saint Gregory.

The latter years of Augustin's life were also years of public achievement; indeed, they can best be chronicled in terms of his dramatic successes, for after 1879 his career became indistinguishable from the life of his theater. His stature on the American theatrical scene was an imposing one. In 1888 George O. Seilhamer dedicated to him thus the first volume, *Before the Revolution,* of his *History of the American Theatre:*

To Augustin Daly, this work is inscribed by the author, in recognition of his rare earnestness as a student of dramatic literature, evinced by revivals of the works of the masters; his faithful adherence throughout his career as a manager and dramatist to the methods which make the drama an art as well as a business; and his enthusiasm in gathering the scattered records of the stage, so that the achievements of the past may do honor to the present, and delight and instruct posterity.

Daly was in Paris on business connected with the lease of his London theater when he died, on June 7, 1899. Among the papers found in Augustin's desk after his death was one dated January 24, 1890, which contained the following memorandum to his wife: "If Brother is so inclined I would like to have him prepare a copyright edition of my favorite plays: those in which I had the benefit of his assistance." To Miss Rehan he left in his will the fine furnishings which had graced his stage. To the public, his death was the occasion of many tributes, of which the obituary from the New York *Evening Post* is typical: "The oldest and ablest of our theatrical managers, he was practically the only man in the country to whom the term of theatrical manager, in its wider and better sense, was really applicable."

Daly was aware, as he confessed in a letter to Margaret Hall, that the kind of existence he chose had resulted in a "life which . . . is not peopled with many friendships." He was described by Charles B. Davis (in *The Adventures and Letters of Richard Harding Davis*) as "a most crusty, dictatorial party."

His personal peculiarities [admitted Winter] were many and striking. . . . In character Daly was self-centered. Toward the world his demeanor, ordinarily, was austere. He believed in himself. He possessed extraordinary power of will and an amazing capability of endurance. . . . I have never known him to be tranquil or to impart tranquillity. He stimulated action. His mind was continuously concentrated on the active business of life. He thought quickly, acted quickly, moved quickly. . . .

The many converging aspects of Daly's career all lead to one conclusion: he was a man dedicated to the theater with a tenacity and a singleness of purpose which drove everything else from the path of his concern. That he failed to achieve the highest artistry is a fault of his intelligence, not of his heart, for on the level of intentions he stands as an earnest and devoted manager. As he said at the Shakespeare Society dinner,

What I particularly observe with regard to a high purpose in theatrical management is that such purposes are formed by study, directed by instinct, and kept alive by inclination; and, in one sense, therefore, the true manager is born and not made.

The opening section of the speech could be his credo, in his brother's words:

If to write the songs of a nation is to exert more influence upon it than to make its laws, then the men who control the amusements of the people have a responsibility in one way as great, if not greater, than the men who fill its pulpits. It is with a sense of such responsibility that I have done what I have done for the modern stage. . . .

CHAPTER 2

Blood and Thunder
Dramatist

Puff: *No, no sir; what Shakespeare says of actors may better be applied to the purpose of plays; they ought to be 'the abstract and brief chronicles of the time.' Therefore when history, and particularly the history of our own country, furnishes anything like a case in point, to the time in which an author writes, if he knows his own interest, he will take advantage of it.*

Sheridan, *The Critic*
Act II, Scene 1.

Although success as a dramatist first came to Augustin Daly by way of an adaptation, and his own original scripts are now deservedly forgotten, it was their stunning theatricality that first made his name significant in the history of the American theater. As a writer he has never had any real stature; as a contriver of effects, however, he was bold and ingenious and occasionally achieved true theater magic.

Daly's original plays are of three kinds. There are the sensational melodramas featuring a trick device: *Under the Gaslight* (1867), *A Flash of Lightning* (1868), *The Red Scarf* (1868), and *The Undercurrent* (1888). Of a different sort is the frontier drama, *Horizon* (1871). And then there are the panoramic spectacles depicting low or unusual life in great metropolitan areas: *Round the Clock* (1871), *Roughing It* (1873), and *The Dark City* (1877).

Under the Gaslight was the first of Daly's original plays to be a success. Initially produced August 12, 1867, at the New York Theatre, this phenomenal melodrama has had a theatrical history almost as sensational as its contents.

The plot is involved and by modern standards frequently absurd. The heroine, Laura Courtland, is a girl of unstained virtue and unbelievable endurance, a sort of Lily Bart, whose behavior is difficult for present-day readers to understand. The villain, Byke, is just as singularly drawn: a man of ruthless and remorseless evil and selfishness. Laura, engaged to the wealthy, socially prominent Ray Trafford, is confronted by her presumably real father, the thief, swindler, and black-mailer, Byke. When Ray learns of Laura's background, he reacts according to his snobbish standards: "What a frightful story.... What would my mother think? my friends? Society? —pshaw! She knows of course that I cannot wed her now!"

His reaction is the same as that of Laura's many other acquaintances. Snubbed, she leaves home and her social sphere, not before having demonstrated her inherent nobility to a messenger, Snorkey, a one-armed Civil War veteran who becomes her protector, and who serves as the playwright's method of keeping the strands of the story together. Being a messenger, Snorkey can enter or leave the stage for almost any purpose, especially the obvious one of delivering a speech of explanation.

In the lowly hovel to which she flees, Laura is cared for by Peachblossom, a girl of the streets whom she has befriended. She is pursued by the now contrite Ray and Pearl Courtland, her presumed "cousin," as well as by Byke and his consort, Old Judas. Snorkey, of course, is in on both sides. The justices of the police court decide that Laura is Byke's daughter and since she is a minor must obey him. Byke and Judas now plan to take Laura to New Jersey whence they will attempt to blackmail Pearl, who is really Judas' daughter. They are foiled by Snorkey and by Ray who jumps into the North River to save Laura, the rescue providing an exciting third-act curtain.

We are next told—and apparently expected to believe—the most extravagant nonsense, namely that Pearl and Ray are now engaged to be married; and we actually see Laura, whom they are hiding at the Courtland summer home at Long Branch, encouraging the two of them. Her nobility and self-sacrificing nature make her a sticky, unbelievable heroine. For the second time, her whereabouts is discovered by Byke and Judas; to avoid bringing trouble to Pearl, she leaves again. She arrives at the local railroad station in the dead of night, and, since she can get no train until morning, talks the signal man into locking her in the shed with the baggage—miraculously including a bundle of axes—for the night. Snorkey arrives, trailed by Byke who trusses the messenger up and ties him to the track. With the sound of the approaching express ringing in her ears, Laura chops her way out of the shed to rescue Snorkey in the nick of time. This scene was destined to become one of the most famous spectacles on the American stage.

The last act, of course, clears up all the loose ends. Laura is established as the true Courtland and is reunited to Ray. Graciously, she still clings to Pearl as her "sister." Snorkey and Peachblossom engage in a lot of silly stuff to indicate that their interests are indeed amicable and their intentions matrimonial; Byke is magnanimously released to "emigrate," and we are told of Judas' death. Everything, in other words, is properly concluded.

Snorkey's rescue from death on the railroad tracks is the central incident of the play and the stage directions are most explicitly written to bring out its effectiveness. It is "Night. Moonlight." with a "View of the Shrewsbury River in perspective." The locomotive lights glare on the scene, followed by a "roar and whistle" as the "Train rushes past."

In dealing with railroads in his sensational scene, Daly was taking as his subject one of the most fascinating topics of the day. The expanding railroad industry in America, with the growth of the great trunk lines leading to the transcontinental linking in 1869, was the source of many New York fortunes. Daly demonstrated here, as he was to do many times in his career, his intense awareness of what would interest and hold the public's taste.

Colonel T. Allston Brown calls the scene the "sensation of the play." Brown also indicates that Daly took the idea for it from an English play entitled *The Engineer; or, the Life of George Stephenson*, which was produced at the Victoria Theatre in London in 1863, and in which "a man was run over." "The play," he adds, "was a failure notwithstanding." No copy of it is now available, but there are in existence many copies of a biography by Samuel Smiles entitled *The Life of George Stephenson, Railway Engineer*, upon which the play must have been based. In this work, Smiles relates the story of the grand opening of the Manchester-Liverpool Railway Line on September 15, 1830. The Duke of Wellington, then Prime Minister, and Sir Robert Peel, then Secretary of State, were on hand, as were thousands of spectators, and eight locomotives and trains, the complete English rolling stock. At Parkside, near Liverpool, where the engines stopped for water, Huskisson, M.P. from Liverpool, rushed over to shake the Duke of Wellington's hand. Caught between two trains, he was vitally injured by the locomotive, "Rocket." Another engine, the "Northumbrian," conveyed the dying man into Liverpool, covering fifteen miles in twenty-five minutes. "This incredible speed burst upon the world with the effect of a new and unlooked for phenomenon."

Dithmar claims that the use of the railroad episode in *Under the Gaslight* was an "afterthought. . . The idea of the exhibition of a moving railroad train on the stage was not new, but the rescue of a human being, as it was depicted in *Under the Gaslight*, from a railroad track, was a novel and patentable device." While asserting that the plot was otherwise completely original, Dithmar does say that Daly's impetus to compose the piece came from Lester Wallack's play *Rosedale*, which was based on a novel, *Lady Lee's Widowhood*, and produced at Wallack's Theatre in 1863.

Daly did not use the incidents in the older play; he merely found in one scene those "elements of suspense and surprise, used in just the right proportions and the vivid pictorial exhibition of the dominance of evil over good" to provide a melodramatic situation which he could use. According to Dithmar, "he resolved to employ exactly the same dramatic elements, with different pictorial adjuncts, and produce, if possible, a stronger effect." Dithmar then praises the climax as a "perfect example of the art of playwriting," quoting as his authority a "shrewd French critic" who said that "the art of preparation is the dramatist's art." In his book, *Techniques of the Drama*, William T. Price agrees with this view, and cites Pearl's account to Ray of Laura's early history as a good example of the proper use of narrative and the rescue of Snorkey as an example of the dramatically powerful use of suspense.

The original run of *Under the Gaslight* at the Worrell Sisters' New York Theatre lasted from August 12 to October 1, 1867. The cast was headed by Rose Eytinge as Laura and J. K. Mortimer as Snorkey; these two had, the year before, created great successes in Daly's *Griffith Gaunt*. On December 4, 1867, the piece was revived at the same theater with the three famed sisters themselves—Irene Worrell as Laura, Sophie Worrell as Pearl, and Jennie Worrell as Peachblossom—heading the cast. This run lasted until January 29, 1868, thereby giving the play over a hundred performances in its first season, at a time when a month's run meant a real hit.

In England, *Under the Gaslight; or, Life and Love in These Times*, "A Drama of American Life," was first presented at the Tyne Theatre, Newcastle, on April 20, 1868, and later at the Pavilion Theatre, London, on July 20, 1868. An adaptation of the play by a Miss Hazlewood, called *London by Gaslight*, was produced at Sadler's Wells Theatre, London, September 19, 1868.

The subsequent history of *Under the Gaslight* is involved and impressive. It continued to be performed in New York and Brooklyn almost yearly until the 1880's. In Boston the first production took place the week of April 28, 1873, at the Boston Theatre. A more important production there was the four-act version which, according to the playbill, was "Re-Written, Re-Arranged and Re-Constructed by the Author expressly for Oofty Gooft." Oofty Gooft (Gus Phillips) played the piece all over the United States; he even had special *Under the Gaslight* stationery printed. Madame Methua-Scheller and Jennie Hight also took *Under the Gaslight* to places far and wide in the United States. It was "probably the most popular drama that appeared on the old Denver Stage," according to Melvin Schoberlin's study, *From Candles to Footlights*, and it had equally great success in Salt Lake according to Whitney's *The Drama in Utah*. David Belasco acted in the piece in one San Francisco production. Numerous burlesqued versions also testify to its popularity.

The final revival in Boston at the Castle Square Theatre in 1900 is interesting because of the reviews which comment upon the play's "undiminished popularity" and speak of the "enthusiasm" of the audiences, for the piece has been "a favorite of its kind for a generation." Another reviewer adds that "if any playgoer is unfamiliar with *Under the Gaslight* his education has been sadly neglected, for he has lost the chance to study a genuine melodrama that belongs to the historical American stage about as completely as does *Uncle Tom's Cabin*." And in the same year, when Theodore Dreiser wrote *Sister Carrie*, he had his heroine turn to theatricals in an amateur production of *Under the Gaslight*.

In 1929, Christopher Morley, instituting a season of beer and drama in Hoboken, revived Dion Boucicault's *After Dark*.

Reversing the order of the 1860's, Larry Fay brought out a production of *Under the Gaslight* at the Bowery Theatre shortly after, complete with beer and peanuts. The audience evidently enjoyed the raucous pleasures of hissing, booing, and applauding. Mr. Atkinson of the *Times* suspected that the excitement was a little "synthetic." But Mr. Lockridge of the *Sun* felt that "not even to *After Dark* need *Under the Gaslight* yield as an example of the strutting, declamatory, deliciously preposterous drama of an earlier day."

The railroad scene was not the only timely aspect which drew audiences to *Under the Gaslight* in that earlier day. The character of Snorkey embodies significant social commentary. He is a veteran of the Civil War who has lost an arm in the Battle of Fredericksburg, and he receives no pension. "Ah! Miss, don't blame Uncle Sam for that [forgetting the veteran], he's got such a big family to look after, I can't find no fault if he don't happen to remember all us poor stumps of fellows."

Though he must therefore work as a messenger, Snorkey bears no malice, even against those who failed to measure up. [To Ray] "Yes, Captain; I remember you joined us in New York and left us in Washington. Real fighting wasn't funny, you thought."

There seems to have been no stigma attached to those who secured military commissions and then deserted when the going got rough. Snorkey's cheerfulness and lack of self-interest seem odd to the modern reader accustomed to huge governmental appropriations for veterans. But in 1867 he was evidently not an anomaly. He is of interest today primarily as one of the first dramatic representations of the Civil War veteran. Also, together with Bermudas, "one of the undercrust," and Peanuts, Snorkey epitomized the New York lower classes. They are in the tradition of "Mose, the Fireman," one of the famous figures in American theatrical history.

Contrasted with these sympathetic pictures of the lower classes is Daly's cynical study of upper-class society. He portrays the socially elite of New York as a pack of wolves.

Society is a terrible avenger of insult. Have you heard of the Siberian wolves? When one of the pack falls through weakness, the others devour him. It is not an elegant comparison—but there is something wolfish in society. Laura has mocked it with pretence and society, which is made up of pretences, will bitterly resent the mockery.

This picture of society as vapid and superficial was, and is, a viewpoint favored by dramatists. Boucicault, Baker, and Daly all presented the lower classes as virtuous, the upper classes as superficial; villains of either class were despised and eventually overcome, while virtue in either class usually received more than its own reward.

One other contemporary note in *Under the Gaslight* concerns women's rights, particularly the right to vote. After Laura batters her way out of the signal shed and saves Snorkey's life, she leans exhausted but triumphant against the switch, as Snorkey admiringly exclaims, "Victory! Saved! And these are the women who ain't to have a vote!" Somewhat later in his career, in 1889, Daly returned to this theme of women's rights. *The Lottery of Love* contains an amusing satire on the bloomer girl in the character of Mrs. Zenobia Sherramy.

A final touch of authenticity, the sets, have frequently earned praise for the realism of *Under the Gaslight*. In all justice, it must be pointed out that realistic scenes of New York had previously been successfully presented by Baker in *A Glance at New York* (1848) and by Boucicault in *The Poor of New York* (1857). These three plays, together with others of Boucicault and Daly, do, however, represent the increasing concern of writers to achieve realism, a tendency which the historians of American literature have generally attributed to novelists of a somewhat later period.

In the chequered career of *Under the Gaslight*, perhaps most remarkable of all is the series of legal disputes which attended the piece. Dithmar referred to the play as containing a "patentable device." And Daly did regard the rescue of Snorkey as his private property. His concern in this instance has ironical overtones inasmuch as he was constantly ransacking old plays, French and German dramas, and novels, for dramatic devices with which to enhance his own pieces. Nevertheless in 1868, he brought suit to protect his rights.

Dion Boucicault, the English playwright who was as much a pirate if not more so than Daly, had on August 12, 1868 produced a "Drama of London Life" entitled *After Dark*, at the Princess Theatre in London. Announced as the "authorized adaptation of Messrs. Grange and Dennery's 'Les Oiseaux de Proie,' " to which it bore little resemblance, the play was a sensational melodrama with startlingly realistic scenery, a rescue from drowning, and a railroad train which roared by just after the hero had been pulled from the tracks. The success of the piece was enormous. Although the reviewers noticed the resemblance to *Under the Gaslight*, nobody else seemed to care, at least in England, and existing copyright laws gave Daly no international rights.

But when Jarrett and Palmer, to whom Boucicault had sold the American rights, produced the play at Niblo's Garden on November 16, 1868, Daly at once started action for an injunction. He maintained that the railroad scene, even though it took place on the underground, was an infringement of his copyright.

Boucicault's reply was that "The Railway effect is not derived from Mr. Daly's 'Under the Gaslight,' but is a London stage machinist's invention of as early a date as 1843." Boucicault probably had reference to Charles Selby's *London by Night* which occupied the Strand Theatre, London, on May 12, 1845, from which he borrowed freely; comparison of a few extant passages of *London by Night* with *Under the Gaslight* certainly reveals direct pilfering on the part of Daly as well as of Boucicault. William A. Brady later asserted in a letter to the New York *Sun*, January 24, 1898, that Boucicault had originally filed an affidavit in which he also claimed that Daly took the scene from a magazine article called "Uncle Tom's Fright" in which "a man was placed on a railroad track at the peril of his life and was rescued in a new and novel manner."

Regardless of the source of the scene, Judge Blatchford stated that

All that is substantial and material in the plaintiff's railroad scene has been used by Boucicault, in the same order and sequence of events, and in a manner to convey the same sensations and impressions to those who see it represented, as in the plaintiff's play. Boucicault has, indeed, adapted the plaintiff's series of events to the story of his play, and, in doing so, has evinced skill and art; but. . . . There is no new use, in the sense of the law, in Boucicault's play, of what is found in the plaintiff's railroad scene.

And Palmer was obliged, therefore, to pay royalties to Daly on every American performance of *After Dark*. The effects of the suit were troublesome for a long time. In 1889, William Brady purchased the rights to *After Dark* and wrote to Daly's lawyers for a definition of Daly's rights in the railroad scene. He then opened the play at the People's Theatre on May 20, making such alterations in the railroad scene as he thought would protect him. But Daly sought an injunction, claiming that *After Dark* had been performed in many places to his great loss. The evidence at this trial was very complex, with witnesses describing the exact way of staging the scene at different performances at various places, and with the defense trying to prove that the railroad effect was not original with Daly anyhow.

Daly's injunction was finally denied by Judge Wallace in June 1889 on a technicality. Ex-Judge Dittenhoefer, representing Brady, had pointed out with keen legal acumen that Daly's copyright was void for the reason that the title of the play as published did not correspond with the title as filed by him pursuant to law, the former being *Under the Gaslight, A Drama of Love and Life in These Times,* while the latter was *Under the Gaslight, A Romantic Panorama of Streets and Homes in New York.* In denying Daly's suit Judge Wallace declared

A verbal difference between the registered title and the published title would not necessarily invalidate the copyright, but when the variance is so material that the substantial identity between the two titles is doubtful, and might deceive the public into the belief that they refer to different publications and themes, it is fatal. It is patent that there is such a material variance in the present case, unless all the title except Under the Gaslight can be disregarded. This is not permissible. It will hardly do to segregate what the author has designated and deposited for registry as the title of his work as a unit, into parts, and treat one part as the name and the other as descriptive matter, and eliminate the latter as part of the title. If such an analysis were ever permissible, it could not well be made in the present case, because it is impossible to discriminate between what is the descriptive matter and what is the name.

Undaunted, Daly sought a new injunction, which was again denied, by Judge Cove, on November 14, 1893. The case was appealed and the Circuit Court of Appeals reversed the decision of the lower court on October 27, 1894, and ordered Brady to pay royalties on performances for which he was liable, estimated at 747. The case was taken to the Supreme Court, which ultimately upheld this last decision. "In the end," reported Brady in his autobiography, *Showman,* "Daly got a judgment for $61,000. But the statute of limitations spared me from having to pay more than $6,000. Licked though I was, I'd made an important contribution to the development of the copyright law."

The final word to this series of lawsuits is not a legal note at all. The situation was reversed in 1929 when Christopher Morley produced *After Dark* in Hoboken, followed by Larry Fay's rival New York production of *Under the Gaslight.*

Twentieth-century rivalry, however, was all in fun and involved no suits of any kind. Following Morley's success, Brady, still asserting his common law rights in *After Dark* thirty-five years later—the statutory copyright had run out— raised the royalties for performances except in Hoboken and himself took the play on the road.

While the involved legal dispute over *After Dark* was continuing, Daly instituted another suit in defense of his copyright in the railroad scene in 1868. *Humpty Dumpty*, a pantomime, was having a successful run at the Olympic Theatre through the summer and fall of that year when a litigation ensued *re* the introduction of a comic railroad effect. Daly proclaimed the comedy a violation of his rights and obtained an injunction. The affair was compromised by a modification of the scene and the payment of a fee to Mr. Daly.

Under the Gaslight was published by three firms: Wemyss (Author's Edition, 1867), French (French's Standard Drama, No. 378, 1895), and Lacy (Lacy's Acting Edition, No. 1201, n.d.). This last version contains a preface which is interesting for the light it throws upon then existing publishing practices. More than anything, this statement of the English publisher was a plea for American adherence to the International Copyright Convention:

This edition is not printed for circulation in the United States— the American copy is published by Mr. Wemyss, 575 Broadway, New York, and permission to perform it must be obtained of the author, Mr. A. Daly. To both these gentlemen, I offer a sincere expression of regret that I have at length allowed myself to follow the disreputable example of some New York and Boston publishers, and appropriate property to which I have, certainly, no moral right. I have for years wholly repudiated the practice of pilfering from Americans, and should never, at any time, have assumed what I consider to be a degrading, if not dishonest, position, had I not been the victim of hundreds of instances of similar delinquency from the other side of the Atlantic. . . . Sympathising with the honest movement now agitating the public attention in

America for a reciprocal protection of literary property—I have taken this step to aid it, and deliberately assert that had Mr. Daly possessed the right to introduce this drama into England and her Colonies—its merit is such that he might have hoped to derive an important pecuniary result therefrom for years—all which is sacrificed by the disinclination of the American Government to believe in the genius and inventive powers of its own citizens.

Daly's second original play was *A Flash of Lightning*, produced at the Broadway Theatre, June 10, 1868, another sensational melodrama. One of the first eccentricities to be noted about this play is that it is everywhere listed, including the title page of the published edition, as having five acts, but the actual printed version contains only four acts. The story is one largely of tears and sensations; it combines the worst features of *East Lynne* and *Uncle Tom's Cabin* in a melodramatic mélange that is improbable, frequently to the point of sheer stupidity. Yet it received a most favorable reception from the press and even during the summer season enjoyed an initial run of seven weeks.

As in *Under the Gaslight*, the plot centers around two sisters (this time, real sisters), one of whom is beautiful, selfish, and snobbish. Garry Fallon, an Irish immigrant who has made good, has spoiled his younger daughter, Rose, while disliking the older, Bessie, for her lack of his kind of driving ambition. Mrs. Fallon, a kindly, quiet woman, must do good deeds on the sly to avoid her husband's wrath; she is even unacknowledged by Rose, who refuses to allow her mother to accompany her to her swank private school (Rose has actually told her girl friends that her mother is the family cook). Rose has met the rich, socially prominent Fred Chauncey, but, sly one, he secretly admires Bessie and clandestinely gives her a pair of gold earrings while Garry ostentatiously presents Rose with a gold necklace. All these activities, it should be pointed out, take place during a violent storm. Garry suddenly discovers that the necklace is missing; at the same time, he finds the earrings hidden in Bessie's room. She halfheartedly denies her father's accusation of thievery, attempting to shield Jack Ryver, whom she believes guilty, but whom she loves. The first act concludes (at last!) with the father turning Bessie out of the house; he gives her over to the police in the person of Skiffley.

One soon realizes that the greatest defect of these melodramas is their involved plotting. Action is more important to them than motivation. The characters must be doing something in order to prevent the play from falling to pieces and to provide a continuing, if sketchy, series of events into which the playwright sets his scenes of spectacular excitement. So, Garry's renunciation of his daughter and his heavy-handed action in turning her over to the police are improbable and absurd; he will repent and be forgiven, we know, but meanwhile the action allows a multitude of tears to be shed by the sentimental audience. American theatrical producers had discovered sentimentality *per se* to be an immensely profitable commodity long before the movie serial or the radio soap opera.

Fred, outraged by Bessie's behavior as Ray had been by Laura's in *Under the Gaslight*, now turns to Rose—a fate no better than he deserves. Skiffley, the villain, tries to get Bessie into his power; by saving her, he plans to gain her devotion and marry her. He gets a street urchin to lure her to a thieves' den, but Ryver turns up also, and with the aid of Mrs. Dowderry he and Bessie escape. The whole focus of this act is upon the presentation of the New York underworld; Daly was well aware of the appeal of the underworld scenes, particularly when enhanced by elaborate sets. Nor is this tendency entirely to be deplored. Although this type of domestic melodrama is, by and large, French in origin, the use of new realms and strange settings did contribute, however slightly, to the gradual emancipation of the drama which was to take place in the following half century.

In Act III, Bessie and Jack are on board a Hudson River steamer. She has turned him down again for absolutely no reason but that the plot must go on. He has taken a job as a fireman. Skiffley, of course, is also on the boat. He handcuffs Bessie to the bed in her stateroom. The boat engages in a race with a rival. As a consequence of getting up too much steam, our hero and heroine's boat catches on fire. Jack, naturally, rescues Bessie. This spectacle must certainly have proved almost as exciting as the railroad episode in *Under the Gaslight*, but the playwright was saving an even greater surprise for the last act.

For the denouement, we return to the Fallon home. Rose and Fred are married. Bessie is locked in her room. Garry Fallon has gone crazy and believes that his coal is pure gold. Meanwhile, Jack announces that he is now a civil engineer. At last, the robbery is to be officially investigated. Skiffley demonstrates that a woman must have perpetrated the crime, but Jack, using his newly acquired knowledge of engineering, shows that the necklace was destroyed by a flash of lightning! All are overjoyed at proof of Bessie's innocence, but are immediately plunged into gloom over her disappearance. She has left a note: "I have no other resource but death! Father, God forgive you! Tell Jack!" But the audience, if it is wise, knows better. Her "insensible" body is carried in and she revives in time for the final tableau.

J. S. G. Hagan, critic for *The Dispatch*, has perhaps best summed up the action. It was, he says, "excessively sensational and bristled with incidents from beginning to end. Its plot was improbable, its dialogue commonplace, but the play hit the public taste." The cast, headed by McKee Rankin and introducing his wife, the "vivacious and elegant" Kitty Blanchard to the American stage, included John K. Mortimer, Miss Blanche Grey, and Mrs. G. H. Gilbert, excellent performers who undoubtedly had a great deal to do with the success of the piece. In addition, the play was handsomely

staged by Mr. Barney Williams under whose management
it was produced.

The only serious complaint seems to have been that the
drama was too long, hardly doing justice to its title, *A Flash
of Lightning.* Despite "too many collateral features," the play
did succeed in presenting "the vices, eccentricities, vicissitudes, dangers, miseries and underground horrors of Metropolitan Life." True to its subtitle, *City Hearthsides and City
Heartaches,* it detailed a series of scenes and personalities
neither new nor different but continually interesting to New
Yorkers, who seem to take a diabolical pleasure in witnessing
their city's weak underside. Indeed, the characters here are
the same types depicted in *Under the Gaslight* and in the
plays of Boucicault, Wallack, and other contemporaries. They
are stock figures of the nineteenth-century stage both in England and America; they are the children of Dickens and Bulwer-Lytton; they are descendants of a melodramatic *Macbeth*
and were born in the gory last act of *Hamlet.* They held the
stage completely until scattered by Ibsen, Wilde, and Shaw,
after which they simply moved into the more expensive
celluloid environs of Hollywood.

In addition to stock characters and more or less standard situations—fires and water spectacles were common theatrical property—Daly even pilfered the major incident from which the
play takes its name. The notion of using lightning as a thief
had already been employed by Sardou in a novelette called
La Perle Noire, which he later dramatized and had produced
at the Théâtre du Gymnase, Paris, April 12, 1862. In Sardou's
version an adopted girl, who had been a thief in her childhood (this situation Daly had utilized as the story of Laura in
Under the Gaslight), is suspected of a robbery, and, like
Bessie, is saved by the ingenuity of her lover, a scientist. The
lightning in *La Perle Noire* not only melts up money, but also
destroys a string of pearls, rips wallpaper from the walls of a
room, and melts a precious memento; in this instance, Daly

had modified the sensational behavior of this strange character.

A Flash of Lightning's opening run lasted from June 10 to August 1, 1868. In September of the same year, Mrs. Conway, always hospitable to Daly's plays, produced the piece at her Park Theatre in Brooklyn. Other New York productions occurred in 1873, 1875, and 1877. A burlesque version, *A Flask of Jersey Lightning,* was performed by Bryant's Minstrels on June 22, 1868, while the original play was still on the boards. The first Boston production, beginning August 27, 1868, closely followed the New York and Brooklyn openings. And the play was twice produced in England: at the Amphitheatre, Leeds, on August 1, 1870, and at the Grecian Theatre, London, on November 21, 1870.

The effectiveness of the spectacles in these first two melodramas undoubtedly encouraged Daly to write a third such "thriller." The sensation in *The Red Scarf; or, Scenes in Aroostook* was an old-fashioned sawmill episode in which the hero, Gail Barston, was trapped by his rival, Harvey Thatcher, and bound to a log about to be sawed in two; as an extra touch, Thatcher set fire to the mill to destroy all traces of Barston. Acting with the same daring and bravery that Laura Courtland had shown in *Under the Gaslight,* May Hamilton, the heroine, was able to foil the dastardly plot and to rescue the hero.

This piece was first presented at the theater famous for melodrama, the Bowery, on November 30 and December 1, 1868. Listed as a "New Drama by A. Daly," it shared billing with *O'Neil the Great,* but its popularity outlasted this second play, for it continued to be performed the rest of the week, on December 2 and 3 with *The Lonely Man of the Ocean* and on December 4 and 5 with *Handsome Jack.* According to the historian, A. H. Quinn, it was performed at Conway's Park Theatre, Brooklyn the following November. It was evidently designed as a vehicle for Sallie Partington, a "peripatetic star," who enacted the role of May Hamilton.

One other melodrama belongs to the same category as *Under the Gaslight, A Flash of Lightning,* and *The Red Scarf.* Since no copy of the play, *The Undercurrent,* now exists, we must depend upon the reviews and the playbill for information about it and on Daly himself. In an interview in the New York *Times* for October 25, 1888, Daly made some interesting comments about the play.

When I was in London ten years ago [he is quoted as saying], I was approached by Mr. Chatterton, who was then manager of Drury Lane Theatre, and asked to furnish him a local melodrama to follow the run of the Christmas pantomime at that house. At that time I thought I was in a position to comply with his request, and we talked the matter over between ourselves. I had an idea of combining in one play the powerful sensations of my two old dramas, "A Flash of Lightning" and "Under the Gaslight," sensations which had made both pieces very successful, and by the combination of which I thought I could produce a melodrama which would be very effective when presented to a London audience. My idea was to mold the effects into an entirely new story, and to build up the sketches of character which were illustrated in my old plays, investing them with a coloring local to London, and making such additions of characters as the situation should suggest.

The Undercurrent was thus a confessed reworking of ten-year-old materials.

These admissions were made when Daly was discouraged by many failures. In 1878 he had gone to England in an attempt to recapture fame and fortune via London and the theaters there. He found, however, that London theaters were generally closed to outsiders, and that English writers and producers were unfriendly to potential American rivals. Since he could get no manager to accept any of his already composed plays—he tried in particular to peddle *Under the Gaslight, Pique,* and *Lemons*—he set about doing a new play for Chatterton of Drury Lane.

On November 15, 1878, he wrote to Joseph from London

that he was busy on the outline of a play, making it a combination of *Under the Gaslight, The Dark City,* and "one or
two other sensations," but "placing the action of all in London." And he added, "when I have completed the *scenario,* I
shall forward it at once to you and I know you will do all
you can as of yore." In January he went to Paris to see
L'Assommoir "for the purpose of adding any of the local
features of that play to the business of my own." One wonders
if he had in mind "patentable" features. Anyhow, on February
10, 1879, he wrote to Joseph acknowledging, "Got your
1st and 2nd acts today; they are splendid."

These letters to Joseph refer to the projected play for Drury
Lane to be called *A Stranger in London* which was to have
been produced on April 11, 1879, but never got into rehearsal
because of Chatterton's financial failure; in all probability
this is the same play as *The Undercurrent.* They also indicate
Daly's procedure in "writing" a play, a method which he had
pursued "of yore," probably with *Under the Gaslight, A
Flash of Lightning,* and *The Red Scarf.* The system was
simply that Augustin prepared an outline of the plot, a description of the characters, an indication of the necessary action—
a *scenario,* in his own words—and sent it to Joseph who did the
actual composing. Later letters show how disturbed Augustin
became when act three was delayed by a storm which severely
battered and delayed the mail boat from America. Mrs. Daly,
who joined him in London in the spring, herself brought over
the last act.

A further oddity about *The Undercurrent* adds proof to
the assertion that it was Joseph and not Augustin who wrote
the play. Several of the reviews of the piece suggest a resemblance between *The Undercurrent* and *The Two Orphans*
mainly because of the two half-sisters. In 1879, according to
letters exchanged between the two Daly brothers, Joseph
was working on an adaptation of the French play, which he
referred to as "The Ducks." The work could not be pro-

duced by Daly, however, because another American manager
had secured the rights in this country.

The fact that *The Undercurrent* is set in London, that it
combines many features of *Under the Gaslight* and his other
sensational melodramas, plus the admission of Daly that he
had originally worked on it in 1878—these facts lead to the
assumption that it was simply *A Stranger in London*, perhaps
revised. The peculiarity is not that Daly should have used
his old work, a practice common to all writers, but that he
should have produced the piece at Niblo's Garden rather
than at his own theater. The reason seems to be that he had
a successful play, *The Lottery of Love*, on the boards, and
had in preparation a revival of *The Inconstant* to follow.
Whatever the reason, *The Undercurrent* was first performed
at Niblo's Gardens and ran from November 13 to 24, 1888.

It is surprising that the play had such a short run, for the
reviews are uniformly flattering. They concede that the play
is simply a reworking of the older dramas. "Instead of treating
life in New York, the scenes are laid in London. Same ole
Snorkey is . . . Ryan, the messenger. . . . The two girls are
sisters; the villains scheme for the same end, but keep one
sister concealed in order that the other may enjoy a fortune
left the first one by her uncle." Old Judas has become Mother
Hundreds and Peachblossom is now "Silenah, a Castaway,"
but "the climaxes are much stronger, and follow each other
in rapid succession." As in *Under the Gaslight*, the one-
armed messenger (he is also one half-sister's father) is tied
to a railroad track by the villain (a wicked uncle), but the
scheme is foiled by the heroine, the daughter, who luckily
happens to be in a blacksmith shop nearby. The great pictorial
scene of the play is an "underground Italian den in Whitechapel." One reviewer indicates Daly's reason for choosing
this locale: "the recent events in that horrible spot where so
many women have been butchered make it seem more horrible." The reviews even stress that the play is "cleverly

written" and that the "curtain always falls on effective situations."

The scene in the All-night den in Whitechapel at the end of the second act, with the cleverly designed staircase by which the heroine, when almost breathing the air of freedom, is dropped back into the arms of her captors by a mechanical contrivance by which half the stairway falls to the floor, is most thrilling, as is the escape over the housetops, while the old *Under the Gaslight* railroad effect—that of the express apparently about to crush the life out of a human being—is as exciting as ever.

Never quite abandoning his penchant for the sensational after the successes of his initial melodramas, Daly also tried writing a play which combined spectacle and history. *Horizon* is probably his best known original dramatic effort. Like the rest of his works, it was in the main topical, designed both by content and theatricality to attract large popular audiences. It was "written, rehearsed, and produced" by Daly for his father-in-law, John Duff, at the Olympic Theatre.

Opening March 21, 1871, the play stands as one of the earliest and, up to its time, most important of our frontier dramas. Its pictures of the west, of the Indians, of contemporary politics and especially politicians, lend the piece interest which overcomes the inanities of its plot and many of its characterizations. Daly was thoroughly aware of his own intentions since he copyrighted the drama as "a play of contemporaneous events upon the borders of civilization."

The young playwright (he was thirty-three when he wrote *Horizon*) had become quite a figure in the theatrical world, and felt his responsibilities. Years later he was to write, "Possibly our national drama, from a literary point of view, will reach its best period when native writers vie with each other in illustrating native characters and contemporaneous fashions and follies." Certainly it must have been with some such intention in mind that he composed *Horizon*. He also realized that plays especially built around one character, "studies of native character—such as 'Solon Shingle,' 'Davy Crockett,' 'Colonel Sellers,' and so forth—have no literary value and serve no purpose in the structure of the national drama, because they perish with the actor who has given them substance." The correctness of his diagnosis here has been verified by time. He sought to avoid that danger by including many types in *Horizon*. Certainly the successful seven-week run of the play justified his efforts, for the piece was itself a pioneer in a pioneer field.

The play is set on the western plains, "pretty well out towards the *Horizon*." Fort Jackson, Rogue's Rest, the Big Run River, Dog's Ears, All Gone, Hollo Bill—these are the "queer names" by means of which the drama achieves local color. To these parts go the central characters of the story: Captain Alleyn Van Dorp, a West Point graduate and the adopted son of the wealthy, socially distinguished Mrs. Van Dorp; Sundown Rowse, Esq., a prominent man with influential Washington connections; Columbia Rowse, his daughter; and the Honorable Mr. Smith, a British subject. Alleyn's job is to fight the Indians and to afford protection for Mr. Rowse's land-grant, an area of some twenty thousand acres, subsidized by Congress for the Union Pacific Railroad. Before Alleyn can get into any real action, however, he falls in love with Med, "White Flower of the Plains." We realize that she is Mrs. Van Dorp's missing daughter, who was carried off years before by a drunken father. Miss Constance Rourke has pointed out, in *Troupers of the Gold Coast*, the similarity of this situation to the actual history of the actress, Lotta Crabtree; she also mentions that Lotta's starring vehicle, *Heartsease*, produced in Boston in May 1870, anticipates some of the effects and has some of the same characteristics as *Horizon*.

Rogue's Rest, at the moment of the arrival of Rowse's party, is undergoing one of those "changes of moral atmosphere" which Bret Harte has described in so many of his stories. Indeed, the situation in Act II of *Horizon* is so similar to that

in the opening of "The Outcasts of Poker Flat" that Daly's
originality at this point becomes completely suspect. John
Loder, "alias White Panther," is Harte's John Oakhurst,
gambler: a noble indifference to their doom is characteristic
of both. "Oakhurst received his sentence with philosophic
calmness. . . . He was too much of a gambler not to accept
Fate." And Loder says, "When Civilization steps in, it's time
for John Loder to make a move higher up. I mean to put for
some infant settlement nearer the Horizon." One remembers
Oakhurst's self-sacrifice at the conclusion of "The Outcasts of
Poker Flat," renouncing his food for the young Piney and
going off alone to take his life. Similarly, Loder surreptitiously
gives Wolf money, as Med says, "just when you saw my dress
was ragged, and my feet were almost on the ground." Although he loves Med, seeing her safely married to "some
young fellow who don't play cards" becomes Loder's aim in
life; after that is accomplished, he will "see them safe off and
blow my own worthless brains out comfortably." Loder
and Whiskey Wolf, a "boozer" (actually Wolf Van Dorp, and
a dead ringer for Harte's "Uncle Billy," sluice-robber and confirmed drunkard), are being run out of town with a Heathen
Chinee and an Indian, Wannemucka.

The plot is now complicated by Wannemucka. He is in love
with Med. To get her in his power, he kills her father, Wolf.
But then that nobleman of the West and of the card-table,
Loder, takes over as her protector; nor must we forget the
hovering Alleyn.

Two Indian raids are next presented on the stage and a third
is described as having occurred elsewhere. Each raid provides
a dramatic curtain for an act. The first takes place in a romantic
setting as a barge containing women and children is moving
downstream. The Indians reach the boat from the water and
from overhead trees; their attack is foiled by the appearance
of American soldiers. The second raid is made on the primitive
stockade while the troops are away. Even so, the white women

hold the savages at bay with guns until Wannemucka traps them by a ruse, pretending to be wounded.

The last act finds the women and Rowse as captives of the Indians. They are rescued, of course, by Loder, disguised as an Indian (a legitimate ruse), and by the American forces led by Alleyn. The final tableau, "a picture of triumph," presents Med in Alleyn's arms, Columbia in Mr. Smith's, and an assorted group of dead Indians lying under the feet of Rowse, Loder, and the soldiers.

Besides his obvious dependence upon the overwhelming popularity of Bret Harte's stories, Daly also leaned heavily upon the current events of the Indian wars for many details of his plot. From 1865 to 1870 there had been constant warfare against the Indians caught in a "gigantic vise" between the pushing Missouri and Pacific frontiers. By the close of the Civil War, there were over 25,000 American troops, similar to those described in *Horizon*, in the field. And although by 1871 there was some lull in the actual fighting, public interest in the West and in the Indian was at an all-time high. It was not until 1874 that Custer published his popular autobiography, *My Life in the Plains*, which was followed, in 1876, by his rival Nelson A. Miles's *Serving the Republic*. By his interest and presentation in 1871, therefore, Daly was actually anticipating along with Harte the great literary interest in the frontier which was finally chronicled and analyzed in Turner's remarkable study in 1893.

It is pertinent to point out that whereas literary historians and critics constantly refer to Edward Eggleston's novel *The Hoosier Schoolmaster* as one of the earliest attempts at a realistic depiction of the western frontier, they generally ignore the drama. Lucy Hazard's *The Frontier in American Literature*, for example, does not mention a single play. The date of *The Hoosier Schoolmaster*, 1871, is the same as that of *Horizon*. Just as much as Eggleston, Daly and other dramatists were incorporating what Jay B. Hubbell described as the "two distinct and important contributions of the frontier to our literature: a vast field of new materials, and a new point of view, American."

Daly's picture of the Indian is one of the most interesting in all dramatic literature. He had a large body of plays, and an even larger assortment of novels, from which to select his materials. His choice of characterization showed the Indian not in any one simple form, but in a variety; Wannemucka is tricky, deceitful, and lazy, yet he is also courageous, strong, and even poetic. The first discussion of the Indian occurs at Mrs. Van Dorp's New York mansion. Mr. Smith, the Englishman, is the first to speak: "Aw—yes—the noble savage. I'll speak to him as his paleface brother. I've read the Leatherstocking stories, and I think I can manage 'em."

Fresh from West Point and Washington, Alleyn takes an attitude that is typically Babbitt: "No quarter to the savages who murder women and children. But to the weak and oppressed, I may be a friend. Duty commands no more."

One must remember that his captaincy has been secured by Rowse as a political plum. That gentleman, a very successful lobbyist, has his own definite ideas about the Indian: "Well, I'm going to take a case of dollar store jewelry out with me, and trade it for furs with the simple-minded red man. There's nothing like carrying civilization into the Far West."

Already Daly has dealt with the conventional attitudes toward the Indian. The first actual encounter with an Indian shows us Wannemucka offering to play poker with Rowse for the latter's watch and chain. The politician is indignant:

Moses in the bulrushes! Who'd have thought of this romantic injun sporting a deck and offering to play poker? My feelings are hurt. If you had offered to scalp me, you red rascal, I might have forgiven you. But Poker! That knocks the romance, and I despise you.

Leatherstocking and Stone's Metamora are in Rowse's mind. He has read of Pocahontas and Hiawatha and finds the reality of Wannemucka disenchanting. Loder, however, is on hand to point the moral

> That's civilization, my friend! When the noble savage was in his native state, he went for the hair of your head. Now he's in the midst of civilization, he carries the weapons of enlightenment, and goes for the money in your pocket.

The Indian, in other words, is presented cynically, like those satirized by John Brougham, whose burlesques, *Metamora* (1847) and *Pocahontas; or, the Gentle Savage* (1855), are among the finest and most successful travesties to be found in the nineteenth-century theater.

Melodramatic demands also focus interest on the savage. At the conclusion of Act II, Wannemucka treacherously shoots Wolf from the rear, and Acts III and IV conclude with sensations in the form of brutal Indian attacks on unprotected women. Act IV continues the disillusionment; now it is Columbia who prates the following schoolgirl nonsense: "I used to think I'd like to have an Indian brave fall in love with me—so romantic," but, "I mean a real noble savage, not a dirty, common Indian." She also, it might be pointed out, prefers an Englishman with an "honorable" before his name to a common lobbyist and profiteer like her father. She too has a literary imagination, for the Indian of her dreams is "somebody like Fennimore [*sic*] Cooper's braves."

Daly's final picture of the Indian is basically poetic. Wahcotah has given Med a potion to make her appear ill, whereby she will not arouse the jealous Indian maidens to harm her. He describes her, saying, "The white maiden is as the leaf upon the ground—as the fallen rosebud." Daly is not only thinking of Hiawatha, he has almost used Longfellow's rhythm. Wannemucka is even more lyrical.

> As the roses on the stalk droop, when one of their number is plucked away, let the fair sisters of our tribe bewail her. She shall be laid under the prairie grass, where the wolf shall not find her, for her grave shall be deep as the red man's love.

Forgotten, for the moment, is the fact that he has tricked Med into her capture, and that he is tricking her "fair Indian sisters" into believing that she has died. Theatricality has the upper hand, as Daly introduces a "low chant" sung by Onata and the Indian girls:

> Let us speak of her:
>   She was white as the white snow,
> And her spirit went away
>   Under the breath of Manitou
> As snow flees before the sun.

The final picture of the Indian is the most typical of the times: "the good dead Indian" crushed beneath the triumphant feet of the American soldiers.

Daly added to the cast of *Horizon* no typical backwoodsman. Colonel Nimrod Wildfire, Buffalo Bill, Kit Redding, Nick of the Woods—these were the traditional frontiersmen of the drama. Instead, he drew a ridiculously comic figure, a satirical portrait of a lobbyist and crooked politician, Sundown Rowse, Esq., destined to become the forerunner of such stage notables as Bardwell Slotes, Colonel Sellers, and Silas K. Woolcott—yes, and even of Senator Claghorn. In answer to his mother's query, Alleyn defines a politician

> Why, they, let me see—they take care of the public's interests. You know the public interest must be cared for. The old adage is: "What's everybody's business is nobody's business." Now the politicians do everybody's business and account to nobody for the way they do it.

In the role of Sundown Rowse, George L. Fox created a great hit. Evidently his scenes with Notah, the papoose who became fond of him and trailed him everywhere, were hilariously funny.

Two other characters of some historical interest are introduced in *Horizon*. Cephas, "a Fifteenth Amendment," is a singing Negro, full of hearty good spirits. The Heathen

Chinee is, again, largely drawn from Harte; he is being deported from Rogue's Rest by the lazy, half-drunk Vigilante Committee because "he works for half-pay. Steals the bread out of honest men's mouths."

On the whole, the play was effective not only for its intrinsic merits but also because of its production and acting. One of its most exciting features was a panoramic background which moved to simulate a drifting boat. Agnes Ethel as Med, J. K. Mortimer as Loder, and Hart Conway as Alleyn headed an exceptionally fine cast. Critics Brander Matthews and Laurence Hutton, and such rival managers as A. M. Palmer, testify to the merit of the play on the stage.

It is curious in the light of its great success that the play has had practically no stage history. Contemporary reviews were generally commendatory. "*Horizon* will have a run," predicted one. "Its merits lie in its sketches of western character and the verisimilitude of its local scenery, and the general vivacity of its incidents. . . . If not equal as a drama to the author's previous plays, it is exciting and interesting, and will be one of the temporary theatrical sensations of the day." Its sensationalism was indeed "temporary," as there are no records of any performances after the initial run.

As a piece of literature, *Horizon* has fared somewhat better. It was privately printed in 1885, and was anthologized by Allan G. Halline in *American Plays* in 1935. In the introduction, Professor Halline indicates the importance of the play "by reason of its literary recognition of the frontier" and expresses his appreciation of the seriousness of Daly's attempt to represent the American scene in *Horizon*.

Since none of Daly's "spectacles" now exists, and no scripts are to be had, they must be dealt with conjecturally on the basis of playbills, reviews, and memoirs of various sorts. All of these plays were advertised as being "original." They all attempted to portray the low life of the times as the titles—

The Dark City, Round the Clock, Life!—would indicate. Although each had individualized characters, the plays were more collections of sketches, frequently with music, than they were actual dramas. After the overwhelming success of *The Black Crook* at Niblo's Garden, on September 12, 1866, revues of this kind had become more and more popular. Panoramic in their method and scope, they were mainly derivative in content. Indeed, Daly drew his ideas and even his dialogue from a multitude of sources, both foreign and domestic. Unless one could bring Parisian, London, and New York music halls back to life, it would be impossible to track down all these sources. It is sufficient to say that these revues were taken from the music hall successes and from the popular burlesques of the day. Brander Matthews condemned these "variety shows" as "purely sensational amusement for the unthinking." He did indicate, however, the importance of these productions as "a nursery for the actual theater" in which actors and playwrights had an opportunity for experience, and he expressed the hope that these artists would "later outgrow the limitations" of the form.

Daly wrote, or adapted, these spectacles primarily to get audiences into his theater. The success of *The Black Crook* had been a lesson in finance to the New York managers. *Round the Clock; or, New York by Dark*, a "local sensational folly in 4 acts and 12 tableaux," was partly based on *La Tour du Cadran*, a vaudeville by Hector Cremieux and Henri Bocage. This vaudeville's viability is attested to by Henry B. Smith in *First Nights and First Editions*, where he relates in 1914 Charles Dillingham gave him an old play to "convert into a new musical entertainment." The piece, called by Smith *Watch Your Step*, with music and lyrics by Irving Berlin, was derived from this same French vaudeville. *Round the Clock* was produced at the Grand Opera House on November 25, 1872, and ran until January 30, 1873. The playbills for that theater the week of January 14, 1873 carry the information that

Round the Clock, referred to as "the most original piece done here for 30 years, brought in one week more money to the theatre than any drama ever before given in this country— that is to say, during the first week of its production, eight performances were given, and the receipts actually reached within a fraction of $19,000."

The contents of the piece and its significance in depicting the New York scene are well brought out in an unidentified review:

A new piece, taken from the French, but extensively altered and localized. . . . Augustin Daly is to be credited with an adaptation which, whatever else may be said of it, includes a great deal of variety. The traditions of "Tom and Jerry" and other choice dramatic translations of "life in town" are liberally drawn on . . . and it is furthermore backed up by an immense diversity in the way of fun and extravagance, marvels, radiant dresses, and pretty scenes. The latter are chiefly pictures of well-known buildings, and places in New York, and are to be praised for fidelity. . . .

One amusing incident relating to the production of *Round the Clock* deserves mention in a theatrical history. Harry Hill, whose combination saloon and dance hall was featured in the presentation, wrote Daly a letter of complaint stating that the representation of his place was not exact. Learning of a revival to be given in 1874, he wrote a second note in which he expressed the "hope that you will improve my place." A third and last revival was in February of 1877 at the Grand Opera House.

Daly opened his new Fifth Avenue Theatre on January 21, 1873, with *Alixe.* The second production, *Roughing It!,* a month later was another of Daly's "original spectacles." Labeled "a dramatic kaleidoscope in four acts and ten tableaux," it, too, was founded on a popular Parisian revue and was "embellished with some of the experiences of Mr. Mark Twain." The piece was distinguished mainly by the presence of the charming Mrs. John Wood in the cast; she played the role of Antoinette McDuffie, "a young lady who carried along a life-sized portrait of her mother, frame and all, when she eloped with a mild young man."

The Dark City and its Bright Side opened the fifth season at the Fifth Avenue Theatre on September 4, 1877; two weeks later, Daly closed the play and gave up the management. It was the last of those spectacular dramas which Daly produced.

Again, as in the case of *A Stranger in London*, there is a series of letters which shows that Joseph Daly was largely responsible for the actual script of the play. Much of the correspondence concerns the casting of the piece. The brothers were especially anxious about Ada Dyas, the English star, James Lewis, who was inclined to be temperamental about his roles, and Emily Rigl, who had just come up from the chorus of *The Black Crook*. Parts were altered and constantly being tailored to suit the player; this practice was a confirmed Daly technique.

Originally the revue was to have been called *Our City*, but Augustin received a letter from "a young lady by the name of Walsh . . . that she writ a play in 1870, called it 'Our City' & it was acted at the Bowery Theatre. . . . And though she is not certain whether *my play* is her play, she *is* certain that her title shall not be mine, so I'd better etc., or she'll etc. etc. etc." Daly, wise in the way of lawsuits, did change the title and heeded Joseph's advice to conduct an advertising campaign to announce the change; further, it was Joseph who recommended the subtitle, "And its bright side," to "relieve the play from any lugubriousness its title may suggest." Daly's play was not based on Miss Walsh's, but it was founded on a French drama, *Les Compagnons de la Truelle* by Theodore Cogniard and Louis Francois Clairville (L. F. Nicolaie).

The plot of this "entirely new drama," as the playbill called it, is the same old story of two half-sisters, one the rightful heiress, separated and ruthlessly victimized by a wicked uncle, who has come into the family fortune by burning up a will—actually the charred paper is still in the chimney. The plot, therefore, is reminiscent of *Under the Gaslight* and anticipates *The Undercurrent;* one of the chief characters, Mother Hundreds, has the same name and the same function in both *The Dark City* and *The Undercurrent.* "To see one of his plays is to obtain an idea of them all," commented one reviewer; "they are all 'frothy,' without the necessary element of solidity." All reviewers alike complained about the unnecessarily complicated plot. "Each spasm or act closes with a bouncing sensation, such as the concealing of a stolen will, or an attempted murder or a suicide; and when art and crime can do nothing further to excite us, nature steps in with apoplexy and fits."

Only William Winter, of all the critics, found some justification for the play, which on opening night ran until one A.M. He begins his review by stating that "truth compels the remark that the play was not received with the usual eclat," but he attributes that "to an oversight on the part of the gifted author in endeavoring to avail himself of too much material." Winter then weasels out of any comment on the plot because "the lateness of the hour prevents an analysis of the theme." However, "it would be unjust to the author to comment too severely upon the manifest faults of the performance until he has had further time to correct his . . . errors of judgment." Why, one asks, should the manager of a New York theater be allowed "time to correct his errors of judgment"? The answer, of course, is that Winter was friend first and critic second. His obvious bias in Daly's favor was the result of intimate acquaintance, of travels together, even of loans of money, rendering him an inadequate reviewer of Daly's plays for all of which he expressed indiscriminate admiration or feeble excuses.

The other critics did agree with Winter in admiring the sets. Not a single review failed to comment upon the effectiveness of scenes of Newspaper Row, City Hall Park, Jefferson Market, and the East River Bridge. These spectacular accents were the only commendable feature of the production. "Whatever merit may be about last night's performance is due to the scene painters and actors." The cast included Maurice Barrymore, John Drew, William Davidge, and Mrs. G. H. Gilbert in addition to the already mentioned Ada Dyas, Emily Rigl, and James Lewis. "The author of the play can claim no share in it."

These spectacular plays, featuring melodramatic scenes strung together on the thinnest of plots, add nothing to Daly's stature as a playwright, and of course he probably wrote only the scenarios anyhow; they show him to have been a producer rather than an author; they indicate that he knew how to stage a play effectively, or he knew what people to secure to do that job for him.

In sum, one must acknowledge that as a writer of original plays, Daly created little, if anything, that was either good or new. These plays are significant by virtue of their use of realistic scenes and because of their popularity; the length of run, which was not long by present standards but impressive in their period, and the number of revivals are the basis of judgment. On the debit side, they helped prolong the reign of melodrama on the American stage. The research revealing that Daly probably did not write these plays does not so much lessen his stature, which has always been based more upon his productions than upon his writings, as serve to illustrate the prevailing method of playwriting in America at the time. Most of our dramas were adaptations or revisions, and originality in the modern sense was an unnecessary qualification for success. The theater was slowly emerging into a new world—the world of Ibsen, Shaw, and O'Neill. Daly's work helped to establish a theater and audiences which these writers could utilize.

CHAPTER 3

Ten Steps to Fame:
Dramatizations

There was a literary gentleman present who had dramatized in his time 247 novels as fast as they had come out—some of them faster than they had come out—and who was a literary gentleman in consequence.

"When I dramatize a book, sir," said the literary gentleman, "that's fame. For its author."

Dickens, *Nicholas Nickleby*

Playwrights have always been attracted by the dramatic possibilities of stories and novels and have successfully adapted them to the stage. Yet only in modern times has the troublesome question of plagiarism been raised. Copyright laws, especially international regulations, are devices of recent vintage. Certainly, in periods when dramas themselves were literally stolen from their authors for re-use, concern for the rights of storytellers was unknown.

In adapting some ten novels for the stage, Daly did as many a successful playwright before him. In England, Dickens and Scott had constantly been ransacked and in this country Cooper and Irving were hardly less pillaged. There are over twenty known dramatic versions of *The Bride of Lammermoor, Ivanhoe,* and *Kenilworth,* and over a dozen adaptations of *Guy Mannering* and *The Heart of Midlothian.* Dickens was subjected to the same "borrowing"; indeed, his

influence on the Victorian drama, as Fitz-Gerald has remarked in *Dickens and the Drama,* can scarcely be overestimated. A new novel by Dickens was eagerly seized upon
and old ones redramatized constantly. By 1886, there were
nine known adaptations of *Pickwick Papers* and at least eight
versions of *Bleak House.* Some adaptors even went back to
scavenge the works of eighteenth-century writers, but in
general it was the contemporary novelists whose plots and
characters dominated the stage.

In America the practice of dramatization had early become entrenched. Our first playwrights were vigorous
adaptors of novels. "The task of compressing Tales of three
volumes into Plays of three Acts is one of merely technical
and mechanical drudgery," wrote one successful though
anonymous adaptor. William Charles White's *The Clergy-
man's Daughter,* which opened the year 1810 at the Federal Street Theatre in Boston, was based on Henry Mc-
Kenzie's *The Man of the World* and *The Poor Lodger* at the
same theater in December of 1810 was taken from Fanny
Burney's *Evelina.* Such a well-known dramatist as William Dunlap based his *Fontainville Abbey,* which played the
John Street Theatre beginning September 16, 1795, on Mrs.
Ann Radcliffe's *Romance of the Forest;* his *The Father; or,
American Shandyism,* at the same theater six years earlier, was
based in part on Laurence Sterne's *Tristram Shandy.* And
James Nelson Barker took *The Court of Love,* produced at
the Arch Street Theatre in Philadelphia on March 26, 1836,
from Pigault-Lebrun's *La Folie Espagnole.* Barker also arranged a very successful version of *Marmion* at the Park
Street Theatre, April 13, 1812, which held the stage as late
as 1848 and was twice printed, in 1816 and in 1826.

Two successful mid-nineteenth-century adaptations radically affected the history of the American stage: *Uncle Tom's
Cabin* and *Rip Van Winkle.* Mrs. Stowe's novel was presented in some seven versions within two years of its publi-

cation in 1852. One of these, by George L. Aiken, had over
two hundred performances within that time. Washington
Irving's short story from *The Sketch-Book* got off to a
slower start, the first dramatization coming in 1828, nine
years after its publication, but the fifth treatment, by
Boucicault and Jefferson (Adelphi Theatre, London, September 4, 1865; Olympic Theatre, September 3, 1866), was
produced with continuing success into the twentieth century.

The extensiveness of the practice of adaptation can be
measured by the successful dramatizations of Daly's most
prolific contemporary, actor-manager-dramatist Dion Boucicault. In addition to *Rip Van Winkle* there were: *Dot*, from
Dickens' *The Cricket on the Hearth; Smike* from *Nicholas
Nickleby; Jeanie Deans* from *The Heart of Midlothian;* all
in the winter of 1859–1860. *Clarissa Harlowe*, eighteen years
later; *Cuisla-Ma-Chree* from *Guy Mannering* ten years after
that, and possibly his two finest plays, *The Octaroon* in 1859
taken from Mayne Reid's *The Quadroon* and Albany Fon-
blanque's *The Filibuster*, and *The Colleen Bawn* in 1860 from
Gerald Griffin's *The Collegians. The Colleen Bawn* ran for
over three hundred and sixty nights in London. Indeed, as one
scholar has said, "Boucicault levied on this writer or that.
He took a lease of Scott and Dumas père. . . . He treated these
authors precisely as people treat a house they rent furnished."

Many adaptations were slavish and less imaginative than
those of Daly or Boucicault, yet they greatly influenced the
stage of the first half of the nineteenth century. Love of
exaggeration in character and incident and fascination for
breath-taking exploits—one thinks of *The Count of Monte
Cristo*, for example—were keeping alive the melodramatic
tradition. Spectacles crowded the stage. Dramatizations
often consisted of stringing together exciting episodes from
current novels, with little concern for realistic characterization or logical sequence. In the later half of the century
fiction itself was developing a different style, evident at any

rate in those stories seized upon by the playwright. In the words of Professor Nicoll, "Love of incident and grotesque characterization had appeared in the past; now a deeper psychological note and a franker treatment of intimate domestic life became the fashion." Ibsen and James Herne were on the horizon.

Certainly it was to novels of deeper psychological insight and of more concern for the problems of domestic life, however faulty they may have been as works of art, that Augustin Daly turned when he undertook the dramatization of novels early in his career. In his struggle for fame, the youthful playwright was here taking the easiest course, the creation of plays based upon someone else's plot and characters. That he honestly endeavored to preserve the original character of the novels is greatly to his credit, and more to be admired than the usual practice of lifting only the more flamboyant dramatic incidents. That he took the novels and added to them scenes, incidents, and characters from contemporary life must also be viewed as a step toward creative playwriting. Joseph Daly regarded their joint dramatizations as "original" plays, for he wrote Augustin on June 28, 1887, "I include dramatizations of novels as original plays because novels & plays are essentially and radically different literary achievements. The only thing they can have in common is a story. The plot has to be changed—the incidents altered—etc. etc."

The complete list of Daly's adaptations from novels includes ten titles, with the date of first performance as follows:

Griffith Gaunt; or, Jealousy from Charles Reade's novel, New York Theatre, November 7, 1866.

A Legend of Norwood; or, Village Life in New England from Henry Ward Beecher's novel, Worrell Sisters' Theatre (New York Theatre), November 11, 1867.

Pickwick Papers, from Dickens, Worrell Sisters' Theatre, January 22, 1868.

Man and Wife from Wilkie Collins' novel, Fifth Avenue Theatre, September 13, 1870.

No Name from Wilkie Collins' novel, Fifth Avenue Theatre, June 7, 1871.

Divorce from Anthony Trollope's *He Knew He Was Right,* Fifth Avenue Theatre, September 9, 1871.

Oliver Twist, from Dickens, Fifth Avenue Theatre, June 3, 1874.

What Should She Do?; or, Jealousy, dramatization of Edmond About's *Germaine,* Daly's Fifth Avenue Theatre, August 25, 1874.

Pique from Florence Marryat Lean's *Her Lord and Master,* Daly's Fifth Avenue Theatre, December 14, 1875.

L'Assommoir from Emile Zola's novel, Olympic Theatre, April 30, 1879.

Griffith Gaunt, a dramatization of Charles Reade's novel which Daly completed in a week for Mark Smith and Lewis Baker, was presented at the New York Theatre, a converted church on lower Broadway, on November 7, 1866. The original production starred Rose Eytinge, whose services Daly borrowed from Lester Wallack, and John K. Mortimer. It ran for six weeks, the last night being Daly's benefit. Six days after the benefit, this same five-act version was produced at the New Bowery Theatre and was to have been repeated but the theater burned to the ground on the afternoon of the next day. Within a month of its New York première, the piece was also being produced in Boston. Daly's version played a week after another *Griffith Gaunt* there, and the *Traveller* compared the two:

One week ago today in speaking of the dramatic version of "Griffith Gaunt" at the Museum, we said it was the "worst dramatization of any book we ever remember to have seen." We had not then witnessed Mr. A. J. Daly's version; but after having seen it at the Boston Theatre last night, we must in candor admit that the production of Mr. Schonberg at the Museum is, in every respect, incomparably superior. . . . Any person who had read the novel . . . would meet with nothing but a sad disappointment.

Other performances of the Daly adaptation occurred while it was enjoying its initial New York run, on December 3, at

Wall's Opera House and on December 10, at Mr. and Mrs.
Conway's Park Theatre, Brooklyn. The many productions
so close together, even simultaneous, show the prevailing
situation: *popular* novels were quickly dramatized. Three
years later on April 14, the play was presented at the Théâtre
Français as a benefit for the widow and children of Humphrey
Bland, the original Squire Peyton. With John K. Mortimer
in his original title part, the play was produced on November
12, 1873 by Mr. George B. Waldron's company at the
Denver (Colorado) Theatre. The production was rated by
reviewers as "fine," but they note that because of the de-
pression of that year it drew only small audiences.

Besides the version by Schonberg which preceded Daly's
in Boston, a third adaptation, perhaps by George Aiken, was
presented at Niblo's Garden on August 11, 1874, eight years
later, but was not successful. The novel continued to tempt
playwrights as late as 1908, when Freeman Wills and the
Reverend Canon Langbridge had a version of it produced
at the Theatre Royal, Margate, on October 19.

The initial performance of Daly's *Griffith Gaunt* in 1866
antedates Reade's own dramatization by five years. Actually,
the author of the novel wrote three dramatic versions of his
own; the first was called *Griffith Gaunt* and played at the
Leicester Theatre, London, October 9, 1871; the second,
entitled *Kate Peyton's Lovers*, starred Ellen Terry and
Charles Kelly at the Queen's Theatre, London, December 20,
1873; and the third, *Jealousy*, opened at the Olympic Theatre,
London, April 22, 1878. This third version was a revision of
the second, and was printed five years after being performed.
The novel originally appeared serially in both *The Argosy*
and *The Atlantic Monthly* December 1865 through the following November and occasioned some bitter comment.
It was generally well-received in England and praised by
Swinburne and Dickens but in the United States it was
strongly attacked as "indecent." The attack led Reade to bring

suit against the New York weekly, *The Round Table*, for libel. He won his suit and was awarded a judgment of sixpence. He brilliantly defended himself and his position in a pamphlet, "The Prurient Prude."

The story, set in the eighteenth century, deals with an involved case of bigamy committed "under a delusion," and consequently not to be judged according to ordinary standards. Although called *Griffith Gaunt*, the novel actually centers around high-born, high-strung Kate Peyton, the daughter of an impoverished Squire. She is sought in marriage by two gentlemen: Sir George Neville, the more prepossessing, is an aristocrat and extensive landowner, and his case is sponsored by Squire Peyton; Griffith Gaunt is a more primitively emotional type, and a Protestant, while Kate and Neville are Catholics; Neville is presumably the heir to the estate of Bolton Hall.

In quick succession two events occur: a duel between the lovers, which Kate dramatically breaks up, and the death of the owner of Bolton Hall, who leaves the estate to Kate. Like Candida she chooses the weaker man. Her choice is also prompted by Father Francis, her confessor, who tells her that Griffith needs a good Catholic wife. Kate's devotion to the Church and to Father Francis' successor, the young, dynamic, and handsome Brother Leonard, gradually breaks up her marriage. In a burst of madness and jealousy, Griffith beats up Brother Leonard and departs.

Some time later, Griffith, through the tender nursing of Mercy Vint, recovers from a kind of brain fever at her father's inn, The Pack Horse. He falls in love with Mercy's sweet nature and marries her, assuming the name of Tom Leicester, his illegitimate half-brother, rather than lose her to her rural swain. Later he returns to Kate but only to secure money; though they are temporarily reconciled, she learns of his duplicity and threatens exposure unless he makes amends. Again he departs. And at this moment, a pistol shot and a cry of murder are heard. Some days later, a disfigured body, believed to be Griffith's, is found in the pond.

Meanwhile, Griffith though absent has inherited a large estate. In order to settle the legalities connected with the inheritance, Mr. Atkins, the agent, persists in finding Griffith, whereupon Kate is accused of murdering him and is put on trial for her life. Her self-defense (she is not allowed counsel) is a magnificent piece of courtroom drama. She is on the verge of being convicted when Mercy and her baby arrive with a letter from Griffith which saves Kate's life; this act of Mercy's prompts a warm friendship between the two women. Mercy's baby conveniently dies, and she then marries Neville. Kate and Griffith are eventually reconciled, and the novel ends with an account of the good deeds, especially for abandoned girls, accomplished by Lady Neville and Mrs. Gaunt.

The theater must be more succinct than a novel. Daly's version tightens up the rather rambling structure of the original. Yet in a play of five acts, with a large cast of twenty-seven, Daly has left out remarkably little of the vital action and none of the important characters. Strangely enough, he omits the greater part of the effective courtroom scene. The play also eliminates, as a concession to the conventions of the time, the fact that Griffith lives with Mercy and has a child by her; the stage Griffith leaves Mercy immediately after their wedding. However Daly uses Reade's lines wherever possible, even where scenes seem undramatic as a consequence.

Daly has added to his play a county fair in Act III which has no place in the novel but which provides him with a spectacle, and makes for a good show, as it allows the real Tom Leicester to confront Mercy in her wedding dress. Much of the final action of the novel is merely summarized in the play, and since the resolution must come in the last act, Griffith is forced to appear at the trial; this is probably the reason for Daly's cutting short Kate's defense. The reconciliation takes place in the courtroom and no marriage between Mercy and Neville takes place or is even indicated. As for changes in the characters, Mr. Atkins, the agent, is omitted, Jane Banister, the cook, becomes Jane Frost, and some six or seven rather flamboyant persons are introduced to act in the Fair scene.

The most striking effect of the play is its succession of dramatically exciting curtains: Act I ends with Griffith's proposal of marriage, taken from the novel; Act II ends with the fight between Griffith and Leonard, and Kate in despair; at the conclusion of Act III, Griffith tells Mercy of his bigamy and she faints; the cry of murder! rings out at the end of Act IV as Kate faints away; and the final curtain falls upon the courtroom scene with Kate saved and Griffith begging for forgiveness.

Rose Eytinge created a sensation in the part of Kate Peyton. The *Times* review said she "plays the part to perfection. . . . We have long considered Miss Eytinge the leading actress on the American stage, and our readers will share the opinion with us after witnessing her performance of the difficult, and, in some respects, embarrassing *role* of *Kate Peyton.*" Even though the play toned down some of the parts to which the critics of the novel objected, nevertheless a degree of courage was required on the part of producers and author even to tackle such a theme. Its success would seem to have justified their efforts though both play and novel have since been shelved.

A clever satire of the novel, *Liffith Lank; or, Lunacy,* appeared in the New York *Times* and was afterwards published by Charles H. Webb in the same year as the dramatization, 1866. The appearance of the parody, which ran to at least three editions, further demonstrates the popularity of the novel and the dramatization.

With his next dramatization, of Henry Ward Beecher's

A Legend of Norwood; or, Village Life in New England,
Daly turned to the native scene as he had in *Under the Gaslight.* The novel had originally been commissioned by Robert
Bonner, editor of *The New York Ledger,* who seduced
Beecher into writing it, his only fiction, by the generous
offer of $24,000. The novel ran serially in *The Ledger,*
and afterward appeared in book form in 1867.

The significance of the novel lies in its treatment of the
Civil War, for it is one of the first serious works of fiction
to deal with the struggle. As James Truslow Adams and
others have pointed out, few of the major literary figures
of America, with the notable exception of Whitman, were
stirred to great output by the war. We have little or nothing
relating to the war and its attendant problems from Thoreau,
who died in 1862, Hawthorne, who died in 1864, Longfellow,
Holmes, Melville, Howells, or Twain, who went to Hawaii.
Whittier and Lowell wrote on the war but produced inferior
work. Only a handful of minor writers—Henry H. Brownell,
E. C. Stedman, G. H. Boker—were successful with war literature.

In drama as well as fiction, there were few good writings
dealing with the war. In his survey of native American plays
to 1870, Perley Reed has made some interesting observations
about Civil War dramatic literature which might be summarized here. He notes that the Roden bibliography mentions
fifty plays of the Civil War decade (1860–1870); not more
than one-third of these significantly reflect American life.
Realistic characters occur in the pieces that treat American
history, political and social questions, and situations arising
from the Civil War, and are only significant in the war plays.
Political and fashionable characters are somewhat the more
numerous. Noting that this is a period of transition and
comparative inactivity in American drama, he concludes that
the decade of the Civil War contributed little of permanence
to native drama.

The truth is that the influence of the theatre was away from realism, and our accepted masters were Kotzebue, Scribe, and Sardou. During the same years also the declamatory school of acting held sway: Cooper, Kean, Macready, Forrest, the Booths, Davenport. These influences tend to suppress realism. The strongest plays were usually the least realistic.

A Legend of Norwood was one of the number that did treat the Civil War; in addition to this fact, and to the political and social prominence of Beecher, according to Rebecca Washington Smith it deserves at least historical fame for beginning the "Lincoln legend in fiction." Daly however omits the scene in which Agate Bissell goes to see Lincoln; Lincoln arranges that her ideas on hospitalization shall take precedence over the stupid bungling of the military system. Lincoln is presented as saintly and calm, with an amazing insight into people and events and the ability to act with courage and dispatch in pressing situations.

The novel opens with a discussion of the charms of a New England village, Norwood. Here we meet the villagers, all sterling, God-fearing people; the only vices among them seem to be gossiping and the tendency of a few to drink. The search for a true religion is carried on endlessly in long discussions beneath Dr. Wentworth's favorite elm. It is a leisurely written novel, with many long passages of description and of philosophy; indeed, one chapter (xxi) is labeled "Mental Philosophy" and the author indicates that it may be read or skipped according to the reader's inclinations. As would be expected, Beecher states in the preface that as he has "the habit of looking upon men as the children of God and heirs of immortality," he can "hardly fail to clothe the simplest and most common elements of daily life with importance and even with dignity." These "simple and common elements of daily life," such as nutting parties and other seasonal activities and church-going and conversation, form the basis of the uncomplicated plot. Beecher's one-time friend and associate, Theodore Tilton, wrote that "Mr.

Beecher had sufficiently atoned for the dramatic character of his sermons by the sermonic quality of his novel." And Beecher himself laughed, "People used to accuse me of being the author of 'Uncle Tom's Cabin'—until I wrote 'Norwood.'"

The story deals with Barton and Alice Cathcart, the simple but intelligent brother and sister who grow up on a farm near Norwood, and with Rose Wentworth, the charming, cultured daughter of the town's doctor and leading citizen. Barton loves Rose; Rose loves Barton. But Beecher forces them to endure many a heartache and even a war before they can enjoy their "boy meets girl, boy loses girl, boy gets girl" romance. Rose is also loved by Tom Heywood, a Southerner; he is, in turn, loved by Alice, but she does not declare her passion until she weeps it out over his dead body on the battlefield at Gettysburg, after which she dedicates her life to teaching in the South. Another of Rose's admirers is Frank Esel, a Boston painter, whose presence allows Beecher to dilate at some length on art and its purpose. But the most extensive digressions deal with the North-South relationships and the conduct of the war. Heywood's return to Charleston on the eve of the conflict enables Beecher to discuss, in calm and considered terms, the various causes of the war and allows him to show that hot-headed passion and pride actually precipitated the conflict. The author relates at length the arguments for states' rights which were the basic issues. And actually we see the war undertaken reluctantly by both North and South. Several battles are analyzed and Gettysburg is completely detailed, both from the military point of view and in terms of the plot. For Barton Cathcart, now a General, is wounded there; Tom Heywood, the Southerner, is killed; and Alice, Rose, and Agate Bissell, their companion, are prominent participants as nurses. The novel ends with marriages all around, a chapter or two upon the goodness and dignity of the Quakers, who have nursed Barton, and a tribute to the heroism of the doctors and nurses who deserve "testimonies of a nation's gratitude." The actual conclusion is quiet and personal.

The people are dispersing. The sun is just setting. Some linger and seem reluctant to leave. If you, too, reader, linger and feel reluctant to leave Norwood, I shall be rejoiced and repaid for the long way over which I have led you.

In making his adaptation Daly worked from advance copies of the serial supplied by Editor Bonner. He had secured the permission of Henry Ward Beecher by means of a letter designed to arouse Beecher's interests and sympathies, and, incidentally, incorporating some of Daly's sincerest ideas about the place of the stage in our national life.

New York, July 3, 1867

Henry Ward Beecher:

Dear Sir:

I have been so much impressed with the remarkable faithfulness to the calm poetry of New England life which emphasizes your story of "Norwood," that I feel a great desire to represent, as far as the dramatic art may help me to do so, some of the pictures that you have created. I have spoken with Mr. Joseph Howard, Jr., of this desire, and he feels confident that you will not withhold your consent. I shall liberally avail myself of Mr. Howard's intimate knowledge of your tastes to produce a faithful reflection of your beautiful story, that we may teach to that great audience which reads only with its ears the royal truths that you have uttered through the entertaining personages of "Norwood." Where the work is done in the proper spirit, the dramatist must always assist the moralist rather than otherwise; and that which is strongly good and really pure—as the lessons of "Norwood" certainly are—must always exert an elevating influence, whether given forth from the newspapers or the stage.

Very respectfully,

Augustin Daly

This dramatization from advance copies, agreed to by Robert Bonner to give Daly "a decided advantage over any party," was not an innovation. Allardyce Nicoll quotes a passage from an anonymous skit, *The Civil War of Poetry* (Olympic Theatre, London, 1846), which indicates that the financially crafty Dickens sold his novels in manuscript form to adaptors, although he wrote some bitter words about the practice in *Nicholas Nickleby*. In America, F. C. Wemyss reports in his *Life* that he secured a copy of Cooper's *The Red Rover* from Carey and Lea in advance of publication and gave it to S. H. Chapman to dramatize.

Daly's version of *Norwood* was in four acts, each of which concluded with a tableau. He utilized all of Beecher's slender plot, leaving out only the long philosophic and political passages. The tableaux show best the progress of the action: Act I, The Nutting Party; Act II, Departure of the Volunteers; Act III, Died on the Field of Battle; Act IV, The Return of the Veterans. The climax in Act III showing the Battle of Gettysburg was effective and rather dramatic and the picture of the battlefield has vigor even if it tends to be somewhat conventional. The description of the scene shows great attention to the total visual effect.

A portion of the field of Gettysburg before last day's battle. The hour is supposed to be about midnight. The curtain rises upon a Tableau. At the back in perspective is seen a disordered field, illuminated in a ghastly manner by the last rays of the moon, which is about setting. On mounds and hillocks are seen dismounted cannon, dead horses, broken wagon-wheels, etc. Tents here and there, from which faint lights are seen. Sentries are leaning on their guns.

Inasmuch as Daly made the adaptation for the three Worrell sisters, who had taken over and renamed the New York Theatre, parts had to be provided for all. Sophie played Rose Wentworth and Irene was Alice Cathcart. For the youngest sister, Jennie, Daly elaborated a character merely suggested in the novel, the Hardscrabble Boy, in which part she achieved the only success of the play. Beecher had indicated that Hardscrabble was a poor farming suburb of Norwood. Daly introduced the Hardscrabble Boy as a character who makes up for the deficiencies of his background by his enthusiasms and who, contrary to the others from his district who are antiwar, volunteers eagerly as a drummer-boy. The part was conceived and played with sufficient sentimental appeal to make it popular.

The dramatization, according to Miss Sturtevant, who edited the volume of Daly's plays in The America's Lost Plays Series, was by Daly and Joseph Howard, Jr. The newspaper critic Hagan also considered both men to have had a hand in the play since his review of the piece refers to the "dramatists" and to "their ability." And Dithmar, who wrote the official *Memories of Daly's Theatres* for Daly, indicated that the "ephemeral glory" of *Norwood* was "shared" by Daly with Joseph W. Howard, Jr. Yet the published version of the play, "printed for the author, 1867," contains only the name of Augustin Daly. From our knowledge of the practices of Daly, it is altogether possible that he had the assistance of Mr. Howard in the preparation of the drama.

The play was produced on November 11, 1867, at the Worrell Sisters' Theatre and ran until December 4, although Judge Daly states that "the dramatization was no better than the novel." Hagan justifies this by stating that the story was "one well suited to dramatic representation," and adds that the "work was evidently induced by the expectation of Mr. Beecher's name alone proving a power of attraction. . . . It was very fairly put upon the stage and commendably acted, but was neither coherent, exciting, nor brilliant in any sense."

"Mr. Beecher's name alone" did provide some of the expected reaction. In his biography of the preacher, Howard indicates that there was a "storm of indignation" against Beecher for his presumed connections with the "immoral" stage. Actually, Mr. Beecher never saw the play of "Norwood" on the boards, but it was read very carefully to him, and he said he saw nothing objectionable about it whatever, and sincerely trusted it would make a success for the dramatist's sake. Mr. Daly expended a great deal of money on it, and procured the services of the best actors he could find; but, as he subsequently said, the country was hardly yet prepared for a war play. The general upheaval had not subsided; passion was not yet gone; bereavements and losses were yet too sacred, and after a brief season the play was withdrawn.

Certainly, neither Beecher nor Daly was averse to the publicity attendant upon the presentation. Paxton Hibben has pointed out that the dramatization proved "good advertising" for Beecher. And the shrewd Joseph Daly in a letter to his brother indicated that the newspapers will "of course" make the piece a "Go." They won't let it "die"; their abuse will make it into a "matter of importance."

The twenty-four-day run of the piece plus a brief production at the Academy of Music, Brooklyn, do not substantiate Joseph's prediction. There is no further dramatic history of the play. Tompkins reports that "H. W. Beecher's drama, 'Norwood,' had a single representation" at the Boston Theatre, January 25, 1868. By "Beecher's drama" he must, in all probability, have meant Daly's version of the novel.

An anonymously written parody, *Gnaw-wood: or New England Life in a Village*, by "Henry W. B. Cher," was published some time after the dramatization; it contains the following sentence in the Preface:

I do not pretend to write as well as Wordsworth, or Tupper, or Crabbe, or Augustin Daily, or Artemus Ward, or Dickens, or Fanny Fern, nevertheless I'm some on a story, as well as on a sermon, at least Bonheur thinks so, he likes my style, "he pays his money and he takes his choice."

The burlesque is a rather clever slapstick version of the novel. A dramatic parody, written by that versatile journalist, Joseph Howard, Jr., was also presented, at Hooley's, a house

of minstrelsy, in Brooklyn; it featured the well-known actor
George Christy in the role of Pete.

The relative unpopularity of *Norwood* did not deter Daly
from making another adaptation for the Worrell sisters. On
January 22, 1868, they produced his version of *Pickwick
Papers.* The production, which ran only through the week
of February 3, was, according to Hagan, "very amusing and
pleased greatly." Only one of the famed sisters, Jennie, the
erstwhile "Hardscrabble Boy," appeared in this play, this
time essaying the minor role of Mary, the housemaid. Other
players of some reputation, however, were cast in the four-
act adaptation including the famous C. T. Parsloe as Sam
Weller, Celia Logan as Arabella Allen, J. B. Studley as Jingle,
and H. C. Ryner as Pickwick. The play marked the first
stage appearance of William Carleton, as Winkle.

The playbill shows that the work contained twelve scenes,
featured the Bardell *vs.* Pickwick trial and Bob Sawyer's
party, and ended with the "Christmas Festivities on Ice at
Dingley Dell." Hagan has indicated that the adaptation was
by Daly, and added that "the piece contained a great deal
that Dickens never wrote."

In the case of *Pickwick Papers,* as with *Norwood* and
Griffith Gaunt, Daly and his producers depended largely
upon the popularity of the novelist and the novel for the
success of the piece. Especially is this true of *Pickwick Papers*
inasmuch as Dickens was at the time enjoying a tremendous
vogue in this country as a reader and earning substantial
sums of money for public appearances. Daly and company
evidently hoped to cash in on some of this popularity.
Wallack had done the same thing; aroused by the renewed
interest in Dickens, he presented *Oliver Twist* on December
27, 1867, with James W. Wallack, E. L. Davenport, and
Rose Eytinge in the cast. Odell reports that the two-week
run was "immensely successful." It is strange that Dickens,
a devotee of the theater, should not have specifically men-

tioned these productions, but in his letters he did remark on the state of the drama in the United States. "At the other Theatres," he wrote (*The Black Crook* had been playing at Niblo's for sixteen months), "comic operas, melodramas, and domestic drama prevail all over the city and my stories play no inconsiderable part in them."

Dickens' "no inconsiderable part" was enriched by Daly's production of *Oliver Twist* some six years after *Pickwick Papers* on May 19, 1874. By this time, Daly had his own company and theater, the New Fifth Avenue, and consequently was his own producer. Whether he made the adaptation of *Oliver Twist* himself is questionable. Generally there is ample publicity to indicate Daly's hand in an adaptation: playbills, Judge Daly's biography, contemporary reviews and notices, the published version of the play. Daly was an able, if misleading, publicist. The lack of such ballyhoo in the case of *Oliver Twist* inclines one to suspect whether he had any part in the adaptation beyond, of course, supervision of the production. Judge Daly refers to the performance as "the final novelty of the season," and Dithmar speaks of it as a "new dramatization," neither mention of which is very enlightening. One piece of evidence has turned up, however, which is quite interesting.

A. Oakey Hall, who had been (1868–1872) the mayor of New York and who was always interested in the theater, had in 1873 been in correspondence with Daly about his own adaptation of *Oliver Twist*. In one letter, dated simply 1873, Hall refers to the "3 first acts" of his version. Hall was himself an actor; his known dramatic efforts include versions of *Humpty Dumpty* and *Fernande*. He was friend, patron, and legal advisor to Daly. It is altogether probable that the *Oliver Twist* produced by Daly in 1874 was by A. Oakey Hall.

Whatever its authorship, the piece did not last long. On the final night, June 3, 1874, only the first two acts were given as part of a double bill with *Monsieur Alphonse*. A year later, in the summer of 1875, Daly took his whole company on a tour to Chicago, Salt Lake City, San Francisco, and other western points, and included in the repertory, according to John Drew, was *Oliver Twist*.

Critical comments on *Oliver Twist* indicate that it was not much more than a stringing together of episodes, designed to show off the versatility of Daly's large company. According to the *Tribune* the piece was "a series of tableaux" in "four acts of some twenty odd scenes with twenty-one characters." The scenes were clumsily pieced together "without coherency or reason" resulting in a "series of pictures . . . rather than a complete play." Although the *Advertiser* complained that the "story" was "slight," the "company supplied a remarkably even and interesting performance." Little Bijou Heron, daughter of the well-known actress, Mathilda Heron, and later the wife of Henry Miller, played the title role of Oliver. She had just created a sensation in the child's part in *Monsieur Alphonse*, an adaptation of a play of Dumas *fils*, produced in April 1874. The *Advertiser* review concluded with praise for the "excellent" scenery. Daly, in other words, was busy laying the foundations, particularly as regards his company and his staging, of future greatness.

Daly's interest in Dickens was not confined solely to these two productions. The year after production of *Pickwick Papers* he projected a dramatization of *The Mystery of Edwin Drood*. In the September 5, 1871 playbill of *Divorce*, he publicized an account of his efforts and reproduced two letters on the subject. Searching for a clue to the novelist's intentions regarding the conclusion to this unfinished story, he wrote Dickens' son who replied that *The Mystery of Edwin Drood* was "as great a mystery" to him as it was to the public at large. A second letter from Dickens' son-in-law, Charles Collins, a brother of Wilkie, stated that "Edwin Drood was *never to reappear*" but "as to anything further, it must be purely conjectional." Daly was evidently dissuaded as *The Mystery of Edwin Drood* never appeared under his aegis. He did, however, copyright "a dramatization in four acts with an original ending by Augustin Daly" on September 28, 1870. Judge Daly states that he got the idea for his ending from the second act of *Le Juif Polonais*, a play afterwards brought out with great success by Henry Irving as *The Bells*.

Partially on the strength of his success as an adaptor, Daly opened his first theater, the Fifth Avenue, on Twenty-Fourth Street, on August 16, 1869. On September 13, 1870, he began his second season there with another popular hit, a dramatization of Wilkie Collins' novel, *Man and Wife*. The original production lasted until November 19, for a good run of ten weeks. Revivals and other productions occurred as follows: Boston Theatre, Boston, week of November 14, 1870, with Mrs. D. P. Bowers; Aiken's Museum, Chicago, December 5–17, 1870; New Fifth Avenue Theatre, January 3–9, 1874, with Ada Dyas as Anne Sylvester; January 22–29, 1877, by the Daly Company at the Grand Opera House, with a repetition the week of February 26, 1877, at the Bowery Theatre; a series of matinee revivals in December 1879, with Marie Wainwright; and at the Girard Theatre, Philadelphia, January 13, 1896, by the members of Mr. Holland's stock company.

On the whole the critics liked *Man and Wife*. "The play is remarkable for the ingenious preservation and continuity of the few really dramatic scenes in the story, and for the retention of the romantic atmosphere with which Wilkie Collins invests his fables." Slowly but surely Daly was achieving a reputation for artistry and already in 1870 one critic could write, "The entire play was presented with that completeness and elegance which is so characteristic of this theatre . . ."

More than the story, the dramatization, or the staging, *Man and Wife* was acclaimed for the acting of Clara Morris as

Anne Sylvester. The role projected her into stardom. Originally the part had been intended for Daly's leading lady, Agnes Ethel, but on the advice of friends she rejected the part, giving as her reason the "immorality of Anne." Ione Burke, ordinarily the next in line, was still on vacation, so Daly, with that unerring instinct which promoted many actresses into stars, selected the unknown westerner, Clara Morris. In so doing he passed over the dazzling and talented Fanny Davenport, who wanted the part, but his judgment was admirably vindicated by Miss Morris' performance. It was her first starring vehicle in New York, the beginning of her impressive career. Miss Morris' interesting autobiography, *Life on the Stage*, records the trials and tribulations of the poor, frequently hungry, young actress, undergoing the rigors of Daly's rehearsals, to the inevitable Cinderella-like triumph of opening night.

One conversation of Daly's which Miss Morris reports is especially interesting for the light it throws upon the authorship of *Man and Wife*. Speaking to the actress in a fit of temper, the manager said, "Good God! everything goes wrong. The idiot that was to dramatize the story of 'Man and Wife' for me has failed in his work; the play is announced, and I have been up all night writing and arranging a last act for it myself." Daly could hardly have been referring to Wilkie Collins as "the idiot that was to dramatize the story." His statement about some hireling who was to have done the work however does fit in with a phrase in Collins' letter to W. D. Booth of September 20, 1870, in which Collins refers to the "absurdities" which "Mr. Baker" and Mr. Daly might introduce into their adaptation. Both these references imply that only a part of the dramatic version is Daly's, perhaps as Miss Morris' account indicates, only the last act; the fifth act is concerned largely with the melodramatic action of the attempted murder, a bit of theatricality which would call for the talents of a producer-director rather than a writer. In other words, there is some question about the authenticity of Daly's authorship not only of his original plays but also of his adaptations.

With its dramatically powerful plot, it is no wonder that the novel was eagerly seized upon by numerous adaptors. Included with the version by Harry A. Webber in *Ames' Series of Standard and Minor Drama*, number 46, 1873, is a strange critique, which purports to be a review of the piece as produced at the Green Bay (Wisconsin) Opera House, January 8, 1870. Since the novel did not appear until June 1870, and the serialization in *Harper's Weekly*, did not conclude until August 6, 1870, no production could have antedated Daly's of September 1870 unless the adaptor had had access to the proofs of the novel or the serial form as Daly had had in the case of *Norwood*. Since Collins, himself, was busy making an adaptation in 1870, which he sent to Daly, and since there is no record of any such arrangement, such a conjecture would seem unlikely in this instance.

A comparison of Webber's and Daly's versions shows an apparently clear-cut case of plagiarism on the part of the former. There is only the slightest alteration in dramatis personae; the titles of the acts are similar; finally, speeches, both those taken from the novel and those invented by Daly, are alike, word for word, throughout the play, and situation follows situation with similar agreement. The connecting link may well have been a member of the theatrical Devere family inasmuch as George F. Devere played Mr. Moy in Daly's production and H. Devere enacted the role of John Thomas, the "traditional footman," in Webber's. But one hardly need to labor the point of theft; it was an established custom of the times in the theater.

Wilkie Collins' own adaptation did not appear on the stage until February 22, 1873, when it was produced by the Bancrofts at the Prince of Wales Theatre, London, with Charles Coghlan as Delamayne and Lydia Foote as Anne Sylvester.

Collins' version was in four acts, with an ending completely different from that in the novel or in Daly's version which closely follows the novel. Collins omits two important characters, Hester Dethridge, the dumb cook, and Mrs. Glenarm. The Collins play, following its run at the Prince of Wales, toured the provinces with Charles Wyndham and Ada Dyas in the leading roles. It was revived at the Haymarket Theatre, March 29, 1887, with Mrs. James Brown Potter ("How high beauty and social reputation are valued above art and skill . . . may be judged by the statement that . . . Mrs. James Brown Potter is to receive a salary of £100 a week."), Mr. E. S. Willard, Mr. William Herbert, and Mr. P. Ben Greet in the cast.

Mrs. Gilbert, in her *Stage Reminiscences*, has an explanation which accounts for both Daly's and Collins' version of the novel. She claims that "Daly had commissioned Mr. Collins to dramatize the book" but that the irascible Daly wanted "everything *when* he wanted it." Since "English people don't work on those lines," continues the English-born Mrs. Gilbert, "at last Mr. Daly got tired of waiting" and made his own adaptation. There was no difficulty about it, she adds, as Daly wrote Collins a "courteous" letter explaining his haste. And when the play proved to be a success, "Mr. Daly sent him a thousand dollars. . . . Just one little point to show how keen Mr. Daly's sense of dramatic values was." True enough, Daly did pay Collins, for the latter referred to the payment in a letter to his agent, J. W. A. Buck, as late as 1885, but Daly's motive for doing so was probably not his "keen sense of dramatic values," but rather the pressure applied in 1870 by Collins' lawyer, W. D. Booth.

Despite the great success of Collins in England and Daly in this country, several other adaptations of the novel are known to exist. *Wife or No Wife* by David S. James, in a prologue and four "chapters," was presented at the Torquay Theatre Royal, May 21, 1883; a second adaptation by James, called

Man and Wife; or A Scotch Marriage, was later given at the
Theatre Royal, Margate, June 29, 1885. Another version of
the novel by Charles Cameron, a drama in five acts called
Matrimony, was produced at the Royal Alhambra Theatre,
Barrow-in-Furness, September 6, 1886. A typewritten manu-
script in four acts based on the novel was copyrighted Sep-
tember 14, 1908, in Marblehead, Massachusetts, by the author,
Philip Henry McCaigue. Finally, the novel was dramatized as
The Indiscretion of Truth by J. Hartley Manners for Harris'
Theatre, London, in December 1912.

The story of *Man and Wife* is a highly dramatic one, involving the peculiarities of Scotch marriage laws. To a modern audience, the problems of marriage and divorce which the
novel poses seem slightly ridiculous. But the well-documented
evidence which Collins introduces into his story via footnotes
to verify his assertions made exciting reading in the Victorian
age.

The central plot revolves around Anne Sylvester, compan-
ion-governess to Blanche Lundie. Anne has contracted an unhappy liaison with Geoffrey Delamayne, an athlete and a
"scoundrel"; she is pregnant and must force him to marry her.
At that very moment, his father who is at the point of death
threatens to disinherit Geoffrey unless he settles down and
makes a good marriage—namely to Mrs. Glenarm, a wealthy,
attractive, and interested widow. Caught between the demands
of Anne and his father, Geoffrey flees, but not before arranging to meet Anne secretly and marry her. He prevails
upon his friend, Arnold Brinkworth, Blanche's fiancé, to
assist him by carrying a message to Anne at her lonely hideout,
the Inn at Craig Fernie. Then, taking advantage of the
peculiar Scotch laws, Geoffrey declares Anne and Arnold
to be man and wife inasmuch as Arnold, per instructions,
had declared himself Anne's husband before witnesses at the
Inn. Arnold has meanwhile married Blanche so that he now
appears a bigamist; the situation is especially bitter to Blanche

since Anne has been her friend and confidante. Further, Blanche is incited to suspicion by her stepmother, Lady Lundie, who dislikes Anne.

Meanwhile, Geoffrey is making headway with Mrs. Glenarm and with his preparations to participate in a great footrace. And the rascally old servant, Bishopriggs, has complicated matters by attempting to use Geoffrey's note to Anne for blackmail. The whole involved situation is settled partly because of Sir Patrick Lundie's knowledge of the law. Sir Patrick is Blanche's uncle. The result of his interference is that Anne is declared Geoffrey's wife. This fact is accomplished by the use of a letter which antedates by an hour or so Arnold's indiscretion. The bases of both these marriages seem quite flimsy, but Collins justifies them by quoting existing Scotch statutes.

By law, Geoffrey is now Anne's lord and master. He proceeds to attempt to drive her to insanity from which only her sweet nature and determination, plus the devotion of Sir Patrick and Blanche, save her. At length, Geoffrey hits upon a scheme of murder, suggested by a confession to a similar crime committed by the dumb cook, Hester Dethridge, whom he forces to assist him. Naturally he is foiled in the nick of time, and all ends happily with Anne's marriage to Sir Patrick.

To set the story, Collins in a prologue goes back to a similar situation in the previous generation when Anne's mother had been deserted by a husband anxious to make a more socially suitable match. This unnecessary and obviously contrived coincidence Daly omits in his dramatization. He likewise leaves out almost all the references to athleticism, which help to make the novel an interesting and important social document. Naturally, he has to include the problem of the Scotch marriage laws, but he does exclude the marriage between Arnold and Blanche, thereby avoiding the discussion of bigamy. This avoidance may seem somewhat strange in light of the success of *Griffith Gaunt*, but he evidently wanted to keep Anne the central character and did not wish any distracting dramatic struggles. Daly further eliminates Anne's pregnancy. By sidestepping the issues of illegitimacy and bigamy, he made the drama more palatable to the public; in the play, then, the basic considerations revolve around questions of "honor." This transfer renders the plot less important as social criticism, deliberate on Collins' part, and makes it more melodramatic, Daly's theatrical intention.

For above all else, Daly was a conscious artist of the theater. He knew how to make a situation vibrate with emotion, shallow or deep. Act I ends with Lady Lundie's abrupt and startling announcement of Anne's disappearance; her satisfaction with the state of affairs only adds to the drama. The curtain of Act III falls on Anne's generous and self-incriminating use of Geoffrey's letter; here is obvious melodrama as Anne flourishes the piece of paper, flaunting it before Mrs. Glenarm, with the stage directions significantly adding "Music. Tableau." And Act IV concludes equally dramatically as Geoffrey "putting Anne behind him" laughs as he asserts his legal, but evil, rights over his "wife."

Daly's version also tends to individualize the characters, particularly the minor ones. A novelist can sketch in his personalities with a leisurely pen, but a dramatist must characterize with bold and frequently obvious strokes. So Daly makes Lady Lundie's maid, Hopkins, a French girl and gives her an accent; he makes Geoffrey's trainer, Perry, a low comedy type with a German accent; and in the casting, he assigned the role of the dumb cook, Hester Dethridge, to Mrs. G. H. Gilbert, who had been a dancer and pantomimist before she became an actress.

Daly also introduces humor wherever possible. The "three choral gentlemen" who are completely innocuous in the novel are given a comedy scene in the play. Sir Patrick is made into a more humorous character as a consequence of which the idea of a romance between him and Anne at the conclusion is not even suggested. Bishopriggs, by being presented as a tippler, is made much funnier and certainly less sinister since this change minimizes his attempts at blackmail. Certain other humorous incidents are also played up, such as the reading of Milton, a rather charming episode, and the addition of a mother-in-law joke, an essential in a Daly play.

The conclusion of the play offers the most interesting study in technique, however. Collins in his dramatic version changed the ending entirely. As Geoffrey and Anne prepare to leave Sir Patrick's after they have legally been declared man and wife, Geoffrey plans to kill her by driving their dog cart off the road into a gravel pit, intending to jump clear himself. The plan is executed off stage but Anne is saved by the railing, whereas Geoffrey is killed by the excitement of his leap. Dr. Speedwell, a moralizing character from the novel omitted by Daly, is on hand to point out that Geoffrey's weakness of the heart is due to overemphasis upon physical training. If one can judge from the reviews this ending, too, was modified in production. Evidently the Bancrofts objected to the melodramatic accident; consequently, Geoffrey simply dies of a heart attack in the library while Dr. Speedwell drives home his point about athleticism.

Daly in his ending follows the novel. Furthermore, he has a five-act structure which allows him more leeway than Collins' four-act treatment. As a consequence, he has made of the last act a melodramatic spectacle. Instead of Collins' involved account, in which Geoffrey finds and reads a confession of Hester's murder of her brutal husband, Daly presents the whole activity—a faked wall, with removable wallpaper and the murder to be accomplished so that it looks like smothering—as a scenic effect. Admittedly this is a rather cheap device depending upon clever staging and perfect timing, but it is theatrically exciting and provided a thrilling climax to the play. The final curtain is thus conditioned by action rather than by plot or character; as a result, although vivid, the conclusion is somewhat vague in meaning. We know that Anne is saved and we see that Geoffrey is presumably dead of shock, but the fate of others is obscure. There is a striking tableau with Hester, who has suddenly spoken, on her knees praying, Blanche and Anne clinging together, and Arnold and Sir Patrick standing over the fallen body of Geoffrey.

Man and Wife was not the only novel of Wilkie Collins which Daly transferred to the boards of his theater. In the next season, on June 7, 1871, he produced a version of *No Name*. According to Judge Daly, the adaptation was the joint work of Collins and Daly; Dithmar lists the authors the same way; but Mrs. Gilbert says that Collins "assisted Mr. Daly in the dramatizing." Odell refers to the piece as "Wilkie Collins' dramatization of his own novel." Nicoll points out that Collins' play was privately printed in 1870, but lists no performances in England. The assumption that the adaptation was Collins' seems valid. We can, knowing Daly, imagine that his activities in all probability consisted of modifications made during the rehearsals designed to make the piece more playable.

Regardless of whose adaptation it was, the play was not successful; thirteen nights after its first performance on any stage, it was withdrawn. Clara Morris, fresh from her triumph in *Man and Wife,* played the lead and Fanny Davenport masked her beauty for the role of the frowsy Mrs. Captain Wragge. But despite their efforts and the

great pains which have been bestowed upon this production, the results do not seen to have justified them. The novel was a strong one, but the play is weak. . . . It aims to do too much. In the novel there is space for the proper development of the characters, for the full statement of the complex circumstances that influenced the heroine and compelled her into crime. In the play there is no room for this. . . . The result has been a skeleton play. . . .

Such criticism sounds like a reasonable indictment of the dramatization.

For the season, 1873–1874, bucking the hard times and financial panic, Daly expanded his management to three theaters: The New Fifth Avenue, The Grand Opera House, and The Broadway. At this last playhouse he produced another of Collins' dramas, *The New Magdalen*, on November 10, 1873. The play was without question Collins' own dramatization; nevertheless, it was not a success. It was in fact Daly's final production at The Broadway Theatre, for he retired from the management of that theatre within a month.

The noteworthy aspect of this production is that Wilkie Collins, then on a lecture tour in America, himself supervised it, as well as a subsequent production of *The Woman in White*, not, however, under Daly's aegis. According to the *Herald* of November 11, 1873, he appeared at the première of *The New Magdalen* and made a speech. Daly, pressed by the demands of three theaters, imported the English actress, Carlotta Leclercq, for the lead in the play, which ran three weeks.

Again it will be noticed how conscious Daly was of the combined effects of theatricality and timely publicity. As he had previously done in the case of *Pickwick Papers*, he again took advantage of the popularity of a visiting English novelist to attract attention for his new piece, this time adding the snob appeal of an English "name" actress. One must not forget that in addition to other rival attractions—and there were many theaters running in New York despite the panic —this was the period of P. T. Barnum, who taught his contemporaries a great deal about promotion.

Daly's love of novelty and daring, already evident in his productions of *Griffith Gaunt*, *Norwood*, and *Man and Wife*, reached its apogee with *Divorce* and *Pique*. Naturally anxious to open his fall season with a success, he was also well aware of the value of a strong initial impact. *Divorce* was a "strong" piece, his choice for the third season at the Fifth Avenue Theatre, where the play began a phenomenal run on September 5, 1871.

For the material of this piece Daly turned to his contemporary, Anthony Trollope, and the long novel with the strange title, *He Knew He Was Right*—parodied by F. C. Burnand in *Punch* as "He Knew He Could Write." In this psychological excursion, Trollope attempts to deal with marriage between an over-jealous husband and a rebellious young wife, resentful of the intellectual and social restrictions of her married state. The novelist's method is analytical sometimes to the point of weariness. Louis and Emily Trevelyan, the young couple, spend hours in minute self-probing. Their marriage has from the first been hazardous. Emily is the naïve daughter of a bungling colonial official and has never before been to London. Once established there, she rashly encourages the friendship of Colonel Osborne, a retired military man, a friend of her father. Because of the Colonel's reputation as a despoiler of young married women, her husband disapproves of the relationship and commands her to stop seeing the colonel. In a fit of pique, Emily obeys his orders so literally that she further aggravates Louis and embarrasses him socially. Eventually a separation results. Although a great many people set themselves to the task of reconciling the couple, the rift between them widens; even their child cannot effect the wanted reunion. In fact, Louis, with the assistance of a "legal advisor" of more than dubious character, finally kidnaps the child and departs for Italy.

Trollope makes an easy transition to the south of Europe via a subplot. We go there with Mr. Glascock, who is the son and heir of Lord Peterborough and is the rejected suitor of Nora Rowley, Emily's sister. Before we can properly be concerned with the Trevelyans, however, Trollope plunges

us into a consideration of English and American society in
Italy, and we meet an American family, the Spaldings, whose
daughter, Caroline, is eventually intended for Mr. Glascock.

When Louis and Emily are finally reconciled, the former
is in a most pitiable state. Overcome by his jealousy, he has
become virtually insane; improper food and housing in Italy
have further contributed to his downfall, and Emily reaches
him only to comfort his last days.

A second subplot revolves around life in Exeter and the
Cathedral set there. This is by far the most interesting part
of the novel since the characters, particularly Aunt Stanbury,
an old shrew with a heart of gold, are alive and fascinating in
Trollope's best Barchester manner; but since Daly uses
little of this section there is no need to give it more than
passing mention here.

Reading the novel gives one the impression that Trollope
is a misogamist; the characters, all of them, spend most of
their time discussing matrimony, but it takes interminably
long for them all finally to marry. And of course the Trevelyans, the one married couple, are an unhappy example of
the married state. Nevertheless, if one can worm his way
through these considerations, the novel has charm and insight:
Sir Marmaduke, Emily's father, is a clever caricature of a
colonial governor; and the gossip and intrigue of the small
Exeter community are brilliantly detailed.

Trollope himself wrote despairingly of the novel in his
Autobiography.

I do not know that in any literary effort I ever fell more completely short of my own intention than in this story. It was my
purpose to create sympathy for the unfortunate man who, while
endeavouring to do his duty to all around him, should be led constantly astray by his unwillingnesss to submit his own judgment
to the opinion of others. The man is made to be unfortunate
enough, and the evil which he does is apparent. So far I did not
fail, but the sympathy has not been created yet. I look upon the
story as being nearly altogether bad. It is in part redeemed by

certain scenes in the house and vicinity of an old maid in Exeter. But a novel which in its main parts is bad cannot, in truth, be redeemed by the vitality of subordinate characters.

Any final comment must consider Michael Sadleir's opinion that

A modern reader must inevitably find the unhappy, haunted creature [Trevelyan] rather pathetic than repellent; but to contemporary criticism he was a monster. This was not the only occasion in which Trollope showed himself in advance of the taste of his time. . . . And from *He Knew He Was Right* has descended quite a family of "novels of the mind."

Turning from Trollope to Daly, one is immediately impressed upon reading the play with the strength and insight of this second-rate novel. For the play is a stagey piece, stiff and contrived and, for modern tastes, vastly overdramatic. What seemed like a tedious and frequently stupid novel emerges as clever, often brilliant and certainly psychologically sound when compared with the play made from it. "It was not," Dithmar points out, "a drama of fine literary quality. Its language was simply colloquial speech. . . . It was a play of quick, nervous action and striking pictures."

Daly transfers the scene from London and Italy to New York and Florida. The central plot is drastically altered by having Alfred Adrianse (Louis Trevelyan) recover and forgive his wife so that all ends happily. To nurse Alfred in Florida, Daly creates Flora Penfield, "a Florida bud," whose nursing role is reminiscent of Emily, but who welcomes Fanny Adrianse, the wife, with the same friendly warmth of manner with which Caroline Spalding became the intimate of Nora Rowley.

The subplot of the play, revolving around Lu Ten Eyck, Fanny's sister, and her husband, De Wolf De Witt, is Daly's invention, except that the characters do bear slight resemblance to persons in the novel, even if the situations do not. A. H. Quinn asserts that "of twenty-four characters in Daly's play, only six are taken from the novel." The actual count is nearer ten. It is in this subplot that Daly discusses the main theme of the play, divorce. There is no divorce in the novel. Lu and De Wolf are divorced primarily as a result of the evil machinations, prompted by greed, of Jitt, the lawyer, and Burritt, the detective, and of Mrs. Ten Eyck, a busybody. Actually Lu and De Wolf have decided not to get a divorce when the writ is suddenly granted. Once having set the machinery in motion, Jitt secures the divorce through chicanery and distortion. The fact that the divorce is granted when the characters no longer want it adds an ironic note to the play and to the theme which the critics have failed to grasp. The divorce is unreal, for Lu simply tries to provoke her elderly husband by her extravagance. Her reasons are never given. She acts completely without motivation; true, she is badly counseled and her husband is rich enough to grant her whims, but these facts hardly justify her silly behavior. And of course Lu and De Wolf are reconciled at the conclusion and remarry. Certainly if satire is Daly's purpose here, he has so exaggerated it as to make it ludicrous.

The Exeter plot, as has been stated, is barely retained. Grace, the niece "for whom we must find something after the dear girls are provided for," is a pale combination of Dorothy Stanbury and Nora Rowley. But her marriage to the Reverend Harry Duncan does provide Mrs. Ten Eyck with this tellingly ironic comment on marriage: "Ah, well, my loves, you will be happy. You are both poor, and therefore dependent on each other. You can't afford to disagree so you will be happy."

As usual with his dramatizations, Daly adds bits of melodrama which are generally directed at eye and ear appeal. He makes Captain Lynde an ex-Indian fighter and not nearly so subtle a character as his prototype, Colonel Osborne; Captain Lynde actually makes love to Fanny. In the play, Fanny and her mother leave Alfred, whereas in the novel Louis

Augustin Daly, about 1875

A scene from The Railroad of Love, *1887*. Left to right: *Edith Kingdon, Otis Skinner, Ada Rehan, James Lewis, Mrs. G. H. Gilbert, John Drew*

Ada Rehan as Katherine, about 1887

Augustin Daly, about 1898

Fifth Avenue Theatre, reconstructed after the fire of 1873

makes all the necessary arrangements for Emily, the child, and Nora to leave his house. In the novel, Louis, already psychologically ill, and the unscrupulous Bozzle steal the child; in the drama there are two "kidnapings": first, Alfred takes the child, and then Mrs. Ten Eyck, assisted by Burritt, carries him off just as Fanny and Alfred are on the verge of reconciliation; this apparent double-cross provides Alfred with a fine mad scene. In the play, Alfred's jealousy is heightened by Captain Lynde's intimacy with Fanny; the audience knows their intimacy is prompted by mutual concern over Lu's unhappiness; in the novel, the intimacy between Colonel Osborne and Emily is more realistically centered around the Colonel's efforts to have Emily's father recalled from his colonial exile. Finally, Fanny makes a melodramatic curtain speech which Emily Trevelyan would have been incapable of uttering. "Just so far as it is right," she asserts, "I will obey his wishes. If I am in doubt, I will give him the benefit of that doubt, and still comply, but if he outrages my feelings, insults my friends and suspects my honor, I will resent it with all my power to the day of my death." The accompanying stage directions indicate the desired mood: *Music tremolo till end*. Fanny's attitude here, says one scholar of the drama, demonstrates the "growing independence of women."

Of course the main interest of the play is focused upon the "divorce." Jitt, the rascally lawyer, significantly poses the issue. "Two daughters—two divorces," he says. "Why can't every family do as well? It would make our profession as lucrative as a politician's."

This characterization of Jitt is one of the most interesting in the play, for the social comment which Daly makes here is significant. The widespread activity of shady divorce lawyers was a general source of annoyance in the last quarter of the nineteenth century. Their unfair advertising practices, their bribing of witnesses, their general lack of ethics, were embarrassing alike to the legal profession and to intelligent citizens.

Daly's treatment of the divorce theme has aroused the unbounded enthusiasm of historians of the drama. It must be remembered that Daly was a conscientious practicing Catholic and that his views on marriage and divorce must have been colored somewhat by his religious beliefs. In the case of religion, as with other personal matters, however, he made a clear distinction between his private life and his profession. A. H. Quinn praises Daly's social criticism thus:

> Daly shows truly that the only happy marriages are those based on mutual forbearance. . . . He shows, too, the futility of divorce as a cure for the difficulties of married life. With this problem the British novel was scarcely concerned. . . . The play may be considered as one of his original productions. The very title . . . indicated the thorough domestication of the drama.

Under Quinn's supervision, Drs. J. G. Hartman and D. N. Koster in their dissertations each credit Daly with being the first American dramatist to deal with the divorce problem. Yet in Quinn's own *History of the American Drama from the Beginning to the Civil War*, he states that Richard Penn Smith's *The Divorce; or, the Mock Cavalier* (1830) is concerned with an actual divorce, and both Koster and Hartman admit that the social problems of marriage for love or for money had been the concern of such dramatists as Mrs. Mowatt, Mrs. Bateman, Boker, and others.

Dr. Koster's minute analysis of the development of American divorce laws and trends shows that following the Civil War years the divorce rate in America increased every year compounding annually at about a 3 per cent rate of increment. Although the ratio of divorces to marriages was still small—only 1 to 33.8 in 1870—the subject was of sufficient popular interest to attract the pen of a publicity-wise dramatist and producer. Certainly, as Koster indicates, there was a growing tendency towards the acceptance of divorce. He cites as underlying social factors the gradually increasing independence of women; the shifting of large portions of the population from a rural to an urban life, with consequent decrease in the size of the average family and relative economic instability; increase in per capita wealth. In addition to these, there was a lessening in the power and influence of the Church, and an increasing public acceptance of the idea of divorce as the number of divorced persons grew, and a change of stress in marriage, from the social institution point of view to the point of view of the individual's happiness.

Koster overlooks another fact however when he comments on the extensiveness of "Daly's knowledge of the divorce laws of New York State," namely that Daly's brother, Joseph, was a New York lawyer, later an eminent jurist, and his acquaintance with the law may well have been the source of Augustin's information—and plot.

But before all else Daly, as a man of the theater, understood his audiences, and with *Divorce* proved again that he could supply the proper means of entertaining them. That the play would not be acceptable to a twentieth-century audience indicates only the vast change in taste between the 1870's and the 1950's; we have our own equally bad, or worse, plays on much less significant subjects achieving success on Broadway.

As might be expected from its daring theme, *Divorce* was an instant success; the company, the acting, the scenery—in short, the production—were the details selected by the critics for praise. Opening on September 5, 1871, the play surpassed in number of continuous performances any comedy previously seen on the New York stage, with the two hundred mark on March 18, 1872. Actually, it ran, with interruptions for other pieces, for an additional thirty-six performances until May 19, when it closed with a benefit for Mr. Davidge.

The stage history of the play unquestionably proves its

tremendous popular appeal. Productions under Daly's management included: April 15 to May 20, 1873; October 13 to 26, 1873, at the Park Theatre, Brooklyn, where during a period of two weeks the Daly company presented seven plays; May 12, 1874, with Ada Dyas; and February 19 to 25, 1877, at the Bowery Theatre, both performances being under Daly's management. On June 23, 1876, *Divorce* was given at the matinee and in the evening occurred the 200th performance of *Pique*, commemorated by a playbill in silk. Both performances were for Augustin Daly's benefit. In *Divorce*, Fanny Davenport played Fanny, Jeffreys Lewis, Lu, and Georgie Drew, Grace. *Divorce* was next presented by Daly during the month of September 1877, when, having given up the Fifth Avenue Theatre, he was on tour with his company in Baltimore and Wilmington. Finally it was staged from September 30 to October 17, 1879, at Daly's Theatre, on which occasion it served to recoup the failure of *Newport*, with the lead played first by Mabel Jordan and then by Ada Rehan.

For those days, the success of *Divorce* was little less than phenomenal. On one occasion, according to Odell, it was being performed simultaneously in New York, Boston, Philadelphia, Buffalo, and St. Louis. Miss Sturtevant reports a performance given aboard ship by officers of the U.S.S. *Macedonian* in Yokohama harbor.

Divorce also had an amazing history in Boston. The first production reported there was a four-week run at the Globe Theatre beginning October 17, 1871. It was played the next year for two weeks commencing December 2, 1872, at the Boston Museum. Evidently this performance began a tradition, for clippings in the Harvard Theatre Collection indicate that the play was used as the opening piece at the Museum every fall for the next twelve years. But in 1884 the reviews—*Gazette, Daily Advertiser, Daily Globe*, and two unnamed papers—are unusually bitter. "A stupid mass of commonplace sentiment . . . descending to ridiculous pathos," says the *Advertiser* for August 26. "Its sentiment is cheap and stilted, its humor is forced and extravagant, its tone is generally sickly and a silly dulness pervades it," reports the *Gazette* on the 31st. Yet, as one anonymous clipping points out, "It is unnecessary for people to ask whether *Divorce* is worth going to see, when every seat in the theatre is occupied each evening." And one classicist, one suspects a Harvard sophomore in the throes of a drama survey course, goes so far as to complain that *Divorce* "conspicuously disregards the unities. That of action is excusably dealt with but time and place are treated with the airiest nonchalance." But *Divorce* survived to a last recorded performance in Boston on November 22, 1898, at the Castle Square Theatre, when the old play not only filled the house but actually drew standees.

Miss Sturtevant records of the performances in Chicago, where *Divorce* had to compete with the great fire, that civic pride in the accomplishment of a performance on November 6, 1871 was "undoubtedly responsible for the uncritical spirit" of the review in the *Tribune*. Later, on June 8, 1874, the play was given there by Daly's own company, but the famous members of the cast got most of the attention and the praise.

In San Francisco one production at Maguire's Theatre, on August 31, 1874, is noteworthy because of the cast, which included James A. Herne, Jeffreys Lewis, and David Belasco. Performances at Denver, Philadelphia, and Cincinnati further attest to the play's popularity. For the 1883–1884 season, John Stetson, a successful Boston manager, secured a contract from Daly for the rights for all parts of the country not covered by a similar contract that Daly had with Jane Coombs.

The only recorded production in the British Isles, strange to say, occurred in Edinburgh, at the Royal Princess' Theatre on December 12, 1881. Linda Dietz was the star. "Of the literary merit of the drama we cannot speak highly," opined the *London Era*.

There remains only the question of authorship to complete our discussion of *Divorce*. The possible connection of Joseph Daly as consultant or co-author has already been mentioned. Referring to the production of the play in 1873, Colonel T. Allston Brown calls it "A. R. Cazauran's play of 'Divorce.' " Augustus R. Cazauran is an interesting ghost-like figure. *The Dictionary of the Drama* credits him with having written *The Esmonds of Virginia* (1886), *The Martyr* (1887), and other pieces. His name frequently turns up as a hack writer; for a while, he was house dramatist for A. M. Palmer at the Union Square Theatre; Bronson Howard has acknowledged his assistance in the revision of *The Banker's Daughter*. Knowing Daly's usual methods we may venture the suggestion that Cazauran could perhaps have been employed in the writing of *Divorce*. One other curious note deserves a word here. A five-act play, *Divorced*, "dramatized from the novel, *He Knew He Was Right*," was copyrighted by Sam Ryan and George W. Murray in Sheboygan, Wisconsin, on August 3, 1872. This play may, of course, have been an imitation of Daly's; such an explanation would account for the coincidence; on the other hand, recollecting Webber's *Man and Wife* one wonders how far the threads of coincidence can be stretched before they break asunder.

For his next adaptation, Daly turned to a French novel, *Germaine*, by Edmond About. The story is involved and rather morbid. The Count Don Diego Gomez de Villanera, "the last scion of a noble Neapolitan family," whose "fortune is the largest in Spain," has contracted a liaison with a Madame Honorine Chermidy, whose husband is in the French Navy; the affair has lasted three years and has produced a son, Gomez, the little Marquis de los Montes de Rierro. Madame Chermidy has the idea of having Don Diego marry in order to legitimize little Gomez; she selects Germaine, daughter of the Duc and Duchesse de la Tour d'Embleuse. Germaine is dying of tuberculosis. The family, thanks to the charming old duke, is destitute. The marriage is arranged by the family doctor, Le Bris.

Germaine marries Don Diego, accepts Gomez as her son, her family gets a million francs, and Germaine, Don Diego and his mother, Gomez, and Dr. Le Bris leave for Italy in the forlorn hope of a cure. Italy is unsatisfactory; they migrate to Corfu. During this time, Germaine wins the love of Gomez and of her dowager mother-in-law.

Meanwhile, the old duke, resuscitated by money, is leading a gay life in Paris; he falls in love with Madame Chermidy to whom he turns over control of his money and the weekly letters from Germaine. Thus she learns that the de Villaneras need a man servant. She has her maid and alter ego, Le Tas, search out an ex-convict, Mantoux, known as "Little-luck," whom she sends out to them slyly offering him a pension after Germaine's death. As a consequence, he gives Germaine doses of arsenic, but since they are small ones, they act as a curative, and she slowly recovers.

When Germaine is well enough to go about, she and Don Diego confess their mutual love; in her haste to get well, Germaine partakes too much of the "iodometer" and is left at death's door. Le Bris writes of her imminent death. Madame Chermidy, her husband having been killed in China, rushes to Corfu to marry Don Diego. She has, meanwhile, completely ruined the aged duke; out of his senses, he follows her.

Germaine miraculously recovers and is completely cured, the overdose having burnt out the disease. So she is on hand to receive Madame Chermidy, who threatens suit, exposure, suicide, and other dire actions to win back Don Diego. Disclosing that she has a fortune with her, she attempts to bribe Mantoux to kill Germaine; he kills her instead. At first the mad duke is suspected, but Mantoux is caught. The duke dies, so does little Gomez, conveniently, of typhoid, and the family, blessed with a baby girl, lives happily on.

Since Daly knew no French, he undoubtedly first read *Germaine* in the English translation of Mary L. Booth. But as no copy of the play *What Should She Do?* exists, it is impossible accurately to judge the adaptation. From the play-bill and the reviews, it is possible to indicate the characters in common:

NOVEL	PLAY
Duc de la Tour d'Embleuse	The Earl of Kenmair
Don Diego, Count Gomez de Villanera	Lord Basil Clavering
Gaston de Vitre (?)	Bob Kenmair
Doctor Le Bris	Doctor Titcomb
Mantoux	Lamech
Mr. Stevens (?)	Mr. Peabody
Duchesse de la Tour d'Embleuse	The Countess of Kenmair
Dowager Countess de Villanera	Lady Clavering
Madame Honorine Chermidy	Dianthe de Marec, Dame de Lannes
Germaine	The Lady Elaine
Le Tas	Letty
Gomez	Basil

Daly did not Americanize this adaptation. Striving to keep the "society" tone, he "Englished" it instead, transferring the scenes from Paris, Italy, and Corfu to London and Jamaica.

The play, we can gauge from the reviews, did clean up the plot. Daly presents Basil as having actually married Dianthe; when they discover that her husband is not dead, as they had supposed, they then arrange the marriage with Elaine to protect little Basil. The shift from the adultery and illegitimacy of the novel to the bigamy of the play may not seem like a great step, but was carefully planned in order not to offend public tastes. "The play is of a strongly melodramatic type," wrote one reviewer, "and is steeped in a feverish unwholesome atmosphere from the first to last. . . . We congratulate Mr. Daly, however, that he keeps himself clear from even a suggestion of adultery or illicit love." Also, Daly renders the situation of Elaine less morbid by having her suffer not only from consumption but also from an unrequited love for Basil, her childhood sweetheart. As a consequence, their marriage becomes not so much an arrangement (a European custom) as a reunion, one might say, of predestined lovers (American sentimentality). As a melodramatic conclusion, Elaine is deluded into the belief that her husband, not the servant, is trying to poison her; desperately she takes the overdose to end her own life. Then the curtain falls on her miraculous recovery and reconciliation with Basil.

The reviews were generally unfavorable. In those days before out-of-town tryouts, the play was not completely "shaken-down" on opening night and it ran until past midnight—12:20 to be exact. Considering that there were five acts and seven tableaux, this excessive length is not surprising.

Of all the criticisms, Nym Crinkle's is the most trenchant. He calls the play

a bad version of M. About's story. . . . It is bad because he [Daly] has amplified and perverted what was originally symmetrical and credible, in order to find showy work for nearly all the members of his large and excellent company.

In this kind of work Mr. Daly shows himself an apt pupil of the Bronson Howard school—a school, by the way, which has the merit of being distinctly American. It was Mr. Howard who first demonstrated to us with admirable boldness the force of that kind of drama in which all the dramatis personae kept coming and going without doing anything. The merit of that sort of thing was its liveliness. Something was incessantly going on—although nobody could tell exactly what it was. . . . Because his [Daly's] is theatrical not dramatic talent, it is small but proper justice to say that he succeeds. The demerits of the play belong to literature; its excellences to the stage. . . . But the playwright proves himself a good stage manager, and if he has not produced a play he has at least trotted out all his people. This, so far as he is concerned, then, is exhibition, not execution.

What Should She Do? is interesting as a study in the process of dramatizing a novel, but more interesting because of letters exchanged between Augustin Daly and Joseph relating to the adaptation, which throw light upon Daly's practices. These letters clearly indicate that the actual composition of this play was the work of Joseph Daly.

First of all, during the early summer of 1874, Joseph had finished his translation and adaptation of *The Two Orphans*. Augustin wanted to open his fall season with this melodrama, but since the management of Niblo's Garden already had an injunction out to prohibit the performance of the play at the "Onion Square" (Augustin and Joseph's private name for the Union Square) Theatre, he decided to do *Germaine* instead. For his final decision, Daly consulted his legal advisor, A. Oakey Hall, who warned him of the consequences should he produce a play owned by another manager. Actually *The Two Orphans* was finally staged by A. M. Palmer at the Union Square on December 21, 1874, as an adaptation made by A. R. Cazauran, and it became one of the great hits of the American theater.

As a consequence of Hall's advice, Joseph, vacationing with his in-laws in Worcester, Massachusetts, began work on the drama which ultimately became *What Should She Do?* The letters indicate the extent of his labors.

Joseph to Augustin

Worcester, July 2, 1874

I do Germaine this month.

Augustin to Joseph

New York, July 4, 1874

Give good thought to Germaine. . . . I shall announce it as an entirely new play & call it *Jealousy*. So work up effectively that subject: in all the phases: and particularly between the principal characters.

Joseph to Augustin

Worcester, July 13, 1874

Today I began on Germaine. . . . I will try to recollect the few hints you have given me for working it up.

Augustin to Joseph

New York, July 14, 1874

And now apropos of "Germaine" You write me that you have begun on it. I am glad. When I see Hall, it may be that the 2 Orphans will be ugly work to get over—after the late injunction, especially after what I hear of it here. If that is the case I will not open till Aug. 24th—and then with Jealousy.

I presume you are following out the last idea of opening the play at the Old Lawyer's office; where all the family secrets may come out one after the other, something after the following order: At the opening let me have the Lawyer (Whiting) and his clerk (Fawcett) preparing the papers which are being drawn up at the order of the family of the Hero:—(I forget his name)—to be submitted to Madame Kermidy, by which under certain conditions she is to renounce her child.

Madame Kermidy enters: she is an old client of the lawyers & he is ignorant that it is for *her* he is drawing the papers. He is the friend & advisor of her passionate jealous husband—whom he tells her is *alive*. The duchess is announced: as in the play of Germaine & the scene between them follows. The Dr. enters then & I suppose the plot may be pursued as in the original.

I think if you will let the Tropical Scene take place in the island of Madeira or the Canary islands it will be just as well as placing it in America or Cuba.

I fancy in working up the last act you can place the scene in some deserted & ghostly or haunted inn, by the river side & work in the character of the Landlord for *Russell*.

I think also we should have a front scene in the last act prior to the Inn Scene—in which Germaine intercedes with the hero (her husband) for Mad. Kermidy & they resolve to go after her.

The fourth act should end with the following (perhaps it does): a scene of endearment between the child & Germaine in which it is shown how thoroughly the love of the child has been weaned from its real mother & bestowed on Germaine:—this should be overheard by Mad. Kermidy—who dashes out & snatches her child from the embraces of her rival, & utters an angry retort as malediction. In her terror Germaine cries out & the hero enters. Faces his Mistress: takes his child from her & drives her forth loveless & childless, spite of Germaines entreaty.

In the tropical scene work in parts for the lesser people. I have cast the play, with its new parts on the accompanying sheet.

Do you understand & will you work ahead?

Write & give me the order of scenes & a description of them so I can set the painters at work at once!

Augustin to Joseph

New York, July 20, 1874

I am sorry the lawyer's scene doesn't come in. . . . Make a *light* & *heavy* contrast in the 2 mothers for Gilbert & Morant.

Joseph to Augustin

Worcester, July 27, 1874

I am hard at Jealousy. The heroine's name I have taken from Tennyson. It is the old English "Elaine." Or the French "Elene." Whichever you prefer.

I think the play will be capital. The first act is in 2 scenes—viz: Kermidy's & Lord Kenmair's & the 2nd is in one scene—Kenmair's new house.

As far as I can now see the scenes will be.

Act 1.

Sc. 1. Parlor at the London Residence of the Dame de Lannes. "The white hair in the locks of brown." (Or gold if Fanny wears a light head.) See?

Sc. 2. Chamber in the house of Lord Kenmair. "A poor Peer and his last Jewel." (Or Jewett—if you want to make a pun on the bills.)

Act 2.

Elegant drawing room in the New home. (The two verses from Jasmin (Longfellow's) should be put here—as Elaine quotes them in this act.)

Act 3.

Sc. 1. Parlor at the Dame de Lannes. Same as in Act. 1. "A Service is exacted of the Faithful Servant."

Act 4.

Sc. Same as last act in Jamaica. "The contract is broken."

Act 5.

Sc. An Inn at Spanish Town. "The landlord has a Guest."

N. B. A Yankee landlord (compelled to leave the U. S. on account of difficulties.)

Joseph Daly's labors for his brother in *What Should She Do?* are abundantly clear from these letters. Following the failure of the piece, Joseph dashed off a note to Augustin which suggests that he may have had a hand in *Divorce* as well.

New York, September 5, 1874
I wish we hadn't overloaded the poor play. After this no more writing in original characters to sink the whole thing eh? Let's keep our own originalities comic & otherwise for our own new pieces like Divorce.

And on January 7, 1880, contemplating the forthcoming production of *The Way We Live*, Joseph harkened back to their old mistakes again. "Two opening pieces of ours have killed by overloading and strengthening. One was 'What Should She Do' and the other of course 'The Dark City.' Now take warning by their fate; make this simple & straightforward."

The joint authorship of *What Should She Do?* is more easily established than is the source from which the brothers adapted it. About's novel, printed by two publishers in 1857, and Mary Booth's translation of 1860 were both available. According to Nym Crinkle, there was a dramatization by Louis Vider which he says was produced in 1873; and in his letter of July 14, 1874, Augustin had referred to the "play of Germaine." But the most conclusive evidence is offered by the following anonymous editorial, dated September 5, 1875, found in the clipping file of the Harvard Theatre Collection.

When we said last week that we thought from the weakness, desultoriness, and inconsistency of "Mr. Daly's last play," that it was indeed his work, we unconsciously erred; and as we see nothing humiliating in a frank avowal of a mistake, we hasten to make the correction. Bad as the play is, we are now convinced by the facts which we shall presently recite, that Mr. Daly had "but little, if anything, to do with the authorship of What Should She Do" and that his pretensions in this regard are as baseless as his claims to other and more meritorious plays.

The Playbill calls *What Should She Do?* "a new and original Drama of the Times, in five acts and seven tableaux, by Mr. Augustin Daly, author of 'Divorce,' 'Under the Gaslight,' 'Man and Wife,' 'Round the Clock,' 'Leah the Forsaken,' 'Madeline Morel,' 'Alixe,' etc."

What Should She Do turns out to be nothing more or less than an adaptation of d'Ennery's play, which was in turn dramatized from Edmond About's novel of "Germaine." Just who translated that play for the Fifth Avenue Theatre we cannot say with accuracy, but it will be conceded by all that it was *not* Mr. Daly, who has the effrontery to claim the authorship.

Daly, it will be noted, claimed not only the authorship, but advertised the piece as a "new and original Drama."

The manuscript of an adaptation of the French play alluded to has been placed in our hands for perusal by a gentleman whose integrity is beyond question, and whose ability, as indicated by his work, is immeasurably above that of many employed in similar pursuits. The manuscript play, which we have carefully read, is entitled Clara, and is in five acts, and is an adaptation of Germaine. Some months ago it was submitted to Mr. Daly. He kept it for a number of weeks and then returned it to the owner, with a curt note saying in substance that he had, locked in his desk, the original French play, and that he considered both unfit for stage representation, and especially unsuited for the Fifth Avenue Theatre. The adaptor pocketed his discomfiture and cast the unfortunate play aside, where it remained until the recent production by Mr. Daly of the adaptation of the same play, ostensibly by himself. Clara and What Should She Do? are substantially the same play. The story is the same; and, in fact, every feature agrees. In the latter play several characters are interpolated, obviously only to complicate and weaken the story. We do not intend to say that Mr. Daly exercised any bad faith toward the unknown individual who placed his manuscript in his hands, or that he appropriated any of that gentleman's original passages; but we do charge Manager Daly with a degree of inconsistency that is apparently inexplicable, in pronouncing the original French play unsuited for his stage and then producing it. Does he think that his patrons will be satisfied with any dramatic *olla podrida* which he may offer them, however distasteful, or is he so hard run for attractions that he is forced to present a play unfit for stage representation, and especially unsuited for the Fifth Avenue Theatre.

It remained for Daly's next dramatization, *Pique,* to evoke real fireworks—and two lawsuits.

The first suit was provoked by Nym Crinkle, pseudonym of the New York *World* drama critic, A. C. Wheeler. After seeing *Pique,* Wheeler confided to the editor of the New York *Dramatic News* that the play was "founded on, if not altogether derived from another play, by a Miss Eleanor Kirk Ames, entitled *Flirtation.*" Such a juicy bit of gossip naturally intrigued the editor and he printed the accusation. Mr. Daly, "who had hitherto been permitting Messrs. Sardou and Meilhac to claim the authority of his dramatic compositions," at once brought suit against the publisher of the *Dramatic News* claiming damages of $10,000. "In other words, while he generously forgave the reckless French pirates who stole his ideas before they even occurred to him, he determined with strenuous ire, that nobody should accuse him of stealing plot and language from one source, when, in point of fact, he stole them from another." For Daly admitted he had "borrowed" his play of *Pique* from *Her Lord and Master* but was suing to prove he had not stolen it from *Flirtation,* a rather delicate and ironic distinction as the editor of the *Dramatic News* was quick to point out.

The case of Augustin Daly *vs.* C. B. Byrne was tried before the New York Superior Court. Fortunately, the editor of the *Dramatic News* had had the foresight to get a signed statement from Wheeler. Sworn to on February 11, 1876, Wheeler's affidavit contained a charge similar to that made against *What Should She Do?,* that is, that Wheeler had read the manuscript of a play which he suggested should be submitted to Mr. Daly; the author followed the suggestion and when Mr. Wheeler subsequently attended a performance of *Pique*, he "recognized it as identical with the play I had read." To this he added, "I am positive that the manuscript play by the lady I have referred to is identically the same in all material respects as *Pique*."

"Thus confirmed and provided," the editor of the *Dramatic News* "calmly awaited the shock of legal onset." But imagine his consternation when upon the day scheduled, A. C. Wheeler could not be found; he was "hid under a friend's bed in a private house on 18th street." Although this may sound like the scenario of one of Daly's comedies, it was nonetheless in earnest—to the tune of $2363.63, the rather exotic damages finally awarded the "outraged and tearful plaintiff."

The *Dramatic News* did not pay the fine, and "doesn't expect to pay it, but will, of course, appeal." Summing up the situation in an editorial, the publisher of the *Dramatic News* concluded, "When A. Cur Wheeler made his statements, we gave them attention, believing him to be a credible and honorable man. We are not satisfied he lied." The barb was still there.

The other lawsuit connected with *Pique* has similar ironic overtones, only this time Mr. Daly sued an imitator. Shortly after the play began its run, a Mr. Abarbarrel wrote a story, "Married through *Pique*, or the Stolen Child," which ran serially in a weekly newspaper published by the defendants, Norman L. Munro *et al.* "They admit publication and appropriation of characters, but deny imitation of plot and incidents . . . and allege that the story resembles the play only so far as both are from a common source, *Her Lord and Master*." This sounds like quibbling, but actually these reservations and distinctions were necessitated by the current copyright regulations which did not protect a published piece, for example, *Her Lord and Master*, but did protect an un-published one, *Pique*, inasmuch as performance of a play was not considered equivalent to publication.

On the first round of the case, the Judge granted a partial injunction against the word, *Pique*. The defendants then completed the publication of the story as "Married through *Spite*, or the Stolen Child," and also changed the names of the characters.

The second half of the case concerns Mr. Daly's request for a permanent injunction and damages. In so doing, he admitted the resemblance of the play to the novel—his phrase was "a legitimate borrowing"—but was suing against the illegitimate imitation of his unpublished work. Mr. Abarbar-rel, in turn, admitted that his story was a "narrative of the play." He claimed he thought he had a right to make such an adaptation, being unfamiliar with the law protecting un-published manuscripts. The result of this continuation of the case was that "the plaintiff," Daly, "is therefore entitled to judgment and a reference must be ordered to assess the damages."

The paths of scholarly research lead one into strange realms. Information about the second lawsuit over *Pique* is taken from the back of a Fifth Avenue Theatre Playbill for March 10, 1877. It appears that Daly was at odds with the Munros over their publication of "Married through *Pique*" by Mr. Abarbarrel; yet the Daly Correspondence at the Folger Shakespeare Library indicates that on September 22, 1875, shortly before the opening of *Pique*, George Munro, editor of *The Fireside Companion*, wrote to Daly, "I would be glad to enter into arrangements with you to secure stories written from successful plays, whenever you have them. Our former engagements were mutually agreeable. I mean in the case of 'Flash of Lightning' and 'Under the Gaslight' etc." And on October 28, 1875, Daly received a check for $200 from *The Fireside Companion* for *Our Boys*, a play which he had produced but which was written by H. J. Byron. Then on January 2, 1877, Munro wrote again, "Will you please to let us know when we can have the first installment of 'Divorce.' 'Pique' is concluded and we would like to follow it with 'Divorce' at once."

Another curiosity connected with *Pique* relates to a second version of the play. Among the Daly papers at the Folger Library is one which contains a copy of page one of *Piqued! A Society Drama in Five Acts* by Col. T. Allston Brown, copyrighted in 1876, on the back of which are the following notes:

Is the child introduced?
Child stolen?
Pursuit of child?
Tramps introduced?
Raitch?
1st act conservatory
    2 proposals together?
2nd act ending
    with husband dep?

From the notations it seems clear that Daly was ready to pounce upon the piece, but the drama was evidently never produced. It is curious that it is not even mentioned in Col. Brown's own *History of the New York Stage*.

The final irony connected with the authorship of *Pique* is revealed in a letter from Augustin to Joseph Daly on November 21, 1875 from which it appears that Judge Daly may have written the play. "I send you the 1st & 3rd acts—Do think over the bits I suggest & work them in," were the instructions of the producer. And in 1876, Daly was working upon a play (perhaps *Life*) in the course of which required "a novel capture and escape." He wrote to his brother for assistance; Joseph replied helpfully,

If you will look in Aunt's old "Mirrors" for a novel called "The Days of Iturbide" you will find some bandit captures. . . .

Also look into one of her little Christmas gift books, "The Annual" or something like "The Keepsake" & find a tale of the bandits of Spoleto which contains a good "escape." If you can't find what you want then make up something on the style of the capture & murder of the 5 young Englishmen by the Greek bandits & lay your scene among the Express robbers of Indiana. Or if that won't do, tell me what you want and I'll see if I can make it up to imitate the real article.

Novels, then, were a constant source of incidents for the playwright; newspaper stories could also be utilized; and when all else failed there was the helping hand, and imagination, of his brother. More conclusive evidence of Joseph's authorship is contained in a letter from Joseph to Augustin, dated January 24, 1890, fifteen years later. The brothers were having a quarrel over money, and Joseph was pointing out his many past, and unrewarded, services.

It goes against me to say a word in reminder of the many years I worked for no hope of reward, only to help my brother in the dark period from 1873 to 1884. If I kept an account of author's fees for many of the plays then written, how would our accounts stand? And as to those particular plays of "Pique" and "Divorce" was I not satisfied to give no thought of my joint interest in the plays but to regard all the royalty as yours to cover your indebtedness?

Evidently the brothers' tried-and-true practice cast Augustin as the "idea" man while Joseph did the drudgery of writing. However, as one clipping asserts, "the controversy as to the origin of the plots and incidents in the play does not seem to affect the success of its performance, and vast audiences gathered at each representation attest its popularity." With the crowds, then, let us to the play.

Pique has two main themes: the first, which is developed in the first two acts and part of the third, deals with Mabel Renfrew and her marriage and is based upon Florence Marryat Lean's *Her Lord and Master;* the second theme is the kidnaping and rescue of Mabel's child, for which Daly drew on contemporary accounts of the mysterious abduction of Charley Ross.

The novel is divided into parts corresponding roughly to the three volumes in which it was published. We are first introduced to Lady Ethel and the man she loves, the Marquis de Lacarras; he loves money more than he does Lady Ethel and consequently transfers his attentions to her widowed stepmother, the Countess of Clevedon. In a fit of "pique," Lady Ethel accepts the devotion and hand of the wealthy, but socially inferior, Colonel Bainbridge, RA. The story of their marriage (volume two) is unhappy; Lady Ethel snubs her in-laws at Cranshaws, the family estate in Scotland. Finally she confesses to her husband that she does not love him. He volunteers for colonial duty in India. The third volume centers interest in Maggie Henderson, Colonel Bainbridge's cousin, who leads an unselfish life devoted to the whims of her relatives. "Her Lord and Master" is Jesus. Her life is dedicated to caring for others. She has recovered from a broken heart (the consequence of her unrequited love for her cousin) through the greater love of God. At the conclusion of the novel, after she has helped reconcile husband and wife, she joins the order of the holy sisters of Saint Ermenilda.

Daly ignores the religious touches of the novel and centers his play around Mabel Renfrew, who in pique over Raymond Lessing's preference of her stepmother's money, marries Captain Arthur Standish, U.S.N. Although Fanny Davenport had been with the Daly company for six years, this was her first starring vehicle. Her success in the part of Mabel Renfrew led to her use of the play for many years. While she was acting the part at the Grand Opera House in April 1879, Daly, visiting the theater on the advice of Mr. Gardner, manager of Mrs. John Drew's Philadelphia theater, saw Ada Rehan who was playing the role of Mary Standish. Miss

Rehan's "intelligence and adaptability, aided by her 'velvet voice,' " so impressed him that he engaged her for a small part in *L'Assommoir*.

The whole first act of the play is drawn directly from the novel, F. M. Lean's *Her Lord and Master*. Even the novelist's speeches are used. The scene is transferred to Mabel's home in New York, and to Old Deerfield, Massachusetts, where Aunt Dorothy Standish and her niece Mary live. By transferring the action to America Daly eliminates the social distinctions so stressed in the novel, but Mabel antagonizes the Standishes at the family estate by much the same heartless and selfish tactics which Lady Ethel had employed. The main difference is one of timing: in the novel we see Ethel's love for her husband emerging during pregnancy, and the birth of the child concludes their story, while in the play the Standishes have been married for some time and the kidnaping of their child provides the interest for the last two acts as well as the means of their reconciliation. Mabel's awakening love for her husband seems forced and melodramatic when contrasted with Ethel's, whereas the earlier scenes of her courtship, "pique," and marriage emerge more clearly when presented "dramatically."

Two other significant character changes are made by Daly. The first is Captain Standish's father, Matthew. In the novel, Mr. Bainbridge dies at approximately the halfway point, but Matthew Standish in the play is presented as a New England Yankee, God-fearing, strict, and pious; his devotion to the grandchild and sense of responsibility over the kidnaping when the child is abducted from his home prompt him to help in the search and to be present at the final curtain as one of the chief actors in the rescue. The other important character change is in the person of Mary Standish; unlike her counterpart, Maggie Henderson, she has few, if any, religious tendencies. For her Daly invents a love story and centers on her the attention of two of Mabel's cast-off college beaux,

Sammy Dymple and Thorsby Gyll. The two of them provide much of the comedy of the play; they are rich, young, silly—and funny.

The kidnaping of little Arthur provides the excitement in the last two acts of the play. Daly takes us to the "underside of the great city" in some startlingly realistic scenes; indeed, the settings, both those in Massachusetts and those in the New York underworld, make this play a milestone in the history of American stage design. In the slum dens we meet the underworld characters in their own habitat and we see the machinations of the kidnapers. By posing as "Mother Thames," Mabel secures entry to the hideout. There too come her husband and her father-in-law. With the recovery of the child, reconciliations are in order all around. This idea of a child or concern over a child being the means of reuniting parents had also served Daly in *Divorce, Monsieur Alphonse,* and *What Should She Do?*

Daly probably went to the newspapers for the sensational crime which he pictures in these last two acts. Charley Ross, a four-year-old child, son of socially promient Philadelphians, was mysteriously abducted from his home on Wednesday, July 1, 1874, by two men in an "old falling type buggy, painted a dark color." The newspapers throughout the United States took up the case as notes demanding ransom began to appear; a total of twenty-three letters was received. The crime was one of the first of its kind in the United States, perhaps in the world, and attracted the attention of every family in the country. Rewards, posters, inducements of every sort, were offered for the return of the child. Mr. Ross even agreed to the exorbitant ransom of $20,000. Police, private detectives, and public citizens in every city, particularly New York and Philadelphia, were organized in the search. Underworld characters were suspected. Hundreds of leads were, of course, suggested and investigated only to be found false. Six months later a thief killed in an act of burglary at Bay

Ridge, New York, made a deathbed confession. But even on the basis of this confession, police were unable to find Charley. He never reappeared.

Among the hundreds of suggestions which were proffered as solutions to the crime we may include Daly's *Pique*. On May 2, "Daly's box was occupied by the widow of the alleged kidnaper. Detectives hoped that the play might induce her to tell where the boy was." Certainly the idea was no more ridiculous or far fetched than many others. For the play appealed to "those interests that are strongest in the human breast," as one critic wrote, and it had further the felicitous notion of providing a happy ending to the problem—a technique still profitable on Broadway and in Hollywood.

Dr. Hartman claims that *Pique*, because of the "social laws which govern the characters, laws which their pride and sense of fitness will not let them break, belongs to the comedy of manners." This unnecessary classification seems to be stretching a label too far, particularly when *Pique* is one of the few of all Daly's plays with really significant social commentary and an almost intense contemporaneousness. The conflict between the idly rich upper class and the *nouveau riche* middle class, the respect for education, the dislike and distrust of expatriated Americans, the praise of simple, well-regulated living are, it is true, typical of more serious remarks in many comedies of manners. But the comments on the underworld, on swindling, on professional detectives without ethics, and the vivid pictures of New York and New Yorkers are historically more important and interesting than in most comedies of manners. Even the posters depicted on the wall behind Trinity Churchyard, offering rewards for the return of the missing child, are authentic. Stage realism can go no further, and did not even under that master of dramatic setting, David Belasco; and for those critics and historians who prefer to call Zola the father of stage realism, it is well to point out that *Pique* antedates the first production of a Zola play in America by four years. Even the incipient labor movement comes in for a few pertinent remarks, notable for a play produced in 1875.

MATTHEW: Well, I'm in your power.

JIM: Of course you are. You're a rich man, governor! Owner of ten mills and factories, worth four or five millions, but just now you're in the hands of the laboring class, the hard-fisted men of toil.

MATTHEW: Thieves, you mean.

JIM: That's right, call us thieves—that's all you can do. We call you rich men thieves—that's all we can do. But now we'll have no hard names. We'll adjust the differences between capital and labor in a quiet way. You hire eight hundred men to work for you. You've made your millions out of them. It isn't fair. Share your profits with them as earned 'em.

These "many telling hits on topics of the day" assured the play of success. Besides its immediacy, the play was "thoroughly clean and wholesome." To these attributes add its "exceptionally well acted" and well-staged production and "in the face of these merits it would be unfair, even if it would be unprofitable, to dwell on its faults." Although the play received notices of varying degrees of warmth and hostility, it enjoyed a run of 238 performances, from December 14, 1875 until July 29, 1876. Burlesques further attest the play's popularity. Two were copyrighted in March 1876, *The Pique Family, A Play on the Daly* by Sydney Rosenfeld, and *Piquet; or, A Plagiarism of Today* by Montague L. Marks; a third take-off by Kenward Philp was called *Peaked: A Burlesque of Tomorrow;* finally, the very popular San Francisco minstrels gave *Peek: A Daily Play.*

Even while the original New York production was playing to crowded houses, Daly had a second company, headed by Jeffreys Lewis (whose New York part was taken over by Georgiana Drew), on the road. The play continued to be produced in New York until as late as October 17, 1900, when it was performed at the Murray Hill Theatre.

There were almost as many Boston performances from the

first at the Globe Theatre, on August 28, 1876, with the New York cast, until the last revival evidently at the Castle Square Theatre in July 1897. Records of productions in Chicago, New Orleans, Denver, San Francisco, and other cities are numerous. Fanny Davenport played the drama in many of these places; so did Jane Coombs and Agnes Booth.

In England the piece was first given at the Brighton Theatre Royal on October 16, 1882, under the title, *Only a Woman*. A London production called *Her Own Enemy*, apparently a stolen and somewhat mutilated version, was presented March 26, 1884, at the Gaiety Theatre.

Although the authorship of *Pique* was not considered a bright jewel in the crown of its composer, to one anonymous reviewer it "proved him to be possessed of considerable ability as a stage manager, a clear perception of the capacities of his company, and a shrewd knowledge of what is likely to please the public." Such attributes certainly make for success if not for greatness.

Two years of failures followed the great successes, *Divorce* and *Pique;* as a consequence, almost destitute, forced to auction his precious books, Daly plunged his meager resources into a European trip. He hoped for fame in London, feeling that such glory would then win him a fortune in a socially and culturally imitative and impressionable New York. As his brother wrote him (February 18, 1878), "One great advantage of your going there and playing a season in London with good notices is to gain prestige in *New York*. The money in theatrical business is to be made in America, the reputation which can make it here is to be made abroad." Success in London, however, proved elusive. Hoping to find something new in the way of a sensational device or idea, he went to Paris to see *L'Assommoir* at the Théâtre Ambigu; the piece, prepared for the stage by William Busnach, Octave Gastineau, and Emile Zola from Zola's novel, was "all the rage."

Daly wrote to his brother from Paris on January 26, 1879 about his reactions to the play. "L'Assommoir is a disgusting piece: one prolonged sigh from first to last over the miseries of the poor: with a dialogue culled from the lowest slang & tritest claptraps. It gave me no points at all that I could use: & the only novelty was in the lavoir scene." He expanded these feelings somewhat in a letter to Olive Logan.

Realism [he wrote] can scarcely go further; for the sensation scene of Coupeau's fall there is a real scaffolding & real ladders; real hot water for the lavoir scene, and the 2 rival washwomen drench each other, & stand with hair, face, & clothes dripping before the audience, while the stage is positively a puddle. But the whole affair is revolting & certainly attracts from curiosity & not from interest. . . .

He was willing to suppress his obvious dislike of *L'Assommoir* for good theatrical opportunism, however. Fortified by £200 from John Duff, his father-in-law, he secured the American rights to the work and prepared "a version of it, considerably denatured," according to William Winter. Daly's authorship is accepted without question by Dithmar, Odell, and Miss Sturtevant as well as by Winter.

But John Drew in his memoirs, *My Years on the Stage,* states explicitly that "Olive Logan made the version American in all respects." And, despite the playbill, "Adapted and Arranged by Mr. Augustin Daly," Judge Daly clearly says that the version was "the French dramatization of Zola's novel done over into English by Mrs. Olive (Logan) Sykes, who, in fact, negotiated the purchase with the play-broker, Mayer." Olive Logan, as letters between her and Daly prove, was in his employ, being retained for the purpose of spotting adaptable French plays. Besides her salary of $25 a week, Daly rewarded her by producing two of her own pieces, *Surf* (1870) and *Newport* (1879). But her role in connection with *L'Assommoir* was that of a paid literary hack;

certainly Daly showed her no other consideration. In fact, she had to bring suit to collect all of her salary.

Here, then, is a clear-cut example of Daly's appropriation, specifically on the playbill and by implication in the newspapers and other contemporary accounts, of someone else's work. His claim to the piece, he seemed to feel, was proprietary and as such took precedence over literary rights, for he wrote (April 21, 1879), "*It is mine* through direct purchase from the authors." The irony is that he then proceeded to defy all imitators.

Indeed so thoroughly distinct is the dramatic work from the other [Zola's novel] while it contains the very life essence of the novel—that its very originality will be its protection against the imitators who are making ready, as usual, to spring their spurious work on the public, if the courts give them any sort of chance.

A week before the production opened he was already attempting to ward off any such difficulty as had happened in the case of *Pique.* One wonders if he were not prompted as much by conscience as by fear of competition.

Not only did Daly not write *L'Assommoir*, but he was not even the producer. According to the playbill the play was presented at the Olympic Theatre, April 30, 1879, "under the management of Mr. H. Wertheimber," although Daly evidently was consulted about the casting. The cast included several ex-members of Daly's company: B. T. Ringgold and Emily Rigl as Lantier and Virginie; and two newcomers destined for theatrical fame with his company, Maud Granger as Gervaise and Ada Rehan as Big Clemence.

Since the adaptation was not Daly's and since Miss Logan's version was admittedly based on the French dramatization, there is no need to point out the many obvious similarities between the American and French plays. The only distinction the American version may claim is that it was the first of some ten plays in English based on the French work.

The most interesting thing about the performance of *L'Assommoir* at the Olympic is that despite Daly's fascination with the realism of the Théâtre Ambigu, his production lacked those sensationally realistic settings which made the Reade-Warner play, *Drink*, and Belasco's later version at the Baldwin Theatre, San Francisco, so successful. The New York version was indeed "a milestone in the line of Daly mistakes," to quote his brother, whereas the London play, says Winter, achieved "immediate and, unhappily, enduring success." Belasco's dramatization was effective because of

the dexterity of his exacting stage management. A single comparative incident is significantly suggestive: in Daly's New York production the fall of Coupeau from a ladder was palpably made by substituting a dummy figure for the actor who played the part; in Belasco's San Francisco presentation the fall was so skillfully managed that it was for several minutes supposed by the audience an actual accident had occurred.

It is reluctantly that one must admit Daly's falling away from the splendid scenic effects of *Pique*, but it is well to remember that in the main *L'Assommoir* was neither his play nor his production. After this fiasco, he turned again to theatrical management with the opening of a handsome Daly's Theatre on September 17, 1879.

CHAPTER 4

German Comedy
and Song

Je prends mon bien ou je le trouve.

Molière

Whister Kate Bateman stepped onto the stage of the Howard Athenaeum in Boston on December 8, 1862, as the chief character in *Leah, the Forsaken,* creating a role she was to play with success for the next thirty years, she and Augustin Daly, the adaptor of the piece, hoped for an artistic and financial stage success. This they indeed achieved. Furthermore, they were following a tradition, honorable and much observed, of the American drama.

William Dunlap, the "father" of the American theater, began this tradition of producing German plays. On May 15, 1795, New Yorkers witnessed his production of an anonymous translation of Schiller's *Räuber* at the John Street Theatre, the first German play performed in that city. Three years later Dunlap presented *The Stranger* at the Park Street Theatre. Based on Kotzebue's *Menschenhass und Reue,* the adaptation had been prepared by Dunlap himself "on the basis of a poor translation from the German." The piece was a success, so much so in fact that Dunlap consequently decided to study German in order to make his own adaptations from the originals.

For the next twenty years, Kotzebue maintained his

popularity as the leading source of German plays for adaptation. Indeed, not only were his plays constantly translated for use on the English and American stages, but they were played with equal success when German-speaking theaters began to spring up in America later in the century. Kotzebue was supplemented in the 1820's by Charlotte Birch-Pfeiffer, an actress-dramatist, whose plays, largely adaptations from English, French, and German novels, became all the rage in America as they were on the continental German stage. These two playwrights dominated German drama in America in both languages from 1800 to 1860. Zschokke and Benedix were poor seconds. Far down the list came Schiller and Grillparzer; Shakespeare's works in German were more popular on the German stage in New York than Schiller's. In Germany itself, after the death of the great figures such as Iffland and Goethe, there was neither unity nor inspiration to fight off the growing French influence. The good mid-century German dramatists, such literary figures as Hebbel, Ludwig, and later Anzengruber, were not popular in Germany nor were they much adapted outside. By the middle of the century in America, too, German plays were losing out to the more energetic and melodramatic works of French and English playwrights. The domination exerted by German drama on the stages of New York through English-language adaptations abated, although German-speaking theaters throughout America continued to be active and successful until World War I.

The great period of operatic drama and musical comedies brought about a renaissance of German theater in Germany itself in the third quarter of the century. The revival was assisted by the famous Meiningen players, who went to Berlin in 1874, later visiting London in 1881 and the United States in 1891. But in America, the most important contributions to the continuance of the German tradition were made by Augustin Daly and by the wave of German immigration in the 1880's.

Four hundred thousand Germans came to the United States in the 1880's; by 1890, they were the most numerous of any alien strain in the country and Chicago was the third largest German city in the world. Such influxes—the Scandinavians, the Irish, and the southern Europeans also came in great numbers—distinctly affected American life, particularly in the cities. The last quarter of the nineteenth century was the great period of growth for metropolitan America. Improved transportation and sanitation, the economic development of the country at large, and technological inventions made possible enormous concentrations of population. Whereas in 1874 New York City's corporate limits were bounded by the waters surrounding Manhattan Island, by 1898 they had expanded to embrace the Bronx, Kings, Richmond, and a portion of Queens.

These changes, naturally, exerted tremendous influence on the theater. The concentration of wealth and population in cities, and the accessibility of metropolitan areas to commuters, vacationists, and pleasure seekers generally, meant vaster audiences to support long runs and more sophisticated plays. In 1869, Daly produced twenty-one plays in six months, and the ten-week run of *Man and Wife* in 1870 was considered phenomenal. Seventeen years later, from October 5, 1887 to April 7, 1888, he produced only three plays whose longer runs accounted for the full six months: *Dandy Dick*, by Pinero, *The Railroad of Love*, an adaptation from the German, and a revival of *A Midsummer Night's Dream*. Certainly the 1887–1888 season would have been impossible in the New York of 1869. *Dandy Dick* and *The Railroad of Love* would have been too sophisticated for audiences which applauded *Frou-Frou* and Boucicault's melodramas, while Shakespeare, although a staple, could not have achieved a run of over two months; in fact, in 1869–1870, Daly had produced *Twelfth Night*, *As You Like It*, and *Much Ado about Nothing*, all with the charming and popular Mrs.

Scott-Siddons, but the aggregate run was only three weeks.

It is interesting to consider Daly's adaptations from the German with these changing, growing city audiences in mind. From 1862 until 1884, he was content to select for adaptation plays which had already proved their popularity on the various German stages of the City. But eventually New York audiences demanded "new" pieces. After 1884, his adaptations were generally produced first, and then the German managers would play the pieces because of Daly's success. Daly's stature as a producer and adaptor had grown and his company had become a national institution; besides, the arrangements he had made with German dramatists gave him priority of presentation in the United States. When he adapted *Leah* in 1862, *Lorlie's Wedding* in 1864, and even *The Big Bonanza* as late as 1875, there was no question of royalty payments to Mosenthal, Birch-Pfeiffer, or von Moser, the German authors.

Such plagiarism was accepted practice. But in March 1883, Daly wrote his brother the following letter: "In re German plays—I have to send an advance draft to secure 3 plays 1 by Moser 1 by Rosen & 1 by L'Arronge to Berlin by Saturday's steamer. The amount will be $569." The tide had turned. And in 1884, on the occasion of his company's first European jaunt, we can assume he must have concluded arrangements with agents to purchase German plays as we know he did French pieces. Certainly, from that time on, he set the style for German farces.

Daly's interest in French and German plays was in one respect typical of his times. A cartoon of the period, in *The Theatre* for March 20, 1886, shows New York's three leading producers, Wallack, Boucicault, and Daly, dressed in costumes corresponding to their chief interests: Wallack is depicted as an Englishman, Boucicault as an Irishman, and Daly as a German in military uniform.

Doubtless, Daly was partly inspired by a certain snobbishness. Being praised on all sides for his theater and his standard of taste, it was incumbent upon him to be genuinely *avant-garde*. Along the east coast of America, in the latter half of the nineteenth century, to be in the cultural vanguard meant simply to be European. Daly's visits to England, France, and Germany with his whole company were not money-making nor even money-inspired trips. They were, quite frankly, efforts to win recognition abroad, but, more importantly, at home.

It is surprising in a way that the German farces being produced in increasing numbers in Germany as the century wore on were not more widely used for American adaptation. But to a public now used to French plays with their cynicism and polish, German humor was generally thought to be coarse and German sentimentality was unendurably silly. Daly's talent was such that he alone recognized the value of the great reservoir of German farce. True, the misunderstandings which formed the basis of their plots were frequently simple to the point of stupidity, but they were innocent, and the pieces were easy to adapt. Nor must one neglect to mention in this connection what Schlesinger in *The Rise of the City* calls "the arbitrament exercised by women." These plays, so clean and wholesome when compared with French plays of more questionable morality, were certainly the "obvious" favorites of ladies of good background. The prevailing middle-class morality of these plays made them standards of propriety; these were plays to which mothers could send their daughters. One must remember too that the theater of the eighties and nineties, while it continued the tradition of high and great art from Euripides to Shakespeare to Shaw, was also called upon to entertain those audiences which today prefer the movie and radio. These adaptations of his were popular and they were no more inconsequential than any half dozen hits by

John van Druten, F. Hugh Herbert, Ruth Gordon, Garson Kanin, and others, which have in the last few years achieved staggering Broadway runs.

Obviously, no one would presume to insist that these German writers of farce—Kadelberg, the Schonthan brothers, Moser, L'Arronge, Blumenthal, to mention only a few—were either intellectually or dramatically on a par with their more distinguished contemporaries, Hauptmann, Sudermann, or the Norwegians Bjornson and Ibsen. But their plays were popular in Daly's hands. These writers were in a sense the descendants on the one side of Bulwer-Lytton, Sheridan Knowles, and T. W. Robertson, and on the other of Scribe and Dumas *père*.

These plays also reflect the conditions of the theater for which they were originally written. Whereas in England, France, and the United States the theater was centered in London, Paris, and New York, in Germany the theater was dispersed: Hamburg, Weimar, Düsseldorf, Munich, Dresden, Berlin, and Vienna were all important and separate centers. This meant the existence of many local companies skilled in ensemble acting, in the many scattered subsidized and unsubsidized theaters. From these companies there was a real demand, filled by the farce-makers, for comedies requiring clever ensemble acting. This is in direct contrast to the nineteenth-century theater of France and England, the period of great stars, Bernhardt, Coquelin, the Kendals, Ellen Terry, Irving, to name only the most famous end-of-the-century group. These stars wanted starring roles, such as *Camille*, *Cléopatre*, *Hamlet*, even trash like *The Bells*.

In America, Augustin Daly had the only company capable of handling these light-weight comedies deftly and with style. As a consequence, from 1875 on, when his first success in the genre, *The Big Bonanza*, opened on February 17, German farce became a staple of his yearly programs. On November 9, 1880, he presented *Needles and Pins*, adapted from Rosen's *Starke Mitteln*. It ran for over a hundred continuous perform-

ances, and, most important, it featured "The Big Four": Ada
Rehan, John Drew, Mrs. G. H. Gilbert, and James Lewis. No
other quartet in theatrical history has been so well organized
or so completely taken into the hearts of audiences. Critics
from George Bernard Shaw and William Archer to the
humblest urchin on Broadway knew and loved them and were
willing to endure the silly plays they interpreted simply to
enjoy them. Such is theatrical history.

None of the critics has ever inquired into the legitimacy of
Daly's claim to the authorship of some thirty-five to forty
German adaptations and a like number of adaptations from
the French, all completed within a busy lifetime of managing
the most popular and respected theater in New York. To these
activities were presumably added the writing of ten original
plays, the dramatization of ten novels, and the revising of
Shakespeare and other classics. Only a Baconian could hope to
substantiate such monstrous claims.

Daly, himself, could not even read or speak German. Mrs.
Gilbert has stated this fact explicitly in her *Reminiscences*.
But his meager educational background should certainly also
have led to doubt about his capabilities as a linguist. He had
practically no formal schooling. Mrs. Gilbert tells quite
honestly his method of adaptation: "He used to have a
literal translation made of the play he wished to use, and then
he would turn it and twist it about, fitting the parts to the
members of his company, and adapting it all to his audience."

The Daly correspondence at the Folger Shakespeare Library indicates clearly that he had a translator who did the
basic work for him. On the backs of three German letters
from Oskar Blumenthal are notes, in Daly's handwriting,
"Miss Houston, translator." A memorandum, dated May
11, 1895, requests Miss Houston to "Translate this at once
& give the reply to Farrington [clerk in the box-office] to
send to me." Many of the letters have typed-out translations

pinned to them. A letter from Gustav Kadelberg, dated July 3, 1894, has Daly's note, "Translate at once," on the reverse side. Letters from Stobitzer are accompanied by typed-out translations as are the letters from Franz Schonthan, one of which has an accompanying note, dated March 21, 1896, requesting Dorney, Daly's business manager, to "have Miss Houston translate this carefully & mail to me at the Aldine, Philadelphia."

The procedure Daly followed in adapting German plays by revision of a literal translation was common enough at a time when plagiarism was one of the standard methods of writing a "new" play. Dozens of dramatic hacks worked as house dramatists for all the successful theaters, and the extent of their so-called literary labors will probably never be known, for they wrote anonymously and left nothing for identification except their trashy ill-printed plays. Boucicault was such a practitioner; so, too, was Fred Williams, who did many adaptations for Daly. On July 3, 1879, Williams wrote, "I shall be most happy to enter into the collaboration you have suggested." And he apparently completed the arrangements a week later for on July 8, he wrote, "If you consider the position worth the salary I expect, namely, sixty a week, I see no obstacle to a satisfactory arrangement," but he confessed, "You remember I presume that I have told you I am ignorant of German, the adaptations I have made from that source were all in conjunction with Dr. Harris."

F. C. Burnand, the editor of *Punch*, was in much the same position as Williams. His German adaptations, *The Orient Express* and *Number 9*, were produced by Daly in 1893 and 1897, respectively, yet on July 13, 1893, he wrote Daly, "I don't know German—never *could* learn it except enough to feed me—so my work would have to be started from a *translation*."

Even William Dean Howells, mighty editor of the *Atlantic Monthly*, was willing to profit from literary hack work. He had sent Daly several of his plays, but they found no favor with the producer. Astute man that he was, Daly recognized in Howells a potential source of help, and having rejected him as a writer of original plays, he was nonetheless perfectly willing to embrace him as a fellow adaptor. Evidently he made Howells an offer, for on March 19, 1884, Howells wrote that "I will nationalize that German comedy for $2000 cash on delivery, if it is to appear *without* my name. If you want my name with yours, you must pay me much more."

This practice of employing as adaptors playwrights who submitted unusable pieces to him became a favorite mode of operating with Daly. After George A. Hibbard had sent him *Jarman's Own* and *A Wayward Wooing*, both of which he rejected, Daly presumably sent him some German plays to consider as potential adaptations, for on June 23, 1893 Hibbard wrote, "I have read the German plays which you gave me and I think something can readily be made of them." Blanche Willis Howard, the novelist, who had sent Daly her comedy, *Wanted, A Companion*, and a one-act play, *Bachelor Ladies*, was, according to letters exchanged between them, engaged in adaptations of German plays during the summer of 1886. And Charles Gayler, having submitted *The Queens of Society*, *Magic Marriage*, and *Kissing the King*, all of which were turned down, ended up, in 1883, doing an adaptation from the German for $100. The play was *Who's Who;* referring to it, Gayler wrote: "In the very short conversation we had in reference to it, you spoke of my accepting a certain sum per week in lieu of royalty. What do you think you can afford to pay?"

Daly followed the same procedure with Edgar Fawcett, although he did produce Fawcett's *Our First Families* in 1880. Fawcett wrote Daly on November 12, 1881, at the time of the production of *The Passing Regiment* ("adapted and augmented by Augustin Daly"—so ran the blurb on the playbill): "I was very nervous during the 1st act, but at the end of the

2nd I felt that the 'Passing Regiment' had come to stay." His nervousness, it seems obvious, could have resulted only from his concern as a participant in the writing of the play. Three years later, he sent to Daly one J. V. Prichard, whom he recommended highly as "a translator of French and German plays."

Another translator who worked for Daly was Alex Seaman, who wrote him November 15, 1894, "As you have undoubtedly forgotten me by this time, I hereby take the liberty of reintroducing myself. In the beginning of this year I made several translations for you, of different plays from the French & German, in London."

On September 17, 1883, Leander P. Richardson, who adapted French plays for Daly, wrote asking "What about the German piece I was to do?" On March 22, 1894, Arthur Law requested, "If you will now kindly send me the translation of the German play I shall be glad to read it and see if I can undertake the work of adaptation." And on May 6 of the same year Fred Horner acknowledged a check for an adaptation of a play by Laufs. A letter from Arthur Pinero (October 20, 1884) indicates that Daly had proposed to send him literal translations of German plays which he would then adapt for a fee.

Thank you for your kind offer. Will you entrust me with literal translations of such of these plays as you yourself believe in? I have no knowledge of the German language, but in any case it would be upon the spirit and not upon the letter of the original that I should found my labor.

During the next few years Pinero followed the practice of registering in his own name German adaptations of plays owned by Daly which the latter wished to have protected by copyright in England.

Perhaps the clearest light on the procedure is cast by Jerome K. Jerome, who wrote the following in his autobiography, *My Life and Times:*

Afterwards Daly asked me to adapt Sudermann's "Die Ehre." I had marvelled up till then at the linguistic range of the average dramatic author who at a moment's notice "adapts" you from the Russian or the Scandinavian, or any other language that you choose. I did not know then very much German and had to confess it.

"That'll be all right," said Daly. "I'll send you the literal translation."

For translations, a shilling a folio used to be the price generally paid to the harmless necessary alien.

The case is clearly stated. For Jerome continued,

Somewhat against my conscience, I consented to bowdlerise Sudermann's play so as not to offend Mrs. Grundy, who then ruled the English and American stage.

In *A Dictionary of the Drama*, W. D. Adams adds that this comedy, called *Birth and Breeding*, was performed, for copyright purposes, at the Edinburgh Theatre Royal, September 18, 1890. A. H. Quinn, by virtue of having seen a collection of "Daly manuscripts" in the possession of Samuel French, lists the adaptation as *by* Daly *with* Jerome K. Jerome; on the same list, Quinn includes *The Test Arrow*, which, as letters show, was prepared for Daly by A. W. Pinero. These are clear-cut cases of mistaken attribution of authorship to Daly.

The most objectionable aspect of Daly's practice is not that he paid for translations and adaptations, but that on playbills and in printed editions he afterwards claimed the authorship of almost all the German and French adaptations that he produced. The great difficulty, of course, is that there is no way of knowing definitely what plays these authors adapted for Daly, since, first, he naturally made some revisions in them during rehearsals, secondly, he copyrighted and printed most of them in his own name, and finally, his brother Joseph wrote or rewrote almost all his plays anyhow.

It would be impossible to overestimate the role of Joseph Daly in the writing and/or adapting of Augustin Daly's plays.

The failure of Joseph even to hint at such a relationship in his biography of Augustin may be attributed to that sincere and brotherly good will and affection which the letters clearly indicate. Covering the period from 1856 to 1899, the letters, frequently dull, never very well written, often annoyingly vague in reference, do testify to a tremendously close and loving attachment, especially strong on Joseph's part, between the two brothers, and they also constitute a complete exposition of the nature of the dramatic composition engaged in by the brothers. Joseph had a hand, usually a major share, in the writing or revising of almost every play produced by his brother. One of the few exceptions was *A Priceless Paragon*, produced February 12, 1890, on which occasion Joseph wrote a note of congratulations, adding, "It seemed strange to me to sit at the first play you ever produced (French German American) in which I had no hand."

Time and again his contemporaries cast suspicions upon the legitimacy of Daly's claims as an author, but still the analysts of the American stage have willingly subscribed to the fiction that Augustin Daly was a prolific and clever, if not a great, playwright and adaptor. The fact, for instance, that a certain C. M. S. McLellan wrote, in *The Theatre*, "It is stated that Mr. Augustin Daly personally adapted his new successful play, *The Railroad of Love*. 'There are more things in heaven and earth, etc.,' " should have tipped off the careful historian. Daly's prompt reply to this charge, "expressing his mystification at the joke" in McLellan's remark, should perhaps have been a spur to doubt. For, ironically, a month before Daly's retort, he had written Joseph about this very play, *The Railroad of Love*, "You know the piece ends abruptly—you did it intentionally I think: deferring the usual ending till I need it. I need it now." As other notes between the brothers indicate, Joseph spent the month of October in "feverish last minute revision" of *his* adaptation of *The Railroad of Love*. Yet the playbills announced the piece as "a comedy by Augustin

Daly" and the manager even dared express "mystification" over a note questioning his authorship. Meanwhile, during the run of the play—November and December 1887—he was paying Joseph regular royalty checks.

The list of German farces which Daly produced should be headed, "plays adapted by Joseph and Augustin Daly." For their correspondence reveals clearly a close collaboration with perhaps the major part of the work being contributed by Joseph. In June 1886, for example, Joseph wrote that he had finished *Silks and Velvet*, the literal title of *Sammt und Seide*, which eventually became *After Business Hours*. In February and March 1895, Joseph was at work on *A Bundle of Lies*, for which he also provided a "tag." And on October 15 of the same year, Augustin sent *The Countess Gucki* to Joseph "to simplify the ultra German names & soften the dialogue"; on December 6, he returned it for Joseph "to go over *again* with a view to making it contemporaneous." On January 23, 1896, Joseph returned the final version with the "tag."

The account of *Dollars and Sense* is even more detailed. Augustin originally sent *Die Sorglosen* to Joseph from Cincinnati May 30, 1883, following it with a letter, "If you are in the spirit do Sorglossen *now*—and I'll send you soon the other piece to do. You remember you promised me two." While on his summer vacation in Worcester, Joseph decided, July 10, "I will do Sorglossen & put the characters in American dress. It is a charming play to do. Easy as far as plot is concerned since it needs no additions: but must have fine work to give epigrammatic dialogue."

Yet Joseph's ignorance of German matched his brother's for on August 4 he wrote, "By the way who or what is Sorglossen? Is it something to eat?" Nevertheless, "it will be as I promised a witty play. The acting parts are good. But most exacting. I am bestowing much care on it." Evidently with "much care," the piece was finished. In September 1883, four letters were exchanged in which the brothers worried about a suitable name. Finally, Joseph suggested *Dollars and Sense* although he later warned Augustin against the pun involved and insisted upon the subtitle, *The Heedless Ones*, to offset the facetiousness. Mrs. Gilbert has corroborated the Judge's responsibility in the choice of title in her reminiscences:

> *Dollars and Sense* was one of his best titles. I know when he was trying to find a name for that particular piece he read a whole list of titles to us once at breakfast, and I said, "Oh, I like that one." Then it was spelled "Dollars and Cents," and it was Judge Daly who suggested the change. "Let the old man keep his dollars," he said, "but the old woman has the sense."

In December 1888, Joseph prepared *Cornelius Voss*, presented as *An International Match*, "a real comedy," for which he received royalty checks in April 1889; and in July 1889 he was working on *Illustrious Woman*, which became *The Great Unknown*. But not all of Joseph's work was accomplished as easily as that on *Dollars and Sense*. He reports to Augustin on May 5, 1890 that he is having trouble with *The Last Word*. "It has to be *adapted* almost word for word and therefore progresses slowly," he wrote. And on May 20, he expressed the hope that "the next play will be easier to do. This one was such a *sauerkraut* (alias German) production that the adaptation was no joke." But the royalty checks in December 1891 helped him to forget the travail.

Another play with which Joseph had struggled was *Quits*. The first mention of the piece occurs in a letter from Joseph dated June 23, 1881.

> I send per Express today the first 2 acts. The First act is entirely remodelled so as to bring all the fun in at the latter part—the entrance of Mme de B & her daughter. The Second Act—with the exception of some verbal alterations—I leave as it is. The 3rd act is to be entirely changed so as to have bustle. I hope you'll like it.

A month later Joseph "sent" act three.

> The Last Act (being Acts 4 & 5 in one) and not hard to do be-

cause they work out the story legitimately to the end & are full of good comedy situations. I will send it along. . . . If you think the 3rd act will be a go then the comedy will be a success.

On July 22, Augustin returned "the entire lot . . . for revision. Let me have the *Revision* as fast as possible," he begged. On August 11, 1881, Joseph wrote, "I sent all of *Quits* to you yesterday." The final reference to the play is dated September 2 (it opened September 7), when Joseph wrote

Here's your Epilogue. I trust this is the last I shall hear of work on that piece. It ought to be a success—ought Quits. It was the toughest job I ever had. And to think of your sending back after all for an Epilogue! . . . If the actors take as much trouble as the authors the play ought to be a stunner.

Occasionally Joseph had to warn his brother about altering his adaptations. The day after sending *The Way We Live* he wrote to remind Augustin not to meddle and "overstrengthen"; yet three months later, Joseph was still working on the piece but "I have an inspiration for a scene of rehearsing private theatricals that should be a go." No sooner was he finished with *The Way We Live* than Augustin sent him (July 1, 1880) "the translation of *Strong Means*" (*Needles and Pins*). "I have," wrote Augustin, "made a suggestion or two on the title, as to cast, and all the rest will readily occur to you." The "rest" did "readily occur" for by August 2 Joseph was on the third act. "I had to press in a new scene for Lewis at the end of the 2nd, & give him a roaring finale as his part peters out so in the 3rd and 4th acts."

When he was working on *Our English Friend*, Joseph sent Augustin the first act on July 19, 1882, and

a word of advice—or several
1. Give it a strong name
2. Don't spend much on it—for by a strange fatality every first piece for several years has been a failure.

Augustin was not satisfied with the play. He returned it in a week saying, "I don't think you have got the *juice* out of the situation for your finale to Act 3. When you go over this whole you'll agree with me. I think 4 acts is enough—& you ought to join Act 4 & 5."

But Joseph was unwilling to accept this last suggestion, and it was Augustin who capitulated (August 2), "If you prefer to run the 4th and 3rd acts together do so," he conceded. "It will be as well. . . . I don't intend to make any alterations when you have finished. . . . Send your altered work & cast as you do it act by act."

In 1884, Joseph prepared *A Wooden Spoon;* during 1891–1892, he adapted and revised *Little Miss Million;* in 1895, he did *The Transit of Leo.* Not only did he do some dozen adaptations of his own, but he also revised the work of other adaptors. For example, on August 29, 1881, he sent Augustin the "altered text" of *Raven's Daughter.* "The play is very concise as it stands now and should play well," he concluded. Despite Joseph's efforts and the work of the original adaptor, Fred Williams, the piece was none too successful.

One other consideration deserves special notice here—the universal practice of labeling adaptations as "new" plays. Daly did it continually. His playbills and printed editions carried such credits as "an original play in four acts by Augustin Daly, partly founded on the most recent dramatic work of Dr. S. H. Mosenthal of Vienna" for *Madelein Morel,* "a holiday comedy in four acts by Mr. Augustin Daly" for *Needles and Pins,* "an entirely new eccentric comedy, in four acts and a Kermess (from a German piece of Jacobson) adapted by Augustin Daly" for *Red Letter Nights!* or such flagrant deceits with no indication of source at all as "an entirely new comedy of contemporaneous interest, arranged in four acts, by Augustin Daly" to announce *The Way We Live,* adapted from *Die Wohlthatige Frauen.*

This practice was a favorite ruse of theater managers. In England it led to a lawsuit when the magazine, *The Theatre,* questioned the originality of a play, *Hester Gray*, by R. Reece and H. Garnie. Described in the programs as "new," the piece, according to *The Theatre*, was, on the contrary, taken from an old English play, *Ruth Oakley*. The authors sued the magazine for libel: they had not plagiarized *Ruth Oakley*; they had adapted *Hester Gray* from a French drama, *La Mendiante*. The case was heard February 20, 1879, with a distinguished array of witnesses—Palgrave Simpson, Tom Taylor, John Holingshead—who came "to prove that it was the practice to term an unacknowledged adaptation a 'new' play." For, it was admitted, it has been the "practice of nearly every dramatic author to call an adaptation a 'new' play and withhold the name of the original." The excuse given for the label "new" was that the play, although admittedly not "original," was "new" to the English stage.

A further complaint against this sort of deception was lodged by the American counterpart of the British magazine. G. E. Montgomery, associate editor of *The Theatre*, charged that "the average dramatist of today is neither an inventor nor a creator; he is a plagiarist. . . . He steals deliberately and without conscience. . . . Accuse him of theft and he laughs." Indeed the American dramatist of the period considered his plagiarism in the tradition of Shakespeare and Molière who wrote, "Je prends mon bien où je le trouve." The judgment of Mr. Montgomery was that there was a distinction between his contemporaries and Shakespeare "who took a crude, ingenious narrative and transformed it into an imperishable work of beauty." The judgment of time has vindicated his conclusion, for most of the plays of Montgomery's contemporaries have, rightly, disappeared alike from the boards and the libraries.

Daly's first adaptation from the German was undertaken while he was a critic on the *Courier*. It was *Leah, the Forsaken* which opened at the Howard Athenaeum, Boston, December

8, 1862; his last adaptation was *The Countess Gucki* at Daly's Theatre in New York, January 28, 1896, and his final production of a German adaptation was F. C. Burnand's *Number 9* at Daly's, December 7, 1897. In the span of thirty-five years, he was associated with the production of some forty-two German adaptations, of which he claimed the authorship of thirty-six, an average of one a year. These figures do not include adapted but unproduced German plays of which there were eleven.

Leah, the Forsaken, an adaptation of Dr. S. H. Mosenthal's *Deborah,* was, like its original, an immensely popular play. From all accounts, H. L. Bateman originally gave the play to Daly to adapt in a translation prepared by W. Benneux. Bateman was the father of the famed Bateman children, Kate, Ellen, Isabel, and Virginia; and their mother, Sidney Frances Bateman, was equally well known, both as a dramatist and later as manager of Sadler's Wells Theatre. He staked all his means on the production, engaged a supporting cast of note, and starred his daughter, Kate. The Boston reception justified his elaborate plans, so the play was taken to New York on January 19, 1863, and opened at Niblo's Garden.

Judge Daly relates that New York audiences were enthusiastic despite adverse newspaper criticisms of the piece. The public kept the house "thronged" during the play's initial five weeks' run. He attributes the bad critical notices to the fact that other drama critics were jealous of the success of one of their number, but another possibility is that some of them may have been sincerely outraged by the excessive melodramatic touches—both in action and language—of the piece. There were, of course, defenders. *The Spirit of the Times* gave it a favorable review, and George William Curtis, editor of *Harper's Weekly,* praised it lavishly. Curtis, seeing in the story of Jewish persecution a lesson for American Christians who were similarly abusing the Negro, urged his readers to "go and see *Leah* and have the lesson burned in upon your

mind which may save the national life and honor." As a foot-
note to this plea, it might be pointed out that *Uncle Tom's
Cabin* had already far overshadowed *Leah* as an incitement for
racial equality; in February 1862, dramatizations of Mrs.
Stowe's novel were playing in no less than four New York
theaters—Winter Garden, Wallack's, and both Bowerys. Miss
Bateman played *Leah* again in New York May 4 to May 24,
1863, following a successful engagement in Philadelphia. On
October 1, 1863, Miss Bateman opened in London at the
Adelphi Theatre. The version of the play used there was
somewhat revised by John Oxenford of the *Times*. Whatever
changes he may have made, the piece was a tremendous hit,
running for over 300 nights, and was generally well-received
by the English press.

The basis for the play's great popularity with audiences
and actresses alike may have been in the flamboyant characterization of Leah herself. In the mid-nineteenth century, a
theatrical period when acting was more important than playwriting, the part of Leah offered an opportunity for an ambitious actress to display all the resources she either possessed
or thought she possessed. This kind of challenge undoubtedly
inspired many actresses—Ristori, Janauschek, Methua-Scheller, Bernhardt, Lucille Western, Fanny Davenport, to mention only the outstanding—to play the role. Emotionalism,
then, rather than morality, explains the play's continued
success.

The story concerns the love between a Jewish maiden,
Leah, and a Christian, Rudolf. He is faithless to his vows.
Leah, along with other Jews, is driven out of Austria by the
edicts of the land. She returns years later to take revenge, but
she discovers that Rudolf and his wife, Madalena, have named
their child after her and that Rudolf is actively engaged in
getting the laws against the Jews abolished. She forgives
Rudolf, she places a withered rose-wreath on little Leah's
head, she curses an apostate Jew, Nathan, and she leaves, "for

this night I shall wander into the far-off—the promised land!" The curtains are effective, melodramatic tableaux. The most exciting occurs at the end of Act I when an angry mob, pursuing Leah to stone her, is halted by Father Herman who "lifts the cross from his neck . . . and at the sight of the symbol the crowd uncover their heads, and bow in submission."

The original German play was written in blank verse. Daly's version is prose and seems, as some critics have implied, rough and somewhat tawdry.

Madame Ristori had played the piece in Italian in London at Her Majesty's Theatre, July 4, 1863, before Miss Bateman presented it there in English. Her version, translated by Sig. Gaetano Cerri, was compared by Professor H. Morley to Daly's, greatly to the detriment of the latter. In his *Journal of a London Playgoer* Morley says, "The charm of the pastoral play has been all trampled out by the hoof of the American adaptor." Sarah Bernhardt also essayed the role in London in a French version prepared by M. Albert Dumont. Both of these distinguished actresses, as well as Madame Janauschek and Madame Methua-Scheller, played the piece in New York, in their native tongues and in specially arranged English translations.

According to one contemporary, Daly's version "was purchased outright by Miss Bateman." The final night of her initial run, February 21, 1863, however, she devoted to an author's benefit. "The act is so generous a one . . . that the bare announcement of it takes away my breath," concluded one critic. But Miss Bateman's generosity did not so completely overcome the young author. For he fell out with Mr. Bateman over the extent of the reward he should receive; the result was a lawsuit in which Daly's case was presented by A. Oakey Hall, then district attorney.

Hall's speech in Daly's behalf was recreated from memory by Daly for an interviewer from the New York *Herald*, in which paper it appeared on April 26, 1866. From the speech, it is clear that Daly received $250 outright for the adaptation, plus $225, realized at the benefit; Hall contrasted this meager sum with the "hundreds of thousands" which "Shylock" Bateman and his daughter had realized. The oration—for such it was—pictured the young artist caught in the tentacles of the clever Bateman; Daly was presented as the typical professional man—"who dies poor." Hall quoted Thackeray, Shakespeare, Sheridan; he mentioned scores of theatrical names of the past and present. He scornfully referred to Bateman as "this Southern Yankee."

From the speech, it is evident that Daly went to Philadelphia in 1863 with the Batemans for a month. During that time, he was employed as a press agent and wrote *A Memoir of Miss Bateman*. For his services he received $25 a week, which Hall also considered insufficient.

On the subject of adaptation, Hall waxed eloquent. (It is well to remember that he himself sought fame as an adaptor—*Fernande*, *Humpty-Dumpty*, and other pieces.) "Mr. Daly," said Hall, "breathed the breath of life into the dead soulless translation of *Deborah*"; in so doing, he "cultivated the gem into a native and original drama." (Judge and jury were not drama critics!) His climax was fitting: "Shakespeare's plays were but adaptations; Boucicault's plays are mostly adaptations."

Hall's emotionalism captivated the court, and Daly won the case. Apparently it was a hollow victory. For Daly's self-styled "chum" Adah Isaacs Menken wrote him in August, 1866,

I cannot fancy you, Gus, being so frightfully "thin-skinned" as to fancy yourself the injured party in this late affair. The Don Quixotic defender of his daughter's virtue [Bateman] has got decidedly the worst of it. Oakey Hall quite settled that. And his very able defence I see has been copied in several journals. I think that it's a fine thing for you. Everybody will be after you now.

Although Kate Bateman owned the play and continued

it in her repertoire for over thirty years, many other American actresses acted in it. As far as the records indicate, *Leah* was played in 1866 by Lizzie St. John, in 1879 by Elizabeth von Stamwitz, in 1880 by Fanny Davenport, in 1886 by Margaret Mather, and as late as 1898 by Rachel Renard and Nance O'Neil; others who took the role at unspecified times were Avonia Jones (who played the part for President Grant), Mrs. D. P. Bowers, and Alexina Fisher Baker. It is impossible to determine whether all these actresses used the Daly version. One clipping relates that Daly sued Mr. Mead, husband of Lucille Western, for unpaid royalties. "For my part," said the anonymous reporter, "I think it the meanest of all mean things to attempt to cheat a poor literary man out of the price of this mental labor. . . . Pilfering nickels off a deceased colored gentleman's optics is nothing to such an act of barbarity."

Shortly after Miss Bateman's run at Niblo's, another version of the piece, called simply *Deborah*, by Isaac C. Pray, was presented at the Winter Garden (May 30, 1863) with Catherine Seldon and Lawrence Barrett. Further adaptations under a variety of titles—*Hager, Lysiah, the Abandoned, Miriam, Naomi, Ruth*, and *The Slave Girl*—are listed in *A Dictionary of the Drama* and *"The Stage" Cyclopaedia*.

Perhaps the most interesting of all is the burlesque of *Leah*, called *Leah, the Forsook*, by Frank Wood, produced at the Winter Garden on July 13, 1863. The cast included "the enormously funny" Dan Setchell as Leah, "a Shrewish maiden," and Emily Thorne, Mark Smith, Sol Smith, Jr., and C. T. Parsloe, Jr. When, later, Wood and Daly adapted *Taming a Butterfly* for Mrs. John Wood, the playbill prominently announced the piece as by the authors of *Leah, the Forsaken* and *Leah, the Forsook*. Another burlesque, in verse, by William Routledge, was printed in 1869 under the title, *Leah, a Hearty Joke in a Cab Age*.

The success of *Leah* led Daly, in 1875, to a new adaptation, presented on November 22 as *The New Leah*. Even Judge

Daly admits that the title was a ruse to avoid paying royalties to Miss Bateman. For the lead of this piece, Clara Morris returned to Daly's to enact "Esther," as he now called the heroine. Undoubtedly, in this production, Daly was attempting to continue the successful business he had just enjoyed with Booth (October 25 to November 20) and which he hoped the reputation of Clara Morris would accomplish. But the piece was a failure and was withdrawn at the end of a week, and Clara Morris received bad reviews for attempting a role in which "she constantly strained for passion and never achieved it." In none of her three autobiographical books of stage reminiscences does Miss Morris mention this fiasco.

When Daly adapted *Deborah*, he had selected, or rather Bateman had chosen for him, the most popular German play of the period. His second adaptation was from the pen of the most popular German dramatist of the time, Charlotte Birch-Pfeiffer. After great success as an actress, Madame Birch-Pfeiffer had in 1828 turned to dramatizing popular novels, *Der Glockner von Notre Dame* after Victor Hugo, *Dorf und Stadt* from Auerbach, *Die Wais aus Lowood* from Charlotte Brontë, and *Die Grille* from George Sand. "She understood how to make plays affecting and exciting . . . and thus won triumphs which in duration and number are scarcely to be surpassed," wrote Witkowski in his study, *The German Drama of the Nineteenth Century*.

Dorf und Stadt was first presented in this country at the Altes Stadttheater the week of October 6, 1854. Based on Berthold Auerbach's tale, *Die Frau Professorin*, the play achieved great success, and continued to remain in the repertoires of the German theaters of New York for a long time. When the charming Madame Marie Methua-Scheller decided to try her fortunes on the English-speaking stage as well as the German, she turned to this favorite piece she had known and played in as a member of the Stadttheater company. Following lessons in English with Professor J. E. Frobisher, she made her debut in Boston; the theater was the old Boston Theatre, the date was March 2, 1864, and the play was *Lorlie's Wedding*, "an entirely new Musical, Pastoral Drama by Augustin Daly." After one more representation in Boston, on March 5, she opened in New York at the Winter Garden on March 28, 1864.

The five-act adaptation ran a week. It was well received by the *Post*, the *Journal*, and the *Boston Transcript* ("Mr. Daly has constructed a charming play"), but the German paper, *Belletristiches Journal*, regarded the English version as "most unsatisfactory." Hagan, who played the male lead, complained that "the play was very bad, being at times utterly stupid, but the actress partially redeemed it." Probably for sentimental reasons, if no other, Madame Methua-Scheller kept *Lorlie's Wedding* in her repertoire, but a letter from her husband-manager indicates that they, too, considered the Daly version unsatisfactory, for he wrote to Daly from San Antonio, Texas, April 7, 1872, "As to *Lorlie* it is an entirely different piece than you originally produced. I had it retranslated condensed & changed. It is a shorter piece now—& yet not fit for the English stage."

The week after Madame Methua-Scheller and *Lorlie's Wedding* left the Winter Garden, Daly's name was back on the programs. This time the star was Avonia Jones and the play, *Judith, the Daughter of Merari*. The play opened April 4, 1864, and was announced as a five-act tragedy, "a new and original" play, written "expressly" for Miss Jones. When she later played the piece in Washington at Grover's New Theatre, January 17, 1865, the playbill stated that *Judith* was "founded on a Sublime Biblical Legend," and was "written by Augustin Daly."

The claims of the playbill are an exaggeration. Judge Daly states that *Judith* was "prepared in collaboration with Paul Nicholson, a fellow journalist." If confirmation is needed, it can be provided by a letter, dated June 16, 1864, in which Nicholson requested Daly to forward his share of the royalties. "What has become of 'Judith' and all the children of Israel?" he queried. "Do they not declare quarterly dividends? I do not desire 'a pound of flesh,' yet we have an honorable bond between us. . . ." Miss Sturtevant adds they had a third collaborator, a man named De Lille, a writer for the New York *Herald*.

The Albion and the *News* attacked the play on the basis of its adaptation, but *The Round Table* was much more specific, for it charged that the Winter Garden and Miss Jones had sought to buy off the critics beforehand by having them write the play. *The New Nation* refuted this charge, admitting, however, that De Lille and Nicholson "had assisted him [Daly] to write acts and scenes for which he had no time," but adding that "they have had no dealings with the Winter Garden management." The question is a delicate one. For obviously, from the letter quoted above, both Nicholson and Daly, and by extension De Lille, drew royalties for the play, and Daly was furthermore Miss Jones's manager. Inasmuch as they were also drama critics, one might question the objectivity of their reviews.

Certainly some of the papers left little doubt of adverse opinion. The *News* stated that "there was much more to condemn than to admire. . . . Ridiculous inventions like those in this 'original play' are monstrous." *The Albion* was more explicit. "*Judith* was made in Germany by an artizan of some local repute named Hebbel. Thence, under the auspices of the great Ristori it was conveyed to Italy; thence to America, where it foundered. . . . " It is on the basis of some such statement as this that Miss Sturtevant must have projected her claim that *Judith* was "probably based on *Giuditta* by P. Giacometti and *Judith* by F. Hebbel."

The important thing is not that Daly and his collaborators should have borrowed—without acknowledgment, of course—

but that for once Daly should have chosen such a distinguished source as Friedrich Hebbel. As far as popularity goes, Hebbel, until the birth of realism late in the century, remained ignored and unknown both in his own country and abroad. And certainly there is no reason to assume that Daly selected *Judith* for adaptation for any reason other than its melodramatic possibilities. Since no copy of the adaptation exists, it is impossible accurately to determine the extent of the borrowing. Hebbel's *Judith*, written in 1839, was according to Witkowski, "the first modern drama of the nineteenth century." Daly, Nicholson, and De Lille, working from a literal translation, may have recognized neither the literary nor the spiritual quality of the drama. Certainly, if well adapted, a play of this caliber could hardly have earned such critical comments as "wearisome," "wretched," "turgid."

The indebtedness of *Judith* to Paolo Giacometti's *Giuditta* (1857) is, of course, equally difficult to ascertain. Giacometti was a prolific playwright. Ristori, Salvini, and others played his works both in Italy and America. Daly probably secured a literal translation of the Italian play (an undated contract shows that he also acquired Giacometti's *Marie Antoinette*) and used it along with the translation of Hebbel's *Judith* to work into the dramatic hodgepodge which he and his collaborators finally produced. The shortness of the run of *Judith*, one week, seems sufficiently eloquent testimony of its lack of worth. The subject of the Biblical heroine has, however, remained an intriguing one for dramatists. Besides Hebbel, Giacometti, Daly and collaborators, T. B. Aldrich, Arnold Bennett, Jean Giraudoux, T. Sturge Moore, and others have used the story; and Carl Van Doren rendered Hebbel's *Judith* in English in *Poet Lore* in 1914.

Daly's early German adaptations, like his versions of French plays, were generally designed for the use of a particular star. The star system was vicious; its worst effects were felt not so much by the theater as an institution, as by its literary record.

In *Madelein Morel,* one of the speeches reveals the current evil. A theatrical producer is speaking:

Bless your heart, you have only to appear and speak to be the rage. You can't do this in the standard plays, because the old dramatists wrote for *actors* and *actresses.* You get a new writer to prepare a piece, in which without having to show any talent, you are made the center of interest, the victim of plots, the incarnation of virtue, suffering, fortitude and propriety; you come on in every scene, and stay on till the curtain goes down. The other subordinate, but clever, artists play other parts—you shine resplendent as the star. You make a furor, engagements pour in, and we all accumulate fortunes and retire.

Stars needed, commanded, and got pieces adapted to their abilities. Avonia Jones, for instance, wrote Daly that she could not play parts of charitable or gentle women. "My style is passionate. When I love, it must be madly. . . . " The ambition of every actress was to play Lady Macbeth, just as the men preferred Iago, Richelieu, Richard III. For such stars as Miss Jones, Daly had fashioned the sensational roles of Leah, Lorlie, Judith. His next adaptation was in much the same line.

Although the critics had been lukewarm about *Lorlie's Wedding,* it had served its purpose well: to introduce Marie Methua-Scheller to the English-speaking stage. Prompted by the success of this venture, Fanny Janauschek, likewise a star of magnitude in Germany and on the German stage in New York, determined to try her fortune on the English-speaking stage. The potential remuneration was sufficiently promising to encourage these actresses to undergo the rigors of English lessons; and, of course, they must have been equally stimulated by the desire to be applauded and appreciated by vaster audiences than the ones at the Stadt, the Germania, and the Thalia.

Daly's piece for Madame Janauschek was a one-act play, *Come Here!* based on F. von Elzholz's *Komm Her!* Janauschek, according to the playbills, began, on October 10, 1870, a week's engagement at the Academy of Music "under the management of Augustin Daly." All of her pieces were done in German—*Deborah, Mary Stuart, Macbeth,* etc.—but on Saturday night, October 15, she participated in an all-English program. The first part of the evening was devoted to a performance of *The Lady of Lyons* featuring Agnes Ethel and Walter Montgomery. After the Bulwer-Lytton drama, Madame Janauschek enacted the leading role in *Come Here!*

The plot is quite simple. A middle-aged actress calls upon a manager who has forgotten her. As a test of her ability he imposes in turn several situations in which the words, "Come here!" shall be used: a woman summoning her own child and then a detested stepson, a mother crying out to her child about to be run over by a carriage, a girl recalling her lover after a quarrel, a virago inviting an adversary to combat; finally the same words are spoken in the actress' acceptance of the now charmed manager.

Janauschek had frequently played *Come Here!* in German; after her successful debut, she did it many times in English. Ellen Terry, in her autobiography, *The Story of My Life,* tells that she, too, acted in the little sketch.

Later, Daly's style of play altered as he became a prominent figure in the New York theatrical world. He had written *Under the Gaslight, A Flash of Lightning,* and *Horizon;* he had dramatized *Griffith Gaunt, Man and Wife,* and *He Knew He Was Right;* he had adapted *Frou-Frou, Fernande,* and *Article 47;* and, on August 16, 1869, he had opened his own theater, the Fifth Avenue. For his final production there, on May 20, 1873, he turned again to the author of his first success, S. H. Mosenthal. *Madelein Morel,* a turgid, melodramatic piece, was the play. This time not the play, nor a star, but the fact that it had a cast of tremendous popularity and great ability—George Clarke, Louis James, Henry Crisp, Charles Fisher, James Lewis, Fanny Morant, Sara Jewett, Fanny Davenport, Clara Morris, Mrs. G. H. Gilbert, and Roberta Norwood were the most prominent—carried the piece for a month; on June 28, 1873, Daly closed the theater.

The plot of *Madelein Morel* is involved and stupid. It centers about a case of concealed identity, and exposes the evil lives led by actresses who have, nevertheless, hearts of gold; it is particularly dated for its defense of the double standard: von Arnim is never rebuked for his obviously wicked life; Madelein is cast out on the mere suspicion of dishonor. The last act was regarded as a sensation. Madelein, having been rescued a second time from suicide, is about to take her final vows as a nun. The procession celebrating her marriage to Christ passes her lover's wedding procession. Whereupon, there in the church she tears off her veil, tramples her cross, offers herself to her lover, and then goes crazy and dies.

In her first book of stage reminiscences, *Life on the Stage,* Clara Morris relates some interesting facts regarding *Madelein Morel* and Mr. Daly. Inasmuch as he was a loyal Catholic, the last act caused him some trepidation, about which he had planned to consult his father confessor; but rumors beat him to the church, and the priest came to see Daly instead.

Had Daly been permitted to introduce the matter himself, no doubt a few judicious words from the priest would have induced him to tone down the objectionable speech and action; but the visit to him rubbed him the wrong way and aroused every particle of obstinacy in him.

Daly pleaded with the priest but to no avail. Finally, the manager reminded the father of the annual orphans' benefit, sponsored by Mr. Daly. " 'If the season ends badly, why, of course, there can be no charity benefit,' threatened Mr. Daly." And the priest succumbed. Miss Morris, who played the title role, was equally fearful of the audience reaction, but opening night dispelled her worry and she proceeded to another triumph.

But it was with *The Big Bonanza; or, Riches and Matches,* opening on February 17, 1875, that Daly moved into that field

of German farces which was to make both his fame and fortune. The play revived the waning 1874–1875 season, running
until June 28, for a total of 137 performances. Its first revival
occurred during the week of August 23 that same summer.
Thereafter, it remained for several years a standard piece: it
was played at Mrs. Conway's Park Theatre, Brooklyn, the
week of March 23, 1875; on the Daly company's road trip to
Chicago, Salt Lake City, and San Francisco in the summer
of 1875; at the Olympic Theatre, January 29, 1877. It was first
given in Boston by the Museum Company on October 18,
1875; a second Boston production took place in 1885, and the
final revival there occurred on July 10, 1899, at the Castle
Square Theatre.

The plot of *The Big Bonanza* concerns the friendly and presumably humorous rivalry between two cousins, Jonathan
Cadwallader, "the representative of Money," and Professor Cadwallader, "A.M., M.S., F.G.S., the representative of
Brains." The comedy deals with the Professor's attempts to
make money on the stock market; the humor is the kind that
was prevalent in America during the New Deal when anti-
"brain trust" jokes became popular. In *The Big Bonanza*, the
plot is complicated by misunderstandings, explained in asides
to the audience, to the point of nausea and tedium. The two
love affairs are silly, but they follow a pattern which has always been successful in the theater: boy meets girl, boy loses
girl, boy gets girl. And yet the long run of the piece, despite a
strongly disapproving press, showed that the public liked the
nonsense; as the New York *World*'s critic put it, "This is one
of the most remarkable instances on record of the appetite of
the average American for 'hash' that is warmed up. The allu-
sions to the stock market threw all the able-bodied men into
paroxysms of pleasure, and the quasi-fashionable dresses and
airs of the female players were accepted as proofs supreme of
histrionic genius."

The cast was partly responsible for this success. Headed by

the veterans Charles Fisher and James Lewis, it included such popular players as William Davidge, B. T. Ringgold, George Parkes, Fanny Davenport, Emily Rigl, and Mrs. G. H. Gilbert; furthermore, it introduced to New York Mr. John Drew, of the well-known Philadelphia theatrical family, a young man destined to become a famous matinee idol. The first revival marked the beginnings of Maurice Barrymore's associations with the Daly organization.

The only interesting thing about the uniformly bad reviews the play received is that for once (and the only time) William Winter was caustic in his review of a Daly play:

> The dialogue drivels through four acts of hopeless commonplace in which there is not one spark of wit, not one bright thought, not even a gleam of smartness. The play can hardly be said to have a plot. The story involves itself without any cause, and is straightened out at the end without any reason. . . .

The Big Bonanza was adapted from Gustav von Moser's *Ultimo*. The German play was called to Daly's attention by Adolph Neuendorff, manager of the Germania Theater, where it had been played on November 20, 1874. It is the first of a series of German plays adapted by Daly on the basis of prior success on the German-speaking stages in New York. *Lemons, Blue Glass, An Arabian Night, The Royal Middy*—in fact, all his adaptations until 1884 were, in a sense, "sure things," as they already had visible results of their success with New York audiences. The farce, *Ultimo*, had "tickled Berliners and Viennese immensely," Judge Daly remarked, "for it ridiculed the passion for senseless speculation which set in with the Germans after their intoxicating success in the Franco-Prussian campaign of 1870–1871."

Although the play was a success in New York, Boston, and Chicago, it failed, as did others presented by the Daly company, in San Francisco in the summer of 1875. Miss Sturtevant attributes the indifference to the fact that San Franciscans had seen Bartley Campbell's version of the same piece just a few weeks before. In his letters, however, Daly has a more reasonable explanation: that San Francisco simply did not care for the style of acting offered by his company. Campbell's adaptation, called *Bulls and Bears,* had been made at the request of R. H. Hooley and was produced June 7, 1875. Winter likewise attributed Campbell's success to "the advantage of prior performance" which "took the wind out of Daly's sails, resulting in less than six performances of *The Big Bonanza.*"

Daly did not ignore Campbell's version. Always ready for a legal skirmish, he sent a Mr. James Morrissey, according to one anonymous clipping, with "the assistance of two phonographers, to take down Mr. Hooley's version." Morrissey "took a proscenium box, and with a lady to disarm suspicion, followed up the piece for some time. They were detected, however, and summarily ejected from the theatre." Evidently Daly did not start a suit, although there is a note on the back of a letter from Wallack asking about the rights to *The Big Bonanza* to "Teleg. Lingard to take down Ultimo shorthand for me." Such instructions usually anticipated a lawsuit. But he was dissuaded from possible legal action in Massachusetts by a letter from his counsel, Mr. Rives, pointing out that "Yankee" law was not favorable to restraining suspected plagiarism and no other suit was projected. Of course, he couldn't stop burlesques. One called *The Two Bonanzas* was produced in Boston with Sol Smith Russell in the cast. And he was equally helpless against the English version of *Ultimo,* entitled *On 'Change,* written by Ewerella Lawrence and produced with some success at the Strand Theatre, London, July 1, 1885.

Lemons and *Blue Glass* followed in the successful wake of *The Big Bonanza. Lemons* was presented by Daly on January 15, 1877; its source, Julius Rosen's *Citronen,* had been given on November 17, two years before. *Blue Glass* followed *Lemons* on March 12, 1877, whereas its German original, J. B. von Schweitzer's *Epidemisch,* had been produced at the Germania on March 2, 1874. The critics, including Odell and

Dithmar, attributed both plays to the pen of von Moser, author of *Ultimo*. The reason for their mistake is simple: Daly advertised both *Lemons* and *Blue Glass* as novelties "by the author of *The Big Bonanza*." He meant, of course, himself. The critics were more literal; they assumed by "author" he meant "author."

Both plays are frothy, silly, and obviously designed merely to amuse. In *Lemons*, all mankind is divided into two parts: the lemons and the lemon squeezers. The humor lies in the fact that all the characters are really lemons! Complications arise from the fact that there are four romances to be handled, but eventually everything is straightened out. To do the piece justice, one must admit that the situations though absurd are frequently amusing, and the misunderstandings are kept simple, are based upon humorously conceived characters, and are, therefore, acceptable as compared with many of the obviously contrived mistakes in other farces. The settings indicate the progress of the action: Act I, Breakfast: The Lemons are Selected; Act II, Luncheon: The Lemons are Squeezed; Act III, After Dinner: Lemonade.

As Mrs. Stark, the mother who complicates the play by her matrimonial plans for her children, Mrs. G. H. Gilbert played a role in which she was warmly applauded. Indeed, the play was in general favorably received by press and public and consequently enjoyed an eight-week run from January 15 to March 10, 1877. According to clippings, it was just as pleasant when played by others: the Boston Museum company in May 1883; at the Girard Theatre, Philadelphia, in February 1893; and finally at the Grand Opera House, Pittsburgh, September 1897.

Daly evidently became interested in *Citronen* soon after its production at the Germania for on July 25, 1874, Joseph, having read the play, wrote to Augustin, "When you receive this sit down & write me out a synopsis of acts, scenery & incidents so that I can begin to get up enthusiasm in the right direction—everything to make the play novel, comic & star-tling." Joseph eventually got up the necessary enthusiasm to finish the piece and send it to Augustin for on July 12, two years later Augustin returned it to Joseph with the following note, "I send you today Lemons. Just to go over localizing it as you go & magnifying the situation at the end of the 3rd act."

The brothers collaborated on *Lemons*, then, and in this case the translator, too, can be identified: Adolph Neuendorff, the manager of the Germania. On February 13, 1877, he wrote a note to Daly acknowledging receipt of $254.82 as royalty for *Citronen* "translated by me and adapted by Mr. Daly under my copyrighted title 'Lemons.'"

Daly's success with *Lemons* inspired another manager. On February 19, 1877, James McVicker, the Chicago theatrical impresario, copyrighted another version of the Rosen farce, adapted by James B. Runnion.

Blue Glass featured practically the same cast and the same plot as *Lemons*. As in *The Big Bonanza* and *Lemons*, concern for money and suitable marriages are primary interests. The complications here are furthered by the old device of having letters delivered to the wrong persons. The piece was unpretentious; "entertaining but unsuccessful," the words are Judge Daly's, it ran only a week.

Before condemning Daly for these shallow farces, it is well to scan the list of plays running at the New York theaters the week of March 12, 1877, the same week as *Blue Glass*. At Wallack's was Charles Mathew's comedy, *My Awful Dad;* at Booth's the Kiralfys were staging *A Trip to the Moon* with "a chorus of one hundred"; at the Union Square Theatre, *The Danicheffs*, an adaptation from a French drama, and the only serious new play on the New York stage, was enjoying a three-months run; Niblo's Garden was closed during March after a disastrous season with *Baba* and *Azurine*, both spectacular extravaganzas; the Grand Opera House was showing one of the interminable revivals of *The Two Orphans;* at the Park was the comedy triumph, *Our Boarding House,* by Leonard Grover; Wood's Museum was having a series of Irish plays including *Inshavogue* and *Kathleen Mavourneen:* "the same old characters for all the Irish plays we ever saw"; at the Bowery was *Nimble Jim,* "a local drama"; at the Olympic, the pantomime, *Jack and Jill;* music, opera, and burlesque filled the stages of the city's other theaters. In such a mélange, *Blue Glass* seems just about run of the mill.

On October 13, 1879, the Germania Theater successfully staged a "Schwank," the popular term for a vaudevillian extravaganza, by von Moser entitled *Harun al Raschid.* The piece was very popular. Six weeks later, on November 29, Augustin Daly produced "an entirely new comedy, adapted from the German" called *An Arabian Night,* based on the von Moser play.

An Arabian Night; or, Haroun al Raschid and his Mother-in-Law is a typical German (and Dalyan) farce. The piece abounds with jokes about mothers-in-law. The story concerns young Alexander Sprinkle (John Drew) whose passion for *The Arabian Nights* leads him into strange behavior. His desire to help others gets him involved with a stranded actress named Rosie, "Wild Rose of Yucatan" (Catherine Lewis). From here on the plot revolves about a series of misunderstandings and false identities caused by Sprinkle's fear of his wife's and, even more, his mother-in-law's discovery of his conduct. The characters flit in and out like butterflies. Because of Rose, we are introduced to Hercules Smith, "Premier Cannon Ball Performer and Strong Man of P. T. Boon's Greatest Show under the Heavens," and in order to show off Catherine Lewis' talents, the plot is arranged to allow her to sing and dance. All, of course, ends happily with the lovers united and the mother-in-law left high and dry.

The comedy pleased sufficiently to enjoy a two-months run. The reviews called it "rollicking" and commented upon Daly's "clever additions" which added "real merit" to the piece. According to Dithmar, the role of Sprinkle was John Drew's first "notable triumph." As he further points out, Drew later recreated the role in Sydney Grundy's "much more compact version of the same German play."

Grundy's adaptation, called *Haroun al Raschid and his Mother-in-Law*, was produced by Daly on March 26, 1890. It ran two weeks. The ten-year interval had improved public taste, for Odell laments the fact that what had been liked before was only tolerated now. The distressing facts are that Grundy did adapt the piece, that Daly did produce it, and that the public did tolerate it.

But to go back for a moment to a première of significance, November 15, 1875, at the new Eagle Theatre: Gilbert and Sullivan's *Trial by Jury*. Even to the city which had long supported *The Black Crook*, the advent of Gilbert and Sullivan was important. And although this first production lasted only a week, it was a harbinger of greater things to come. For by February 1879, *Pinafore* was running simultaneously in half a dozen New York theaters (one under the management of Mr. Duff), and on December 1, 1879 Gilbert and Sullivan, with their manager and director R. D'Oyly Carte, presented *Pinafore* at the Fifth Avenue Theatre, to be followed on December 31 by the world première of *The Pirates of Penzance*, under the direction of the masters themselves.

The vogue was set, the epidemic was begun. The theatrical world gave itself over to light opera. Daly wrote from London (February 18, 1879) that

At every theatre they are doing a play which is more or less musical—and I am convinced that the coming success with us will be a genuine comedy: something less extravagant than *Round the Clock*, but really a true comedy interspersed with *songs*, duets and *choruses*: I shall spend the rest of my time here trying to engage about three clever and pretty women & as many men who can sing & act.

It was natural that Daly, keenly conscious of the success of the Gilbert and Sullivan type of musical, should nevertheless have remembered that he was partly responsible for the fashion. As he wrote his brother on February 20, 1879, "It is the novelty of the Gilbert extravagances that takes. They are precisely like *Round the Clock* and *Roughing It*." Indeed, he had produced musical comedies before 1875, not only the two mentioned, but also Olive Logan's *Surf* and his own adaptation of Sardou and Offenbach's *Roi Carotte*. And when he opened his new theater—Daly's—on September 18, 1879, he put these beliefs to the test. He opened with Olive Logan's musical comedy, *Newport*, an adaptation from a French play, *Niniche*, featuring Catherine Lewis and the whole company of Debutantes, including Estelle Clayton, Blanche Weaver, and others. *Newport*, however, was not a success, so Daly had to revive *Divorce* (October 1); then he tried Bronson Howard's *Wives* (October 18); finally he won favor with *An Arabian Night*.

In the interim, at the Thalia Theater, as elsewhere, there had been a shift to the popular style of musical comedy *à la Pinafore*. On October 18, 1879, under the direction of the renowned Conreid, *Die Fledermaus* was presented. But the great success of the season was Richard Genee's comic operetta, *Der Seekadet*, which took to the boards on October 27, 1879, and played intermittently until May 21, 1880, featuring the popular Fräulein Mathilde Cottrelly.

Der Seekadet was the answer to Daly's search. Three months after its successful première at the Thalia, he produced the piece under the title *The Royal Middy*. It began on January 28, 1880, and ran until April 10. The Debutantes made a great hit in their uniforms as naval cadets.

Although Miss Sturtevant claims that *The Royal Middy* was by Daly in collaboration with Fred Williams, the playbills state that the piece was adapted to the American stage by Fred Williams and Edward Mollenhauer, the leader of the orchestra at Daly's, "under the direction of Augustin Daly."

One year later, on January 18, 1881 ("comic opera was to become the raging, devouring element of the theatrical history of the 80's," states Odell), Daly produced his second adaptation from Genee called *Zanina; or, The Rover of Cambaye.* For this piece he had contracted with Mr. Harry W. French for the services of a troupe of Nautch dancers from India. The remarkable scenic effects, including a tropical tornado, and these exotic foreigners, dancers, snake charmers, and musicians, combined to give the piece a run of a month. Judge Daly has an interesting discussion of the troupe, telling of the difficulty of smuggling cobras through the American customs and of arranging a suitable place for the Indians to live during the uncommonly cold winter of 1880–1881. "All that can be said of *Zanina*," commented one reviewer, "is that for elegant and artistic costuming its like has not been seen on the New York stage." In addition to the Nautch dancers, the cast included Laura Joyce as Zanina, Ada Rehan, May Fielding, and Digby Bell.

As Miss Sturtevant points out, Genee was only the composer of *Nisida,* the original name of *Zanina;* its libretto was the work of F. Zell, Genee's collaborator on *Der Seekadet,* and A. West. On the playbill Daly claimed the authorship of the adaptation, but a few lines lower credit is given where it truly belonged: "A Musical Comedy with an original East Indian Interlude by Mr. Harry W. French; several Original Musical Numbers by Mr. E. R. Mollenhauer; the words of all the songs by Mr. Fred Williams; and to be produced with Every Scene New by Mr. James Roberts and Hughson Hawley, Esq."

As had been the case with *The Royal Middy, Zanina* had been seen before its production at Daly's by the audiences of the Thalia. It had been produced at the German theater on December 7, 1880, under Genee's title, *Nisida.* Its long run there, featuring Mathilde Cottrelly, overlapped the production at Daly's.

The last of these musical pieces from the German which Daly produced was *Cinderella at School* which ran for two months, from March 5 until April 30, 1881. The play was an adaptation by Woolson Morse of Benedix's *Die Aschenbrodel*, which also had been the source of T. W. Robertson's *School* twelve years earlier. With the close of *Cinderella at School*, and of the 1880–1881 season, Daly abandoned musical comedy until the nineties when, again prompted by popular taste, he presented *The Gaiety Girl*, *The Geisha*, and others.

After this brief flurry with German musical comedy, Daly returned to his profitable dealings in adaptations of German farces. These plays, all insubstantial in plot and characterization, were successful primarily because they sought to do no more than amuse. The ridiculous situations and absurd complications which made these pieces three-act plays rather than one-act comediettas seemed not to insult audiences so long as Ada Rehan and John Drew, Mrs. Gilbert and James Lewis, were the principal participants. Writing of *The Countess Gucki*, William Archer has stated the case quite clearly:

> The play deserves to rank as a curiosity. It is not a play, it scarcely pretends to be a play; it is simply a contrivance for bringing Miss Rehan on the stage and enabling her to exercise those arts of fascination to which we are all such willing slaves. . . . Mr. Daly has realised the ideal of what may be called absolute action—action unconditioned by either plot or character.

Daly, himself, seems not to have been concerned about the content of these pieces; he was theatrically astute enough to tailor them to fit the particular capacities of his stars and there his responsibility ceased. Over and over again the critics complained of the impossibility of one of these hodgepodge adaptations only to have to relent, halfway through the review, to shower praise upon the performers. As for the public, the audiences of Daly's Theatre projected play after play into the over-one-hundred-performance category, thus insuring success and continuance of the genre.

Besides the brilliance of the acting and the handsomeness of the settings and costuming, these pieces owed success to at least two other factors: the skill with which they were localized to American scenes, and the wholesomeness of the comedy situations. From *The Passing Regiment* (1881) on, reviewers constantly complimented Daly upon his feat of "Americanizing." "To translate the characters from a German to an American atmosphere successfully was no easy task, but Mr. Daly has succeeded admirably in the work," wrote one critic of *The Passing Regiment. Dollars and Sense* (1883) evoked praise as

another proof of the richness of the dramatic mine that Daly struck when he began adapting German farces to his own stage. It is not that Mr. Daly discovered this mine as that he knew so well how to work it. His ability as an adaptor, and the clever way in which he localizes and fills in with new material is the secret of his success. It is no easy matter to make a New York comedy out of a Vienna vaudeville, and it is because this requires a thorough knowledge of both German and English stage, that Mr. Daly has been left in undisputed possession of his field.

Of *A Wooden Spoon* (1884), one critic stated that it showed Mr. Daly to be a "master hand at localizing . . . for no playwright of the present has so well painted for us pictures of contemporaneous metropolitan society." *Love on Crutches, A Night Off, Nancy and Company, The Last Word*—all these and more prompted the same, frequently delirious, comment. Odell summed up the attitude when he wrote that "Daly's adaptations from the German were usually so transfigured that characters and episodes seemed wholly of the American scene."

And for audiences revolted by Ibsen and French "problem" plays, Daly's farces, rightly or wrongly, provided a world of "wholesome reality." Judge Daly, Dithmar, Odell, even John Drew, have commented upon the social distinction and importance of the audiences that thronged Daly's magnificent theater. New York society could indulge itself there without blushing or excuses in a period when conventions and a social code dominated the best society. "The play [*The Way We Live* (1880)] has a motive," suggested a reviewer, "which is to show vice its deformity and to inculcate domestic virtue. For this reason alone the public should go see it." These German farces are "vastly more wholesome than French adaptations" was the compliment directed to Mr. Daly by one of the audience at *Seven-Twenty-Eight*. The observation was, of course, correct. These farces always ended in marriage for the unmarried characters and in reconciliation for the already married ones. Complications and suspicions were always supposed to be funny, and were never indecent. Indeed, the New York public which praised these "pure" plays seems to have forgotten that Daly had also given them *Frou-Frou, Fernande,* and *L'Assommoir.* But then one expected immorality of the French; and these German farces, cleverly interspersed with French plays, gave the Daly Theatre a tone of "wholesomeness."

If some of the critics did approve of the acting, the settings, even of the Americanism and wholesomeness of these farces, the great majority of them were constantly critical of the shallowness and complicated nonsense of the plots. Shaw wrote of *The Countess Gucki,* that it "ought to indicate that the manager is in his second childhood. But I suppose it only indicates that audiences are in their first childhood." As he had pointed out of *The Railroad of Love,* in the old days of the seventies and eighties Daly's sentimental German farces had been "natural, frank, amusing, and positively lifelike in comparison with the plays then regarded as dramatic masterpieces"—*Diplomacy, Our Boys, Forget-Me-Not.* But in 1889 Ibsen "smashed up British drama." Not that the public liked

Ibsen—"he was infinitely too good"—but how they disliked H. J. Byron, Sardou, Boucicault, and Daly after Ibsen! If the answer to Shaw is to be in terms of attendance, then the public still liked Byron, Sardou, *et al*. Henry Irving successfully revived *The Bells* almost every year until 1905! But if the answer is to be provided by the history of the drama, then we know that Daly with his superficial farces was hanging on to an outmoded fad. Plays by Shaw, Ibsen, and Hauptmann were gradually thrusting their way into the repertories. The old order died slowly, and with a smile.

The reviews of *The Great Unknown* in 1889 well illustrate this cross current of attitudes. One exasperated critic wrote, "I do not ask why such adaptations are made by Daly's, but why are they so well received?" Nym Crinkle described the piece as "loose in structure and verbose in treatment." Commenting upon the tag of the play, "And learn a lesson from *The Great Unknown*," another reviewer added that "the lesson chiefly imposed was that it is possible for good acting to carry a bad play." Still another paper complained of the "feeble humor" and many "tedious spots." Yet, despite adverse reviews by every one of his contemporaries, William Winter wrote in the *Tribune*, "It is a good comedy, good because copiously fraught with action, interesting in story, abundant in diversified character, cheerful with humorous traits and amusing dialogue, pungent with playful satire." Winter's position and predilections typify the times; as a critic, he achieved everlasting fame for his violent outbursts against Ibsen. A good example of his extravagant style is the following purple passage from the *Tribune* about Daly's production of *After Business Hours* (1886):

All things concurred to accomplish an auspicious opening of the new season at Daly's Theatre last night. The day has been beautiful, and the evening closed in calmly and softly—a benediction of loveliness and peace. The theatre, swept and garnished as for a festival, was cool and comfortable. A brilliant company filled it in every part, and whichever way an observer might look he saw cheerful colors and happy faces. Such an audience, notable for refinement, taste, and the youthful life and gay fashion of the capital, is seldom assembled. The actors, naturally excited and stimulated by the touching sense of being newly come home to scenes of past success and to admiring and sympathetic friends, were in that fine flutter of awakened sensibility which is always so propitious to artistic expression. . . . The picture disclosed within a picture of talent and beauty, ambition, skill, high purpose and fine achievement touched every heart and elicited a tumult of acclamation. The new play proved congenial alike with the mood of the actors, the temper of the house, and the spirit of the occasion, and the performance of it was almost incessantly piquant and delightful. Even the incidental music, chosen with judicious care by Mr. Henry Widmer, was performed with a gentle moderation benefitting a select and refined entertainment.

Another critic (*The Sun*) stuck closer to the facts: "Later a great issue of gas into the auditorium caused a spell of discomfort."

In general, adverse criticism of the Daly plays employed such epithets as "complicated," "improbable," "dull and insipid," "exaggerated," "empty," "musty and infantile," "trivial and undramatic." A reviewer of *An International Match* (1889) in the *Times* called the play

weak, plotless, wishy-washy without rhyme or reason, and full of offences against average intelligence. In fact, it typifies the most serious of the defects of the Dalyan school of comedy: it assumes that the audience is not at all disposed to view a play from any standpoint of reason, probability, appropriateness of scene or situation, or genuineness of character.

The main point of interest about these plays, however, is not their contemporary reception. As Odell made clear, from 1883 on Daly's was the most popular theater in New York and visitors to the city went there no matter what the play. The playhouse and the Daly Company had become the vogue, and audiences were never lacking. The magnetism of Daly's was perishable, however, and ceased when the curtain closed forever. Acting, before the days of the films and recording machines, was a singular art, for it had to be seen to be appreciated and it left nothing but a memory. So with Daly's players: they are names, or at best wooden pictures, in the annals of the stage. His plays, those ephemeral German farces, however natively and brightly they sparkled, have disappeared from the stage, along with the audiences who loved and applauded them. Only the inanimate record remains.

Of all the German authors Franz von Schonthan was most drawn upon by Daly; six of his pieces were adapted and two others of which he was co-author. Von Moser and Julius Rosen each contributed four farces for adaptation. Two plays of Blumenthal were made over and two on which he collaborated. In the whole list not one is known today, although *A Night Off*, based on the Schonthan brothers' *Der Raub der Sabinerinnen*, was played in Boston at the Castle Square Theatre in 1912 and at the Copley Theatre in 1930, and was adapted for the moving pictures as *Lonely Wives* in 1931.

Daly's final production of a German play was *Number 9; or, The Lady of Ostend*, anglicized by F. C. Burnand. As Augustin had written Joseph, Burnand, who was the editor of *Punch*, "works remarkably cheap & he carries influence"; inasmuch as Augustin was in a hurry to produce the piece in London, he had Joseph stop working on his version. The play was presented in New York from December 7 to 26, 1897, a poor showing, and in a letter to Joseph, Augustin attempted to analyze the cause of the failure. "The radical fault with No. 9—as in The Bundle of Lies—both follow old and familiar lines & introduce no new situation as a climax." Perhaps the explanation was that Blumenthal and Kadelberg, the authors of the original German play, *Hans Huckebein*, Burnand, the adaptor, and Daly, the producer, were simply unaware of the great changes in taste affecting theater goers in 1897.

There are, however, several mitigating factors to take into

account. One is that Daly was also producing other plays of literary and historical value; he could recoup by means of a German farce the enormous expenditure involved in staging Shakespeare and the old comedies in lavish style. A second excuse is suggested in an article by John Drew in *The Ladies' Home Journal* in 1921, and is an explanation already mentioned above. Referring to *Needles and Pins* the actor said that "its most conspicuous merit was that it was unlike anything to be seen elsewhere in New York at that time." True enough, the rival attractions in New York in November 1880, were in general melodramas or else comedies of even less sophistication than *Needles and Pins:* E. C. Lankester's comedy, *The Guv'nor*, at Wallack's; a translation of Sardou's *Daniel Rochat*, at the Union Square; the second year of *Hazel Kirke*, at the Madison Square; *Norah's Vow*, at the Fifth Avenue; a burlesque, *Revels*, at Haverley's; a melodrama from the French, *The Legion of Honour*, at the Park; a comedy, *Sharps and Flats*, at the Standard; and *My Partner*, at Niblo's Garden. The third justification of these farces of Daly's—a justification in terms of pure entertainment—is made in a review of *Seven-Twenty-Eight*, characterized as "a good example of the farcical comedy—in other words, the comedy without purpose other than to excite laughter or without plot more substantial than a mere film upon which to hang a series of mirth-provoking situations."

CHAPTER 5

The Same Old French Melody

*French thought, French plot, French wit, French moral, cast,
And Published, probably, by French, at last.*

John Brougham, *Columbus el Filibustero*
Act I, Scene 2.

F rench drama of the nineteenth century was *the* drama of the western world. Allardyce Nicoll estimates that fully one-half the plays written in England between 1800 and 1850 were suggested by Parisian models, and many were simply literal translations. As for the American drama, Howard Mumford Jones in surveying the interrelations of American and French culture has indicated that "the subject of the character and amount of French adaptation on the American stage should furnish material for two or three monographs." Waldo's excellent study, *The French Drama in America in the Eighteenth Century*, has brilliantly traced this influence from its beginnings to 1800, and two University of Pennsylvania theses, by Harold Schoenberger and Ralph Ware, carry the work on in some degree to the Civil War.

Although French influence on American drama had a less auspicious beginning than the German, it grew more steadily. Dunlap adapted eight French plays between 1797 and 1828; John Howard Payne was the most prolific adaptor of French plays in the early period, having twelve adaptations to his credit between 1816 and 1826; of the twenty plays written by Richard Penn Smith, half were from the French. These three playwrights accounted for practically all the American adaptations in the early period. In the three decades from 1834 to the Civil War, however, some eighteen American playwrights prepared versions of French plays.

Later American dramatists were more industrious than the English in their search for adaptable plays; indeed, they availed themselves not only of French models, but also of the London versions of French plays, and their exposure to French influence was consequently both direct and indirect. Reviewing the theatrical season of 1869 in *The Atlantic Monthly*, William Dean Howells complained that all the musical pieces were French, and all the plays were English, "so there is nothing American on the American stage." And even as late as 1897, Edward Morton was still hopefully predicting in *The Theatre* that "the scramble for French plays will soon be over."

The use of French dramatic material on the English stage has of course a long history. When the English theaters were reopened at the time of the Restoration it was King Charles himself who sponsored the copying of French drama. The Earl of Orrery wrote, "I have now finished a play in the French manner because I heard the King declare himself more in favor of their way of writing than ours." And in a prologue Dryden cynically added,

> French farce worn out at home is sent abroad
> And patched up here is made our English mode.

Cynicism was not Dryden's only attitude toward the French plays; for he copied them assiduously, and finally in defense of his own practice wrote,

> He used the French like enemies
> And did not steal their plots, but made them prize.

Wycherley, Vanbrugh, Cibber, and Fielding carried on the practices of Roger Boyle and John Dryden. In the nineteenth century English drama became so derivative that the faults outweighed the benefits of borrowing. The famous incident from *Nicholas Nickleby* has been much quoted in this connection. Dickens well knew the facts when he had the theatrical manager, Vincent Crummles, ask Nicholas,

"Do you understand French?"

"Perfectly well."

"Very good," said the manager, opening the table-drawer, and giving a roll of paper from it to Nicholas. "There! Just turn that into English, and put your name on the title page. Damn me!" said Mr. Crummles angrily, "if I haven't often said that I wouldn't have a man or woman in my company that wasn't master of the language, so that they might learn it from the original, and play it in English, and save all this trouble and expense."

"All this trouble and expense," however, stopped neither Crummles nor others. Dutton Cook relates in *On the Stage* that *The Era* advertised adaptations from the French at a few pounds, even a few shillings, as a result of which *Don Caesar de Bazan* was shortly running at seventeen London theaters at once. And in 1881, Percy Fitzgerald stated that "the English stage is virtually subsisting on the French."

One reason for the vogue of French plays has been advanced by Brander Matthews in *The Development of the Drama*, when he states that "during the middle fifty years of the nineteenth century it was only in France that the drama was able to hold its own as a department of literature"—a view heartily endorsed by Henry James in his many articles on the theater. Professor Matthews is referring to the *pièces bien faites* of Scribe and Sardou and the *pièces à thèse* of Augier and Dumas *fils*. The acknowledged literary quality of works by these writers and by other favorites, Dumas *père*, Belot, Rostand, was not, however, the quality which attracted adaptors. Rather, it was the style, the theatricality, the dramaturgy, and particularly the skill of construction, which made these plays easy to translate because the dramatic skeleton of the play came through intact, and hence they were desirable from the adaptors' point of view.

The two most important movements which characterized French drama in the nineteenth century were the influence of Scribe and Sardou, which brought technical proficiency to French drama; and the school of Augier and Dumas *fils*, which, adapting the machinery of its predecessors, added a consideration of psychological problems as a function of drama. With these factors Filon, in *The Modern French Drama*, would include the spirit of naturalism and experimentation as exemplified in the Théâtre Libre. Filon also notes the return to the dramatic conventions, as a reaction against the romantic excesses which followed in the wake of Hugo and Dumas *père*, and the end-of-the-century revival of romanticism *à la* Rostand and Jean Richepin. All of these movements gave strength and variety to the drama; above all, the French dramatists of the nineteenth century were men of the theater, familiar with both the human and the mechanical problems of the stage and hence able to create effective plays. Their success was apparent in the theaters of France, Germany, England, and America.

The commercial reasons for this extraordinary dependence upon the French drama are simpler. In a now famous bit of stage history, Boucicault told how in 1841 he received £300 for *London Assurance*. But three years later, a manager offered him only £100 for a new play. Boucicault objected.

The manager replied, "I can go to Paris and select a first-class comedy; having seen it performed, I feel certain of its effect. To get this comedy translated will cost me 25 pounds. Why should I give you 300 or 400 pounds for your comedy, of the success of which I cannot feel assured?"

"The argument was unanswerable," continued Boucicault, "and the result inevitable. I sold a work for £100 that took me

six months' hard work to compose and accepted a commission
to translate three French plays at £50 a piece."

Boucicault's position was that of practically every English
playwright. Recounting the career of his father, James Albery, Wyndham Albery says that after 1880 the dramatist
confined himself almost entirely to the role of adaptor, for

he could adapt a play with more speed than he could write an
original one. As only plays which had been proved successes in
the country of their origin would be chosen for adaptation, there
was the more probability of their obtaining a good "run" in England. He found it, too, easier to get commissions to write adaptations, and was disinclined to work on what he was not sure of
getting placed.

F. C. Burnand, Charles Reade, Sydney Grundy, and scores
of other English writers who were successful both as playwrights and adaptors have substantiated Albery's conclusion.
At the simple task of adaptation, wrote Burnand,

the competent adaptor but incompetent dramatist may make a
little fortune, as he can safely set the pecuniary results of two
adaptations, which may have occupied his leisure for a month,
against those of an original piece, which has cost three or four
months', or it may be a year's, close study, constant labour, and
great anxiety.

"To invent good pieces," Reade pointed out, "is very hard . . .
to adapt them is quite as easy as shelling peas. . . . I can lay
my hand on a dozen adaptors of French pieces who know
neither French or English nor the Stage."

The situation in America was equally deplorable. "Substi-
tute for the manager's statement, 'I can go to Paris,' the
declaration, 'I can go to London,' and the argument of the
American manager is exactly stated," explained Boucicault.
Lewis P. Waldo has demonstrated the truth of this assertion.
For in addition to the French troupes acting in Charleston,
Baltimore, and New Orleans, and to the American dramatists
who were shaping adaptations from French originals, "French

drama became very widely known here through the large number of English adaptations of French plays produced in our country."

Daly exploited and contributed to the French fad in large measure, and produced works derived both from the French sources and the English versions. From the Civil War period until the turn of the century Daly was responsible, in whole or in part, for forty-four adaptations of French plays; in addition, he produced twenty-one plays adapted by others, a total of sixty-five productions of French pieces in thirty-five years, an average of almost two a year. Among these adaptors who worked for Daly were both Englishmen and Americans: Bronson Howard, Dion Boucicault, Charles Fechter, Robert Buchanan, and Clement Scott, men who were among the most prolific and popular dramatists of the times. Practically every American and English playwright, in other words, was engaged in the practice. The American adaptors were unfortunately no better than the English, according to Dr. Ware, for they "had only a fair knowledge of the French language; in translating, they were adequate but not distinguished."

That their adaptations were both simple and lucrative has been amply confessed by Albery, Boucicault, and Burnand. Daly's position is therefore remarkable. According to Daly's playbill for *Our Boys* (September 1875), "The first American manager who treated honorably and justly with French authors for their pieces was Mr. Daly, and he has paid more money for Parisian plays than all the other managers in this country combined."

The ease with which a French play could be pirated demonstrates the inadequacy of the existing copyright laws, and is a basic reason why French plays were exploited during the period.

It is important to understand Daly's position; he was truly a pioneer and a man of honor in his dealings with foreign playwrights. When he produced *Roi Carotte* in 1872 he evidently made royalty payments to Sardou, for the Count de Najac, the American representative of the Société des Gens des Lettres, wrote him,

> You are the first American manager who has fittingly acknowledged that a dramatic work is the property of the author, and that it is his right to be remunerated for it as if it were a fine painting or engraving. By your recognition of the artists' claim you have become our most valuable partner in our effort to secure an international copyright law . . . which would contribute to the development of the genius and the literature of your beautiful country.

Besides the advantage of having already been tried out, another asset of a French play was that it was generally written for a "star." To enumerate some of the titles of the successful pieces is sufficient: *Frou-Frou, Fernande, Camille, Zaza, Madame Sans-Gêne, Cyrano de Bergerac, La Marquise, Denise, Odette, The Count of Monte Cristo, The Corsican Brothers, Don Caesar de Bazan.* As a consequence, one notices in this light that the distribution of French adaptations on Daly's production schedule falls into two major periods: twenty-five productions from 1864 to 1874 when, as a young man, he was attempting to get a start in the theatrical world by attracting such stars as Mrs. John Wood, Avonia Jones, the Conways, Agnes Ethel, Clara Morris, and Charles Fechter; and later the ten productions from 1890 to 1899 when, attempting to ride the waves of theatrical tastes in the Nineties, he reluctantly starred Ada Rehan in *Madame Sans-Gêne* and even in *Cyrano de Bergerac*, tried to introduce French pantomime with *The Prodigal Son* and *Miss Pygmalion*, and revived melodrama in *Roger La Honte* and *The Queen's Necklace*, and musical spectacles in *Heart of Ruby*. During the eminently successful years between these two periods, that is from 1875 through 1889, the French adaptations he used were mainly the one-act curtain raisers, *Love's Young Dream, A Woman's Won't, A Wet Blanket, A Sudden Shower, The*

Wife of Socrates, The Prayer, designed to show off the talents of Ada Rehan and John Drew, or Mrs. Gilbert and James Lewis, before these actors fell back into the ensemble acting required by the adaptations of German farces and revivals of the classics which were the main attractions.

The reasons why Daly as well as the rest of the world was presenting French plays are then quite obvious: production of a proved rather than a problematical success; ease of making a successful adaptation, even by an incompetent; low cost of royalties, generally no fees to foreign authors, and only nominal payments to adaptors; the appeal of French plays for "stars"; and the appeal of French plays to the American public. On this last point some discussion has already been advanced in connection with adaptations of German plays. Certainly American audiences in the nineteenth century were prejudiced in favor of things European. A vast section of the public liked anything French because it was supposed to be civilized. Above all, Daly sought audiences that were cultured and socially elite. First nights at his theater were events of importance to New York's Four Hundred. As a corollary, one might add that long runs depended upon transients, who were no less snobbish in their tastes than native New Yorkers. And of course in this connection French pieces were good drawing cards on the road. As an editorial in the New York *Herald* says on January 21, 1873, "These French plays have a strong fascination for American playgoers."

Mrs. Gilbert has indicated that Daly neither read nor spoke German; she was just as positive about his lack of knowledge of French. John Drew has also stated clearly that "Daly knew no French"; in his memoirs, Drew relates how he was accustomed to read Daly the French newspaper reviews of their productions while the company was playing in Paris. This deficiency on Daly's part was no more a handicap than his ignorance of German. His method of adapting French plays was the same as with German pieces; he generally had a literal translation prepared, which he then adapted, or, more accurately, which Joseph adapted, and which he subsequently announced as his own.

In 1881, Joseph worked on *Girouette* "act by act." In January, 1882, he sent Augustin a plot outline of *Odette*. During the summer of that year he was engaged in translating *Heloise Paranquet*. From his statement regarding this piece—"If you would like to play it, I will translate it"—it seems that Joseph knew French well enough to read and translate the language, an accomplishment which he evidently could not equal in German.

As with the German correspondence, letters from French authors and agents ordinarily have translations attached to them. On the reverse side of a letter from A. Belot is a note in Daly's hand, "Dear Joe, what is this? A. D." Letters from Sardou, Barbusse, Belot, Cadol, and Mons are accompanied by translations. The translations of letters from Adrien Barbusse relating to his play, *Duc Vertige*, were made by someone named Mandrell. Letters from the agents, Porel and Chizzola, are rendered into English for Daly, whose ignorance of the language extended also to matters of spelling: for example, he always spelled Coquelin "Coquelan" and he wrote "Blouett" for Blouet.

There are many letters from playwrights with whom Daly dickered for adaptations. In 1890, Joseph Hatton, referring to a French play that he was adapting for Mr. Lewis, Mrs. Gilbert, Ada Rehan, and John Drew, wrote, "I find the literal translation very good." In 1897, together with an agreement to work for $175 weekly as an adaptor, J. W. Herbert sent an adaptation, "entirely away from the English version." There are several letters from Edgar Fawcett. In 1886, he refused to adapt *Extravagances* as "it is too forced"; yet he did many another French play for Daly and although few of them were produced, Daly paid him for the adaptations.

Paul Blouet, who under the pseudonym of Max O'Rell and with the help of Jack Allyn wrote *Jonathan and His Continent*, also translated for Daly. In 1890, he sent Daly an adaptation called *Clarissa's Young Man* and in 1895 another, *The Duchess of Glamorgan;* that year, while working over *Duc Vertige*, he seems to have been receiving a regular salary of £25 from Daly. It was Blouet who called Daly's attention to *Madame Sans-Gêne*, Sardou's *chef d'oeuvre*. "Would you like to trust me with the adaptation?" he queried on September 7, 1894. Although Daly did not produce the play until 1899, it is possible that Blouet may have been responsible for the adaptation, for the playbills carried no name of an adaptor. The version was ridiculed by the critics for its inadequate and "absurd" translations, which may indicate that they were made by a Frenchman not fluent in colloquial English.

Leander P. Richardson was another adaptor who worked on both German and French plays for Daly. On August 2, 1881, he wrote "I will come on Friday with half of the adaptation as suggested in your favor of today. It is going to make a 'ripping' good play, I think, but it is very difficult to adapt, owing to the big infusion of smut which Mr. Sardou seems to be particularly fond of." The only play of Sardou's which Daly produced about this time was *Odette* (February 6, 1882); the playbill announced the piece as "an original adaptation by Augustin Daly." Evidently both parties were satisfied with Richardson's work, as later in 1882 he served Daly as a London scout for English and French plays and again in 1883 and 1885 he was busy on other adaptations for the producer.

Others who worked on French adaptations for Daly included Dion Boucicault, John Brougham, Robert Buchanan, Clo Graves, Brander Matthews, and Justin McCarthy. Although he wrote, "I fail to find much in The White Crow," Boucicault nevertheless finished the piece "in good shape."

He also prepared a version of Sardou's *Seraphine*. But the most interesting note is about Boucicault, not by him. On April 10, 1872, a certain Harry Woll wrote Daly from London about *Roi Carotte;* he told Daly he controlled two versions of the play, one by Henry S. Leigh, the other by Boucicault, either of which he offered to sell. The lure was that "the piece can be registered in your name in America as your own *property & translation* if you desire it." The italics are Woll's and are self-explanatory.

When he sent *Corinne* to Daly on April 4, 1875, Robert Buchanan included the following note, "Will you go through the piece, add any humorous touches such as you suggest, & then return it to me for final revision. I can thus have your name as joint author, & I have every reliance in your discretion." Such were the ways of adaptors. Again, although Daly copyrighted *The Princess Royal* in 1877 as his own, and although the playbills named him the adaptor, yet a letter from Bronson Howard offers evidence to the contrary. On November 26, 1879, Howard wrote Daly from London about an occasion during which he had done hack work for Daly and "during this short service, I was at work on an adaptation from the French of the 'Officier of Fortune' afterwards produced by you as the 'Princess Royal.'" From all appearances, Daly regarded any work done by persons in his employ as his own.

An interesting problem in Daly authorship is presented by his production of *Article 47* at the Fifth Avenue Theatre, April 2, 1872, an adaptation of a play by Adolphe Belot. The playbill credits Daly with having "authored" the adaptation. Judge Daly says nothing about the authorship; he simply refers to the piece as "the greatest sensation of the management." And although she discusses the performance at length, Clara Morris, who achieved fame in the leading role of Cora, makes no mention of an adaptor. For some reason Daly did not copyright the play, a custom he ordinarily followed with care, even entering his versions of Shakespeare. The U. S. copyright volume does contain an entry by De Witt, the publisher, who on July 8, 1872, three months after Daly's play opened, copyrighted *Article 47; or, Breaking the Ban,* by Henry L. Williams. The published version of the play, issued by De Witt, contains a revealing list; printed side by side on page two are the original cast as played at the Théâtre Ambigu-Comique, Paris, October 20, 1871, and the cast of Daly's production, complete and exactly matching the playbill. Naturally, such an entry does not prove that Williams was the adaptor, but it does cast some suspicion upon Daly's claim to authorship, for might not an adaptor list the cast of the production of a play because he happens also to have authored that play?

Sardou's *Fernande* offers another peculiar case study, perhaps involving Williams. Daly produced the piece on June 7, 1870, announcing on the playbills that it was an adaptation by N. Hart Jackson and Myron A. Cooney. When the play was given at the Union Square Theatre, "by special permission of Augustin Daly," on June 4, 1873, the bills there named only Jackson as adaptor. And when the piece was revived at Daly's in 1879, the playbills again carried only one name, but this time it was that of Augustin Daly. The confusion or deceit evidently bothered Dithmar for, when he wrote *Memories of Daly's Theatres* in 1896, he listed no adaptor at all for *Fernande;* nor did Judge Daly when he wrote the biography of his brother in 1917. One can at least express wonder at these strange omissions; a critic or historian who saw only the playbills of 1879 would, of course, be completely deluded. A provocative corollary to this account is added by the fact that several other adaptors copyrighted and published versions of the Sardou play. Henry Williams' adaptation was copyrighted by De Witt and published in 1870. James Schonberg, who had dramatized *Griffith Gaunt,* made a version which was also published in 1870 by R. Burton. There was also one by Belasco, entitled *Clothilde*. And according to the *Dictionary of American Biography*, *Fernande* was one of "lesser" dramatic writings of A. Oakey Hall. All these versions make one thing clear, however—the popularity of Sardou in America.

As in the case of the German plays, the correspondence between Augustin and Joseph reveals clearly that it was the Judge who produced the majority of the French plays "adapted by Augustin Daly." The record ranges from 1864, when Joseph helped Augustin with *The Sorceress*, through 1898, when Joseph was at work on an adaptation of a play about Navarre. On April 19, 1864, Augustin wrote Joseph thanking him for "having finished up *The Sorceress* so finely and in such good time." The next memorandum is dated December 21, 1873, and deals with Sardou's *La Maison Neuve*. "I am hard at 'Claire,'" wrote Joseph, "and will come in tomorrow afternoon & talk to you. This piece is full of strong situations & *brand new ones* which I will explain." The *Youth of Louis XIV* engaged the brothers' attention the following summer. On the 17th of June Joseph asked, "Would you like me to send you by express the translation of 'The Youth of Louis XIV'?" And on the 21st, he explained "It may not read smoothly as yet, because it is the pure translation. . . . My belief is that it will make an elegant & powerful comedy." But on August 24, Joseph wrote, "I shall cut the piece considerably." Throughout this same summer of 1874, Joseph was at work on the "Ducks," his name for *The Two Orphans*, but an injunction prevented Augustin from producing the piece, which became one of the great successes in American theatrical history. On July 25, 1874, Joseph dropped a note to Augustin that he was "going to Coudert's [an agent's] office to read Les Frères d'Armes," which he considerately translated for his brother as "The Brothers at Arms."

Rose Michel, by Ernest Blum, next took up a great deal of Joseph's time. On June 27, 1874, he wrote, "I shall begin to work on Rose Michel this evening. I don't like the finish of Act 1 but all else is superb." A year later he complained, "I am much & most inconveniently overworked now with Rose Michel. . . . It employs me every night. I have three of the original acts done." To Augustin, who was in Chicago at the time, he then sent "the balance of Rose Michel. Thank goodness that job's jobbed." Augustin never produced the piece although he announced *Rose Michel* as a "forthcoming novelty" on the playbill of *The Big Bonanza* for April 21, 1875. He did copyright it, however, on October 13, 1875, "A drama of vivid passion by Augustin Daly."

A clear view into Joseph's wholehearted labors for Augustin appears in a letter he wrote in July 1874. "I send you the King's Guardsmen (Le Mousquetaire du Roi) which I have translated for you—that is the first 4 acts. You will find it as dashing & absorbing a romance as you ever read & I believe you will want it as 'A Grand Romantic Drama'—by the author of the Duke's Motto—adapted & augmented by A. D.—for your fall opening. I put in pencil how I think the parts might be cast. . . ."

The summer of 1879 was again a busy one for Joseph. From the letters it is clear that these vacations, spent with his wife's family near Worcester, Massachusetts, were invariably devoted to literary labors for Augustin. On July 8, 1879, Augustin sent Joseph two French plays "to amuse your woodland hours & wilt do them for me immediate if not sooner?" They were *Le Mari de la Débutante* and *Bocquet Père et Fils.* Joseph, as his letter of August 25, 1879 reveals, was already at work on *Roi Candante, Bottes de Capitaine*, and *Le Petit Hôtel.*

Daly's procedure with plays is interestingly spotlighted by the history of *Tiote*, from Maurice Drach's *La Petiote*. On May 20, 1880, Joseph wrote, "I suppose Williams has translated it. Work on that as the original is full of 'colloquialisms' which he has already looked out & rendered into English."

But Augustin evidently did not do the work, for on July 1, 1880 he acknowledged receipt of three acts of *Tiote* from Joseph, "& have read the first act which I like very much." Ten days later, Joseph sent the "balance," adding "If you wish to leave to me the general shortening, then send the whole mss. back with your mems." Still concerned for the play, on July 17, Joseph suggested a "new face" for the leading female role. "I would be in favor of a novice—as you were when you had Frou Frou in view and tried for Laura Keene and had to take Ethel." On July 20, Augustin complimented Joseph, "I think you did your share on Tiote admirably." The final word on the piece was in Augustin's letter of July 28, 1880. "I like your ending very much. What is your idea of the 'business' for the gypsy ceremony which Jack & Isobel go through? Write me full particulars." When the play was produced on August 18, 1880, the playbill announced it as "a novel and picturesque play, adapted by Augustin Daly, from a translation by Mr. Fred Williams."

By August 1882, Joseph had almost finished the German comedy, *Dollars and Sense*, and so Augustin sent him "a stunning French play," evidently *Serge Panine*, about which on August 12th Augustin wrote that it had "outrun *Odette* in Paris." Joseph was much attracted by the play and worked on it with great dispatch, so that twelve days later Augustin was writing, "I was surprised to get the two acts of S. P. tonight. I had been looking anxiously for the comedy *Our English Friend* but I suppose you feel *Serge*—& so you have surged. I have only just glanced through it & I confess I think it surprisingly strong." On September 3, Joseph confessed that he "greatly liked" *Serge*.

The next few plays that Joseph adapted were German farces. Then in the spring and summer of 1885 he was at work on *Four Temperaments*, the original nationality of which is uncertain. And by September 10, 1885, he "had finished 2 comediettas"—probably *A Wet Blanket* and *A Sudden Shower*. In the summer of 1887, Joseph was again adapting a play the origin of which is unknown; this one he referred to as *Fleet Manoeuvring*. In October 1887, five years since *Odette* was finished, he started *Un Conceil Judicaire* which became *Samson and Dalilah*. He projected in it a court-room scene admired by one reviewer as "the most respectably truthful of any similar play on the stage." Then, from Paris on September 8, 1888, Augustin wrote, "I want a tag or Epilogue for Surprises [*The Lottery of Love*]. You left it unfinished."

For this last piece, Augustin sent the "usual" 2 per cent royalty, writing on October 15, 1888, "Here is your check for last week. Of course I owe you the $1000 promised on completion of the work—but that I must defer paying till I get these summer bills off my hands." A thousand dollars seems to have by now become the standard fee which Joseph received for his adaptations, plus a 2 per cent royalty on the receipts during the play's run. In April 1889, he acknowledged receipt of royalty checks for *Cornelius Voss* (*An International Match*) and *Un Conceil Judicaire*. Also in April—the 2nd—he stipulated that he must get $500 "preliminary to a play to be done this summer," and he added, "I am to get the usual 2 per cent on the latter week by week—that is understood." In June, though, Augustin reduced Joseph's royalty fee to 1 per cent. In August he sent Joseph *The Marquise* and a check for $500. These payments are most convincing proof of Joseph's authorship of Augustin's adaptations of French and German plays.

Letters relating to *The Marquise* show the brothers doing a real job of collaboration upon *ideas*, but indicate that as usual it was Joseph who did the actual writing. On August 9, Augustin wrote

My hope is that something good will come out of the Marquise. If the set of characters in act 1 & 2 can be concentrated and put into 1—to make better parts & be Americanised, I think that will be the best *opener*. Will you see what you can do in the matter, so I can have it by Sept. 15. It needs a deal of boiling down and much "brilliant witicism."

Joseph agreed and managed to meet the deadline. On September 17, Augustin returned the last act for Joseph "to go over the part of Augusta & to alter the end: which I have sketched out on a sheet. It is no use ending the piece after the Sardou fashion & I have suggested the alteration which won't take much time to do." Again Joseph completed the assignment on time and the play, called *The Golden Widow*, "a comedy adapted by Augustin Daly," opened on October 2, 1889.

Garrison D— and *Neighborly Love* engaged Joseph's energies during the spring of 1890. Having finished *The Last Word* in May, he was at work on *The Grass Widow* when Augustin wrote him from London May 23, "I trust you're well into *The Grass Widow*. So far I think that promises the liveliest opening. I think if you arrange a grand *ball* for the second act—instead of a dinner party—it will give a chance for a dance & a bit of show."

By February 1891, Augustin was inquiring "How is Vie a Deux [Love in Tandem] getting along? I'm ready for it." A year later, just in time for its opening on February 9, 1882, Joseph completed the tag "incorporating all the love plays." The next week he acknowledged his first royalty check for the piece.

An unproduced play, *Chic*, was Joseph's next French adaptation. He sent the completed version of it to Augustin in London in July 1894. Augustin replied "I am very pleased with your share, though the end is not as I want it yet." On another European trip, in 1897, Augustin acquired two new plays, one German, the other of "a higher order," French. "They are very well translated & would require but little work in adaptation—would you care to touch them up?" The

French play was *The Law of Man*, another unproduced work.

Joseph's comments on the next play, *Dupont's Daughters*, are interesting for they reveal a quality of mind generally described as "typically Victorian." Such opinions as he voiced may account for some of the absurdities and omissions the critics objected to in Daly's French and German adaptations, and, more seriously, in Shakespeare and other English classics which he produced. Augustin sent *Dupont's Daughters* (presumably Eugene Brieux's *Les Trois Filles de M. Dupont*) to Joseph from England. "I believe it will be a sensation in New York—and a Novelty," he opined. But Joseph objected to the play and wrote, on November 23, 1897, that it was

a "problem play" of the ultra type. What there is objectionable in it appears to be not merely in the dialogue but in the whole theme and plot and is therefore ineradicable. Thus, you may soften many of the expressions in the talk but there is no way of altering the story so that "young people" could discuss it.

So much for *Dupont's Daughters;* the play was never produced by Daly.

Instead of the "objectionable" French play, Joseph went to work on *Friends from Youth*, "a comedy," he admitted, "of light texture but fresh & original with strong contrasts of character." That he could have preferred such a play in 1897 shows the extent to which the Daly brothers, toward the end of the century, were falling behind in their judgment of public taste. Although he was offered plays by Ibsen and Shaw, Daly never took advantage of the opportunity to introduce these dramatists to American audiences. Daly's repertoire in the nineties—the silly German farces, the "fricassees" of Shakespeare, the trivial French plays—was that of a time already passed. Shaw, Archer, and Huneker were just in their condemnation. By the end of his career, Daly was a monument of conservatism, blind to the great changes going on about him.

The final French adaptations which Joseph did were unimportant. He worked over *Madame Sans-Gêne* in 1898. And in August 1898 he read through Augustin's version of *Cyrano de Bergerac* "to make any corrections or suggestions that might occur to him." Finally, in the fall of 1898, he was at work on a French play about Navarre. On October 7, Augustin sent him the translation of *The Tales of Navarre* "to go over it and see what may be done towards boiling it into 4 acts or 3." On November 26, Augustin wrote asking about *The Queen of Navarre;* and on November 30, he requested Joseph to send him *Margaret of Navarre.* The name of the piece is unimportant; it was not produced. The play was simply an anticlimax to Joseph Daly's active career as an adaptor of French plays.

Daly's productions of French plays were neither significant in themselves nor unique. With few exceptions, his adaptations were almost completely literal translations. Whereas, after 1884, Daly was ordinarily the first to produce his German adaptations in America, with French plays he was simply one of the many who tried to recapture in this country the popularity a piece had already enjoyed in Paris and perhaps in London. Whatever successes he had were due to the inherent merits of the plays themselves, or of such performers as Clara Morris and Ada Rehan.

Of the sixty-five French plays produced by Daly, only two, *Frou-Frou* (1870) and *The Lottery of Love* (1888–1889), achieved initial runs of a hundred performances, whereas of the forty-two German plays during the same period, six attained that distinction. *Camille* and *The Two Orphans*, probably the two most popular plays in America of the nineteenth century, he did not produce. Of the more "distinguished" "literary" dramatists, Daly produced Molière's *École des Femmes* as Bronson Howard's *Wives*, Coppée's *Le Pater* as M. F. Egan's *The Prayer*, and Rostand's famous *Cyrano de Bergerac.* He produced twelve Sardou plays; after

Sardou, Dumas *fils* was most drawn upon, for four pieces. Scribe, Belot, Meilhac and Halevy and Dumas *père* contributed two each.

One of the most popular French playwrights of the nineteenth century not only in France but throughout the western world was Victorien Sardou. Daly's first French adaptation was *Taming a Butterfly*, a version of Sardou's *La Papillonne*, which he and a fellow journalist, Frank Wood, prepared for Mrs. John Wood. The actress staged the piece at the Olympic Theatre on February 25, 1864, where it ran until March 19. Frank Drew was Mrs. Wood's leading man; the distinguished cast included Henrietta Irving, J. K. Mortimer, and William Davidge. Reviews were generally enthusiastic; in fact the New York *Transcript*, in a burst of misguided nationalism, went so far as to call Daly and Wood "our New York Beaumont and Fletcher." Although the translation was uniformly approved, the play itself was treated somewhat coldly because of its "Gallic indelicacies." Yet only a few reviewers were actually hostile; one claimed that Daly and Wood "pirated the dialogue almost *verbatim et literatim* from Horace Wigan's adaptation *Taming the Truant*" but others sprang to their defense, pointing out that the Americans hadn't known of Wigan's "dull" production which had failed in London. "Native dramatists," added one critic, "need encouragement, and where this may be honestly given, 'twere stupid to withhold it." Daly devoted his own review space in *The Sunday Courier* to a letter signed "The Native Dramatists," in which two columns of praise were lavished upon the performers.

Some seven years later, Daly "rearranged" *Taming a Butterfly;* it emerged as *Delmonico's; or, Larks up the Hudson* and enjoyed a life span of three weeks, from June 20, to July 9, 1871. The major change was the dropping of Frank Wood's name from the playbills and from the royalty fees.

As was the case with his German adaptations, the initial success of *Taming a Butterfly* led Daly to adaptations for other stars. For Avonia Jones he prepared *The Sorceress*, *Garcia*, and *La Tireuse des Cartes*, all performed in the spring of 1864. For the Conways Daly rendered Sardou's *Nos Bons Villageois* into *Hazardous Ground*, produced at their Park Theatre, Brooklyn, in 1867. Agnes Ethel, who came to Daly upon the recommendation of Mathilda Heron, her teacher, was such a hit in Daly's *Frou-Frou* and *Fernande* in 1870 that she shortly thereafter left Daly to become a star. Daly's version of *Frou-Frou* had a sensational initial run of 102 performances; it was the first, but not the only, version of the play to be produced in New York. Crowds were so great that the musicians had to be placed underneath the stage to provide extra seats. In 1883, Modjeska used Daly's adaptation, and William Brady produced it successfully with Grace George as late as 1902. Fanny Davenport, Clara Morris, and Agnes Leonard also used the Daly vehicle.

Following in the wake of Agnes Ethel, whose role she took over in *Man and Wife*, Clara Morris likewise achieved significant successes in French adaptations by Daly, notably *Article 47* in 1872 and *Alixe* the following year. Particularly in the former did she display her own brand of emotionalism. On opening night at one point in the action, she threw herself down on the stage with such abandon that her bracelets lacerated her wrists and she took her curtain calls with both arms bleeding.

An innovation of the Daly management was his production of Sardou's daring *Uncle Sam* (1873). Banned in France on the grounds that it would wound the feelings of a "proud and friendly people"—so ran the playbill—the New York production was the first on any stage. "Mr. Daly," it continued, "placing a just estimate upon the strong common sense of the metropolis," produced the piece without changing a single word. According to Judge Daly, Sardou had envisaged the play simply as a comedy of manners, his comments upon American society being no more injurious than similar criticisms of French eccentricities in *La Famille Benoîton*. By present-day standards the plot appears perfectly harmless. American elections are ridiculed by having an educated seal who smokes a pipe almost win an election for the Democrats. The central character, the Honorable Samuel Tapplebot (L'Oncle Sam), is a typical American. He is described as a man

who sold brooms at the age of twelve, was pork-packer at seventeen, manufacturer of shoe-polish at twenty, made a fortune in cocoa, lost in tobacco, rose again with indigo, fell with salt pork, rebounded with cotton and settled definitely upon guano. He rises at six, rushes to his office in an omnibus, is greedy, extravagant, cunning and credulous; without scruples, yet a good fellow; will throw you overboard for a hundred dollars and spend two hundred to fish you out; a perfect type of the American whom nothing discourages, always at the front, his eyes fixed upon his three beacons—wealth for an end, cunning for the means, and as for morals—success!

The best touch is the portrayal of the typical American girl, Sarah Tapplebot; she is presented as an early edition of Anne Whitefield of *Man and Superman*. Sardou has almost completely anticipated Shaw's reversal of the love chase except that he allows Sarah to relent at last; she finally takes refuge in flight.

A. H. Quinn in his *History of the American Drama* has noted that the year 1880 marks a change in Daly's French adaptations. Before that time, says Quinn, his versions retained their French or European settings; after 1880, "he changed the atmosphere entirely and made as little of the original setting as possible." Quinn makes no conclusive deduction from his observation other than to say that "whether the growing sense of the importance of American plays being laid in America caused this change . . . is a matter of speculation." The fact is that the change noted by Quinn did not take place. For, *The Royal Youth* (1881), *Odette* (1882),

Serge Panine (1883), *Denise* (1885), *Roger La Honte* (1889), the two pantomimes, *The Prodigal Son* (1891) and *Miss Pygmalion* (1885), as well as *Cyrano de Bergerac* (1898) and *Madame Sans-Gêne* (1899), all retained their original French settings. Only the "eccentric" comedies—*Love in Harness* (1886), *The Lottery of Love* (1888), and *Love in Tandem* (1892)—were Americanized; and they were localized because they were specifically tailored to the requirements of the Daly company. They were out of the same cloth as the bright, but intellectually shallow, German farces which Daly was producing concurrently with them. Besides, audiences knew they were adaptations and came to see their favorite actors on display regardless of the nationality of the piece.

Daly's most successful French adaptation was *The Lottery of Love*, which from October 9, 1888 until January 7, 1889 achieved a total of 107 performances. The play was based on Alexandre Bisson and Antony Mars' *Les Surprises du Divorce*. Its success was due to the fact that it was exactly tailored to the members of the Daly company. The comedy hinged on the antics of a mother-in-law (played by Mrs. Gilbert) and her skill in handling her daughter's two husbands (John Drew and James Lewis). In his thesis, *The Theme of Divorce in American Drama*, Dr. Koster has pointed out the significance of *The Lottery of Love* inasmuch as it marked the "first appearance in American drama of the female parasite who makes her living through alimony." It is doubtful whether New Yorkers who witnessed the comedy were aware of participating in a historical event. They went to be amused; as one reviewer, C. M. S. McLellan, wrote, "It makes a sensible man laugh, but makes him despise the childish weakness which permits him to do so." Other critics were not so discerning. Boucicault wrote that "the dialogue is the best I have listened to for many years," and Brander Matthews indicated in a note to Daly that the play was delightful enough to make him forget the pain of a toothache.

The basis for laughter in this play, as in all of Daly's farces, lies in the situations, not in the characters. So the mere idea of a mother-in-law, especially as Daly adapted her to American life and made her an ex-bloomer girl, struck nineteenth-century audiences as funny. Her appearance in bloomers was as hilariously side-splitting as the similar incident in *A Night Off* when one of the characters was discovered in his long winter underwear. Another situation undoubtedly considered a "scream" was the one in which a silly old man brings home his young wife only to discover that she is the ex-mate of his new son-in-law. In 1888, when divorce was much less common than today, this predicament was an amusing one. Theatrical fashions and audiences change slowly: *Bloomer Girl* was a successful Broadway comedy in 1943 for much the same reasons that *The Lottery of Love* succeeded in 1888.

The Lottery of Love has a historical interest besides its slapstick humor, however. For at the same time that Daly was presenting his adaptation, the renowned Coquelin, on his first visit to America, was appearing in the French original at Palmer's Theatre, diagonally across Broadway. The critics preferred Coquelin to Drew, but Mrs. Gilbert and James Lewis were awarded the palm over their opposites. During their visit to Paris in 1891, the Daly company further courted comparison by presenting *The Lottery of Love* at the very theater where it had been originally played. When Mrs. Gilbert appeared in her regulation bloomers and little round hat, the French, she reported, were "surprised and puzzled by the change"; but "the genuine dash and fun" carried the play to success. In *Les Surprises du Divorce*, the mother-in-law is an ex-ballet dancer and appears in the picture-taking scene in her old ballet costume.

Agitation for women's suffrage had been an active force for over thirty years in 1888; Mrs. Gilbert indicates that "the woman's right movement was then in full swing." So in *The Lottery of Love*, as in *Leah, the Forsaken, Divorce*, and *Pique* before it, Daly was utilizing a contemporary situation for purposes of theatrical exploitation. That he succeeded so well guaranteed to his pieces a popularity which was, however, but momentary. As did several of his other eccentric comedies, *The Lottery of Love* held the stage for about fifteen years; then it disappeared alike from the boards and the libraries, even before the piece of clothing it ridiculed. But by all standards it stands out as the best of Daly's adaptations from the French.

Samson and Dalilah was another "eccentric"—Daly used the word on his playbills—comedy by Bisson, this time in collaboration with J. Moineaux. Again, marital difficulties (an extravagant wife is taken to court by her husband) constitute the major theme. In defense of the superficiality of *Samson and Dalilah* one has only to look at the rival New York attractions in April of 1889: Academy of Music, Denman Thompson in *The Old Homestead;* Casino, Lillian Russell in *Nadjy;* Niblo's, Mrs. Brown Potter in Sardou's *Cléopatre;* Lyceum (Frohman), an adaptation of Sardou's *Ferreol* called *The Marquise;* Union Square, Helen Barry in *A Woman's Stratagem;* Park, *The Grip;* Palmer's, De Wolf Hopper in *The May Queen;* Madison Square, Maurice Barrymore in *Captain Swift;* Fourteenth Street, *The Iron Creed;* Star, Rose Coghlan in *Jocelyn,* a romantic play of the time of Louis XIII. The incomparable Daly company, that is, the "Big Four" plus a charming newcomer, Kitty Cheatham, made *Samson and Dalilah* a satisfying play and preserved for Mr. Daly the appellation of "the most decently successful of all American managers."

After launching the melodramatic *Roger La Honte* at Niblo's on October 8, 1889, for which he imported the two popular British stars, William Terriss and Jessie Millward, Daly turned to his final eccentric piece from the French, *Love in Tandem* (1892). In reply to a query about this play's source, Mr. Dorney, Daly's business manager, answered that the names mentioned on the program were the right ones, but he could not recall them. They were, of course, Henri Bocage and Charles de Courcy; but they might just as easily have been Franz Schonthan or Gustav von Moser. As one reviewer indicated, "There is not a vestige of the Gallic profanity left, which undoubtedly saved the French original [*Vie à Deux*]. *Love in Tandem* is thoroughly imbued and subdued with the spirit of Dalyesque decency and sanctimonious merriment." But, "as a duet between the only Ada Rehan and the only John Drew, *Love in Tandem* will always be worth hearing," was the forced conclusion.

Daly utilized here the ancient device of having a servant explain the situation. A man and his wife are bored; they deliberately try to irritate one another, he by taking fencing lessons, she piano. He complains of her frivolity; she retaliates by accusing him of more loyalty to his club than to his home. After a series of mere charades, they are reconciled; so are two other couples (pretending to be in love with someone else, the resulting jealousy drives all the lovers into the proper arms). The play ends with a tag in which all of Daly's "love" plays (*Love on Crutches*, *The Lottery of Love*, *The Railroad of Love*, *Love in Harness*) are referred to, for "love," according to Daly's canny view, was the one constant of life.

> Fashions may come or go, as Fashion wills;
> But nature is as changeless as the hills!
> Single or double, may men and women abide,
> But if they go double, then ever side by side.

One curious experiment which Daly attempted was the production of pantomime. The two French pieces which he presented were *The Prodigal Son* (1891) and *Miss Pygmalion* (1895). In America pantomime had never achieved the status it had in France and England. In the first place, American audiences were not educated to it; and, in the second,

American performers, with few exceptions, were not qualified to perform in it. Daly had, it is true, employed the Lauri family of pantomimists in *Roi Carotte* (1872), but their role had consisted more of dancing and pageantry (portraying the daily life of Pompeii, for example) than of acting. Daly had also staged *Humpty Dumpty Abroad* (1873), featuring the only really great American pantomimists, George L. and C. K. Fox. But the Fox pantomime was also entirely made up of humor and ballet.

In Paris during the summer of 1890, Daly had witnessed a French pantomime, *L'Enfant Prodigue*, featuring the artiste, Felicia Mallet, as Pierrot. The piece had been "written" by Michel Carré *fils* and the music was composed by Andre Wormser. "He was so impressed with the charm of the performance," relates Judge Daly, "that he acquired the American rights to the play." Brander Matthews was equally thrilled with the art of *L'Enfant Prodigue*. "Here was a true play," he wrote, in *A Book about the Theatre*, "moving to tears as well as to laughter, holding the interest by a human story of universal appeal."

The Daly production, a version adapted by the producer and called simply *The Prodigal Son*, was not, however, a success. Judge Daly accounted for the failure by the excuse that his brother was "in advance of his time." But Brander Matthews, while praising Charles Leclercq and Mrs. Gilbert, indicated that the major deficiency was the Pierrot of Miss Rehan who, as a pantomimist, was "inferior." "Now the convention underlying pantomime is that we are beholding a story carried on by a race of beings whose natural method of communicating information and idea is gesture," he explained. "But more than once Miss Rehan appeared as if she wanted to speak. . . . Her gestures seemed like afterthoughts; they lacked spontaneity and inevitability." Odell, ordinarily so full of liking for Daly, was unusually blunt. "Daly must have been distressed," be surmised, "even shocked and confused at finding there was one thing, at least, that Miss Rehan could not do. And one thing he could not direct!"

In 1893, Daly brought over a French group—the Cleary company—to interpret *L'Enfant Prodigue* at his theater while his own dramatic troup was in London. The success of M. Courtes and Mademoiselle Pilar-Morin called up further comparisons with the Daly fiasco of 1891.

For his next excursion into pantomime, Daly took no chances with his own company, but brought Mademoiselle Jane May from Paris to star in *Miss Pygmalion*. Again the story was by Michel Carré *fils;* his collaborator was "Jean Herbert," the *nom de plume* of Mademoiselle May. The music was by Francis Thome. *The Dramatic Mirror* found Jane May without the "magnetism" necessary for a panto-mimist; as a consequence, "the audience was not enthusiastic." Vance Thompson of *The Commercial Advertiser* exclaimed that "after the loquacity of the spoken drama, how beautiful is this silence!" But he, too, found Jane May "a trifle hard in outline, a trifle stiff in expression," inferior to her pred-ecessors, Felicia Mallet and Pilar-Morin.

One of the most interesting aspects of *Miss Pygmalion* was that it introduced Isadora (called on the playbills "Sara") Duncan to New York. Her performance was greeted without fanfares but in her autobiography she has dramatically recalled the event. She had first managed to see Daly in Chicago; her approach was typical. "I bring you the dance," she an-nounced. "I bring you the idea that is going to revolutionize our entire epoch. . . . I am the spiritual daughter of Walt Whitman. . . . I bring to your theatre the vital soul that it lacks, the soul of the dancer." Surprisingly enough, he hired her; she accepted a part in *Miss Pygmalion* even though "pan-tomime to me has never seemed an art. . . . The whole thing seemed to me very stupid and quite unworthy of my ambi-tion and ideals." However, youth is adaptable, and she managed to adjust herself to Jane May's "extremely violent temper" long enough to endure six weeks of rehearsal, three weeks in New York, and two months on the road—at a salary, she reported, of $15 a week. "The whole venture," she concluded, "was a distressing failure for Mr. Daly."

Daly produced Rostand's famed *Cyrano de Bergerac* in Philadelphia (Chestnut Street Theatre) on October 3, 1898. His version was based on a translation by Gladys Thomas and Mary F. Guillemard and must have been somewhat distorted as it starred Ada Rehan as Roxane. Charles Richman, who played Cyrano, was merely her leading man. According to Clapp and Edgett's account, the piece was "hastily put together to compete with Mansfield" who opened on the same date at the Garden Theatre, New York. Indeed, Mansfield seems to have complained about the situation beforehand, for in September 1898, Daly had his brother, the judge, write to Mansfield pointing out that Rostand had not copyrighted *Cyrano* in the United States (he could not, under existing regulations), hence anyone was free to produce it.

The Daly version was definitely not a success. Norman Hapgood, in *The Stage in America*, has indicated that it was inferior to all the numerous productions, including the German version (by Fulda), produced by Conreid at the Irving Place Theater. "Prudery," the "mediocre leading man," and "poorly chosen lines" characterized the Daly version. The *Sun*, never very favorable to Daly, printed (on October 28, 1898) the following "Ballade" by "R. A. W.," inspired by "the massacre in Philadelphia, wrought by Augustin Daly, who cares for naught":

> I gayly doff my "Daly" hat,
>   That famous, weird chapeau,
> For I and the Greenroom cat
>   Must wrestle with "Cyrano."
> I am armed with my snickersee;
>   Shall we leave him whole? Not much!
> And now in a trice you shall see
>   How he crumbles at my touch.

How shall I treat this Gascon wight?
  Banish him! Out he goes!
I'll hack the play as I did "Twelfth Night,"
  And Ada shall wear the nose!
This butchering task, I vow,
  I have not enjoyed so much
Since "Merrilies" made her bow
  And was slaughtered at my touch.

Ho! for the music I threw in free,
  When I gave you "Merry Wives"!
The plays that are writ by Shakespeare and me,
  Saw you ever such plays in your lives?
They are tortured and spangled and dressed
  In opera and burlesque and such;
And since William has gone to his rest
  I may mangle all I touch.

ENVOI

Author, beware that your play
  Comes not within my clutch.
I have made for myself a record today
  To mutilate all that I touch.

The account of Daly's French adaptations ends on a note
of failure. Like *Cyrano*, Daly's final French piece, *Madame
Sans-Gêne*, did not achieve success; it ran only two weeks,
from January 3 to 15, 1899. Most of the reviews blamed the
acting of Ada Rehan for the fiasco; theatrical gossipers were
sure that she disapproved of the play and so her bad acting
was a deliberate neglect of preparation. Daly himself presented a different view in a letter to William Winter (January 12, 1899):

I am sorry that you are not to see *Sans Gene* but perhaps you
would care as little for it as the rest. Ada has rehearsed it and
played it through pain & nervous tension: and yet has given some
lovely glimpses of her view of that big natural woman such as no
one else has shown—& I have seen the play with her in Paris,
Munich & London.

Since he produced so many Sardou plays, it is interesting to consider his relations with the French dramatist. A letter from Sardou's agent, C. A. Chizzola, discloses that in 1890, for example, Sardou refused to accept a royalty payment of 10 per cent; Sardou preferred fixed payments on the following plan,

```
frs.   30,000—already paid
       20,000—upon acceptance of scenario
       50,000—upon delivery of manuscript
       50,000—on first performance in America
       ───────
      150,000
```

to this sum Sardou added,

```
frs.   50,000   on first performance in London
       25,000   on 50th performance in New York
       25,000   on 50th performance in London
       25,000   on 100th performance in New York
       25,000   on 100th performance in London
```

Chizzola pointed out that the outright purchase guaranteed by these figures gave Daly the right to sell the play for production elsewhere in America and England, whereas a 10 per cent royalty meant that Sardou still owned the piece and could himself dispose of it to others.

This last point was a ticklish one in those pre-international copyright days. Daly's relations with Sardou became more and more strained, especially when Daly felt that his contract had been circumvented by Sardou's sending a play to Daniel Frohman. The result was that Sardou, in pique, canceled all contracts and all friendly relations, and kept the 30,000 francs advance payment. The letters make it obvious that the great displays of temper on both sides interfered with any rational arrangement to overcome misunderstanding. The result was that thereafter Daly produced only one Sardou play, *Madame Sans-Gêne*, in 1899, for which he had

to pay no royalty since the play, having been published,
was "free" according to existing regulations.

Alongside Daly's many French and German adaptations
stands one Spanish play. On December 5, 1874, at the New
Fifth Avenue Theatre, he produced *Yorick: A New Play*,
from *Un Drama Nuevo* (1867) by Manuel Tamayo y Baus
(Estabanez). The playbills announced it as an "entirely novel
and romantic play by Augustin Daly from the latest literary
and dramatic sensation of the Spanish stage." But, as usual,
there was a translator, perhaps the adaptor, in the background.
In the Daly Correspondence at the Folger Library is a letter
dated December 21, 1874, from J. de Armas Cespedes in
which Señor Cespedes wrote, "I would be very much obliged
to you if you send me the original Spanish piece I delivered
to you with the translation; I mean: Un Drama Nuevo. I
would be likewise grateful to you if you send me today the
amount of the money you have to pay me according to our
agreement." On the back is a note in Daly's handwriting:
"Make out check for $100." Whether Daly was induced to
produce *Yorick* by Señor Cespedes or simply because of its
reputation (it had been tremendously successful in Madrid
and the printed version ran to four editions), its failure probably caused him never again to produce a Spanish play, even
though in 1884 Howells urged him to do so. For Howells
wrote that he knew some modern Spanish and Italian comedies
"far funnier, livelier & better" than the German play which
Daly had sent to him to "naturalize."

Yorick is a play about Shakespeare's "old acquaintance,"
the comedian who aspired to tragic roles. He persuades Shakespeare to allow him to play the dramatic lead in "A new
Play"; in gaining this favor, Yorick acquires also the hatred
of Walton, the company's tragedian. And so, when the
mock play discloses the infidelity of the hero's wife, it is really
of the infidelity of his own wife which Yorick learns,
through Walton's treachery. The comedian then rises to

heights of tragic pathos before killing his rival and himself. The play seems stupid, but Daly felt that it had unquestioned appeal. He secured Louis James to play Yorick and Charles Fisher, made up after the Chandos portrait, enacted Shakespeare. Sara Jewett was the wife, and Frank Hardenbergh the villainous Walton. Despite his efforts at accurate and elaborate settings and the ability of the cast, the play failed. "Disgusted with the desertion of the public, after the trial of one week, the manager indignantly tore off the play and consigned the manuscript to his library," states Judge Daly.

The withdrawal of *Yorick* was not, however, to conclude the history of *Un Drama Nuevo*. Judge Daly says that "Lawrence Barrett applied for the right to produce it. . . . In later years, as *Yorick's Love*, it had a fixed place in his repertoire." The important detail which Judge Daly omitted is that the *Yorick's Love* in which Barrett acted was not Daly's version but a new adaptation by William Dean Howells. Barrett first presented *Yorick's Love* in Cleveland (Euclid Avenue Opera House, October 25, 1878), where John Hay saw it, and wrote to Howells, "You made a great improvement in keeping Shakespeare behind the flies. He was so grotesque in the original. . . ." (Howells substituted Thomas Heywood for Shakespeare.) Further, added Hay, "it was a very different play from the one I saw at the Fifth Avenue Theatre some years ago, improved almost beyond recognition." Howells' answer reveals that he was a much more conscientious adaptor than Daly, "I blank-versified the more touching and noble speeches," he confessed, "and here and there I helped the Spaniard out a little." Barrett later presented the adaptation in Boston (1879) and London (1884). True, *Yorick's Love* remained in Barrett's repertoire for many years, but it was not Daly's unfortunate and badly done version.

CHAPTER 6

Shakespeare, New Style

Marplay, Junior: *Why, sir, would you guess that I had altered Shakespeare?*
Witmore: *Yes, faith, sir, no one sooner.*
Marplay, Junior: *Alack-a-day! Was you to see the plays when they are brought to us, a parcel of crude, undigested stuff. We are the persons, sir, who lick them into form, and mould them into shape.*

Fielding, *The Author's Farce*
Act I, Scene 6.

Students of the nineteenth-century drama come sooner or later to the realization that the most important dramatist of the period was Shakespeare. Any adequate account of the number and quality of the productions of his plays between 1800 and 1900 would require a full study in itself. For one thing, every actor of the period seems to have aspired to play Shakespeare, if not legitimately in tragedy or comedy, then at least in burlesque or operatic version. As a consequence, a study of Shakespearean presentations would have to refer to practically every volume of theatrical autobiography, biography, reminiscence, letters, and criticism written during or about those times. A few standard works do exist, such as George C. D. Odell's monumental *Shakespeare from Betterton to Irving*, William Winter's three series of studies, *Shakespeare on the Stage*, Arthur Colby Sprague's *Shakespeare and the Actors;* and, for works specifically concerned with the United States, there are Esther Cloudman

220 THE THEATER OF AUGUSTIN DALY

Dunn's *Shakespeare in America* and Alfred Westfall's *American Shakespearean Criticism, 1607–1865*. The New Variorum and other editions contain valuable notes explaining the methods of actors and managers; and, finally, there are the acting editions of the plays themselves, as well as prompt-books of various sorts.

The tradition of producing Shakespeare on the American stage dates from March 5, 1750, when *Richard III* was presented by a company under the management of Thomas Keen and Walter Murray. Since that presentation, one of the earliest professional stage productions in North America, Shakespeare's plays have consistently maintained their popularity on the American stage. During the nineteenth century, Shakespearean productions were the one constant in most repertories, and the names of the greatest American performers of the period—Hackett, Forrest, Charlotte Cushman, Booth—are inextricably bound up with the Shakespearean roles in which they achieved fame. Indeed, these roles were the measures of greatness by which an actor laid claim to immortality. For as William Archer has observed, "All we really know about the great actors of the past is the effect they produced upon their audiences." And no plays, as the actors of the nineteenth century were acutely aware, were so rich as Shakespeare's in opportunities to produce "effect."

Ada Rehan's Katherine, Rosalind, and Viola, and Daly's productions of *A Midsummer Night's Dream, The Taming of the Shrew*, and *The Merchant of Venice* are landmarks of theatrical history, though the names of Daly's German and French adaptations have been forgotten. Augustin Daly brought to Shakespeare the attitude typical of his times. He may have made money more easily by producing German farce or French problem plays or English and American melodramas, but it was by presenting Shakespeare and Old Comedy revivals that his theater achieved its fame and reputation.

The truth is that the nineteenth century was fond of

Shakespeare because it made Shakespeare over into one of its own. And the principal tailor of the period, where Shakespearean productions are concerned, was the ghost whom Daly hired to make all his adaptations of Shakespearean plays, the writer of the commendatory prefaces for all these Daly adaptations, the man who edited Booth's acting versions, and the senior New York drama critic, William Winter. To speak of Daly's Shakespeare is always to include Winter's large part in it. Winter has explained "after long musing" the treatment which Shakespeare's plays "ought" to receive, and did at his hands. "Each of them," he insisted, "should be so condensed that the performance will not occupy more than about three hours." To achieve this condensation, Winter recommended three kinds of expurgation: first, "the text should be relieved wherever possible (and as to this point good taste is the right, and should be the final and inexorable, judge) of all foul or vulgar language"; next, "descriptive passages" which are "manifestly superfluous when the scenes which they describe can properly be shown" had to go; and, finally, "passages of literary quality which neither facilitate exposition of character nor expedite movement, and by which sometimes the action is impeded, also can be spared, without injury to the effect of the play, and there should be no compunction about excising them."

Clearly, for Mr. Winter, the play was the thing. About Daly's agreement with Winter's statements there can be no doubt. He proclaimed in a letter to Winter, dated June 9, 1870, his belief that "the stage should hold the mirror up to Nature"—a belief which he promptly qualified by adding, "I veil in delicate language and soften by gentle contrasts the terrible lessons which everyday life teaches." In a word, he confused a mirror with pink glasses.

Ellen Terry, herself involved in Irving's elaborate staging, complained that Daly "had no artistic sense" so that "his productions of Shakespeare were really bad from the pictorial point of view." Shaw, commenting on Daly's *The Two Gentlemen of Verona,* called it a "vaudeville." That Daly, Irving, Tree, and other nineteenth-century producers preferred the painted opulence of an elaborate picture set to the imaginative beauty of Shakespeare's lines indicates the justice of Shaw's bitter criticisms.

In a cogent essay on "Shakespeare and the Modern Stage," Sidney Lee made a plea for the exclusion of embellishment in the production of plays, still the mode in 1906. He pointed to the misleading impressions engendered by current presentations and argued wisely that the result was not Shakespeare but spectacle. Such productions, added Strang in *Players and Plays of the Last Quarter Century,* "really did more harm than good by inculcating a false notion of what a stage representation of Shakespeare should be."

Daly himself was not without the critical faculty, but it was turned toward the audience. On January 23, 1878, he wrote to Joseph from Syracuse that

> The enthusiasm of these inland cities over Shakespeare is very interesting. The people turn out in their best attire, & in their best humors. They come early & never stir till the curtain falls. They yawn under their fans & in their handkerchiefs, & doze under the disguise of intense thoughtfulness & wake up with a start & applaud vigorously, and give "recalls" after every act, & murmur to each other, as they pass out, finally, "superb, exquisite, nothing like Shakespeare, sir, after all"—but dear me, how restless and uneasy the poor bored souls seem to be while it's all going on.

Of course, other commentators were not so outraged as Shaw, Lee, and Strang, or so bored as the poor dozing Syracusans. On the contrary, both Winter and Odell found Daly's productions "magnificent." Clement Scott was an apologist, albeit a lame one, excusing Daly's bowdlerising of Shakespeare by asserting that Daly's acting versions were no worse than those of English producers and adding that at least Daly did not "tolerate" David Garrick's *Katherine and Petruchio.*

Miss Amy Leslie, in *Some Players, Personal Sketches,* has further exonerated Daly. "The subservience of literary immensity to scenic paint and la belle jardinière is not a question of taste, but a sign of the times," she averred. With gaudy abandon and evident relish, she then described Daly's "sumptuous boudoirs and jeweled robes, gardens of Oriental magnificence, and forests which fairly reek with luxurious beauty and painted favors of nature.... These gauds of vesture seduce audiences into admiration for the poet beautiful whose thoughts lie buried in spangles and artificial bay leaves." Such effusions make one pause for reflection before accepting Miss Leslie's pronouncement that "Mr. Daly is a scholar to begin with; furthermore, he is distinctly a dramatic scholar of highest attainments." If Daly's mirror was a pink glass, Miss Leslie's pen, like that of William Winter, was dipped in purple ink.

In a consideration of Daly's Shakespeare productions the figure of Joseph again looms large. The letters between the two brothers are an almost limitless source of information about Daly's versions of Shakespeare. On May 30, 1883, for example, Augustin wrote Joseph from Cincinnati that he was at work on *The Merry Wives of Windsor* and indicated that he hoped to have the revision ready for Joseph's scrutiny upon his return from the western trip. Joseph was paid royalty fees for many of the performances. In January, February, and March of 1893, Joseph acknowledged payments of royalties for *As You Like It, The Taming of the Shrew,* and *Twelfth Night.* It is probable that he received other royalty checks for which he made no written acknowledgment inasmuch as the brothers met almost every day. during the winter months. The final word in the letters relating to a Shakespearean play was written by Joseph on February 23, 1895. He found, he reported, "only two expurgations to be made" in the text of *The Two Gentlemen of Verona,* both of which were examples of "coarseness."

Joseph was more than a collaborator here; he served his brother as a source of information and scholarship, acting in effect as a mentor or personal manager. On September 10, 1874, Joseph wrote Augustin from Worcester in answer to a request for assistance. "I got your memorandum yesterday about O'Kelly & the Shakspere interview," he replied, but "I can't do it out here." The story can easily be pieced together. O'Kelly, a journalist, had asked Daly for "a three column interview" in which the manager was to discuss "the subject of the authorship of Shakspere's plays." As Joseph was quick to warn, such a statement on Augustin's part would be

equivalent to an essay by you on that subject. It would be read by every Shaksperian scholar as a new contribution to Shaksperian literature. It would hurt your reputation more than a thousand bad plays to have you give a poor essay. The leading manager, ex-litterateur, dramatist, bibliographer, like you ought to make a most entertaining as well as erudite conversationalist upon such a topic.

As a result Joseph cautioned Augustin, "Tell O'Kelly that as soon as you get over your present rush of business you will give him an interview." By that time, in other words, Joseph felt that he could get home to the "books of reference I want" and could instruct Augustin on the "points I would like to get in." He then listed the following items which he deemed essential to discuss:

I. The adverse criticisms on Shakspere in the 18th century.
II. Dramatic criticisms generally.
III. Contemporaneous abuse of dramatists.
IV. Shakspere as a *manager* looking out for a full treasury.
V. Shakspere as a poet—unconscious that he was writing for posterity.
VI. Shakspere as an adaptor.
VII. Shakspere as an augmenter of the plays of others placed in his hands and claiming & publishing them as his own.
VIII. The immorality of Shakspere's tolerated Plays.

An impressive list, certainly. No wonder Joseph wanted to consult his reference books. But the main interest centers in the last four items. One can read into these subjects Joseph's— and by extension, Augustin's—justifications for their revisions of Shakespeare. Furthermore, one sees here the same kind of reasoning and the same arguments which their friend, William Winter, set forth in the prefaces for the individual plays.

Joseph again came to his brother's assistance in connection with Shakespearean scholarship some twenty years later. On April 22, 1896, the eve of the anniversary of Shakespeare's birth, the Shakespeare Society of New York honored Mr. Daly with a dinner at Delmonico's. Augustin wrote to Joseph from Washington on April 3, "You know you engaged to write me the speech I should make. Let me have it as soon as you can—and don't make it too long. Fill it with sage remarks likewise with brilliant witticisms." The *Tribune* of April 23, 1896, in an article evidently written by Winter, contained a glowing account of his speech, and *The Dramatic Mirror* for May 2, 1896 also wrote up the dinner at length and quoted extensively from Augustin's remarks. When Joseph published his biography of his brother, he included long excerpts from the speech he had written. The subject was the endowment of a national theater, a project he opposed.

The speech represents perhaps the ultimate in coöperation between the brothers. The irony connected with the event is nowhere more markedly to be observed than in Augustin's letter of acceptance to the Shakespeare Society. All that tends to keep the stage up to the highest standards must be "agreeable to me," he wrote, "although I may for the moment be asked to sacrifice a reserve more congenial to me than applause."

Whereas he had hired any number of hacks to ghost-write his other adaptations, in the case of Shakespeare Daly reserved that distinction for only one, William Winter. The record of Winter's emasculations of Shakespeare covers sixteen years, beginning in 1882 with *All's Well That Ends Well*. On November 27 of that year Winter wrote Daly,

Here are the other acts of "All's Well." I will, if you like, pass a day with you shortly, & we will discuss the piece, scene by scene. You will observe that I have cut the text very freely, & made several transpositions, etc: but I have not added more than ten lines, altogether. The scenic part will be easy & not expensive. We can have a fine military pageant, & a beautiful moonlight view of Florence.

Despite these blandishments Daly did not produce the play even though Winter acknowledged, on June 21, payment for his work on it. "Your remittance is welcome," he told Daly; "and I thank you for such a practical mark of appreciation and remembrance." In the same letter, he agrees to undertake the new "commission," and "will furnish new stage versions of The Merry Wives and The Two Gentlemen before December first, this year."

Winter was not as good as his word. Although he sent the prompt-book of *The Two Gentlemen of Verona* by December 20, 1883, it was not until the summer of 1884 that he had *The Merry Wives of Windsor* ready. He wrote, on June 18, that " 'The Merry Wives' is done. I have been over it again —the fifth time—from cover to cover. The text is now all right, for your purpose. There must in the representation be many changes of scene—*sixteen* in fact." Before he had finished *The Merry Wives*, Winter had undertaken, on May 25, 1884, to do *The Winter's Tale* for Daly. "With 'All's Well,' " he indicated at that time, "you will then have four of Shakespeare's Comedies as arranged by me; and some day they may prove useful. It seems presumption to touch, even in the most reverent spirit, the work of 'the divine William.' But, as we both are full well aware, it cannot be acted as it stands. So I suppose we will be forgiven."

In 1885, Winter was still working on *The Two Gentlemen*. "I have been through it again & again," he wrote on

December 12, "& I have reduced the text and made the piece practicable." Two years later, on November 5, 1887, he sent a long list of suggestions to be added to Daly's own revision of *A Midsummer Night's Dream*. In 1891, he was at work on *Love's Labour's Lost;* "send me the book," he requested, "and I will see to the text if you wish me to do so." On January 18, 1893, he sent suggestions for emendations in the text of *Twelfth Night*. And on May 30, 1895, he wrote, "I have begun to make a stage version, for you, of Henry IV, & I hope to have it ready for you, by your sailing-day—so that you can have it, for examination & amendment, during the voyage."

Much Ado about Nothing was Winter's next assignment. Letters in the autumn of 1896 show his concern for this play. As in the case of *All's Well*, he wrote to arrange a conference in order to go over his suggested changes in the text. A year later he helped Daly with *The Tempest*. "I have carefully read the text of your Play-Book," he wrote, "& I have noted various points for your consideration." The last of the Shakespearean plays for which Daly sought Winter's assistance was *The Merchant of Venice*. "I have been at work all night upon 'Cyrano de Bergerac,'" he complained to Daly on October 4, 1898, "& I am exhausted & sick today. . . . The piece, to me, is an infernal bore—one of the dreariest things I ever was condemned to endure." But at the same time, he was pinning his hopes on the Shakespeare play. "I want the Merchant of Venice to be a great hit," he confided, "as I do not expect to see a long continuance of Cyrano." As late as January 11, 1899, he was still sending suggestions for changes in the text of *The Merchant*, and it is clear that he was the one who suggested Sidney Herbert for the role of Shylock.

The correspondence establishes the fact that Winter worked on eleven of Daly's Shakespearean texts and there may have been more revisions of which no record exists. For these labors, which are startling because they are so extensive, he was evidently well paid. All the revisions except *All's Well That Ends Well* were privately printed by Daly with his own name as revisionist on the title page. All were entered for copyright by Daly under his own name. For all of them Winter wrote Prefaces. For all of the productions, moreover, he wrote criticisms, frequently glowing, always commendatory, in the New York papers. It is interesting to note in passing that all of his letters or papers that survive are in purple ink in a most fragile hand.

In all, Daly produced sixteen of Shakespeare's plays. His first production was *Twelfth Night,* in which Mrs. Scott-Siddons starred as Viola on October 4, 1869, at the Fifth Avenue Theatre. His final Shakespearean venture was a magnificently spectacular production of *The Merchant of Venice* which ran from November 19, 1898, until January 2, 1899, at Daly's Theatre. From 1869, when he opened the Fifth Avenue Theatre, until he gave up the management in 1877, "for some years at least, and, most likely, forever," he produced thirteen Shakespearean plays, starring such famous performers as Adelaide Neilson, Mrs. Scott-Siddons, Fanny Davenport, Carlotta Leclercq, E. L. Davenport, Charles Coghlan, and, greatest of all, Edwin Booth.

He reëntered management at a new Daly's Theatre on September 17, 1879, but a six-year hiatus occurred before his next Shakespearean production, a presentation of *The Merry Wives of Windsor* on January 14, 1886. From then until his death in 1899 not a year passed without a Shakespearean production, usually a newly adapted version, magnificently staged, and featuring Ada Rehan. The galaxy included:

1885–1886, *The Merry Wives of Windsor*
1886–1887, *The Taming of the Shrew*
1887–1888, *A Midsummer Night's Dream*
1889–1890, *As You Like It*

1890–1891, *Love's Labour's Lost*
1892–1893, *Twelfth Night*
1894–1895, *The Two Gentlemen of Verona*
1895–1896, *Romeo and Juliet*
1896–1897, *Much Ado about Nothing*
1897–1898, *The Tempest*
1898–1899, *The Merchant of Venice*

Of these productions, *The Taming of the Shrew* (January
18 to April 30, 1887) and *Twelfth Night* (Daly's, London,
January 8 to May 4, 1894) had consecutive runs of over a
hundred performances. During the two seasons when no
new productions were featured, revivals of earlier productions (*The Taming of the Shrew* in 1888–1889; *As You Like
It* in 1891–1892), or an elaborate production of an old English play (*The Inconstant*, 1888–1889), or of a distinguished
new piece (Tennyson's *The Foresters*, 1891–1892) were offered. The 1893–1894 season was spent in London, where
Daly presented *The Taming of the Shrew*, the very successful *Twelfth Night*, and *As You Like It*. The contemplated
production of *Henry IV* was to have taken place during the
1896–1897 season in New York.

Daly's early use of Shakespeare was a part of his effort to
establish himself in New York as a manager. In the first
six months of the opening season at the Fifth Avenue Theatre,
he included, besides *Twelfth Night* (October 4, 1869), *As
You Like It* (October 18), and *Much Ado about Nothing*
(November 8) in the twenty-one plays produced. All three
featured Mrs. Scott-Siddons, an Englishwoman, a member
of the famous Siddons and Kemble families, and a most charming actress. From letters she wrote to Daly, it is clear that the
versions of the plays she used had already been prepared for
her. Daly's principal function, to provide a supporting cast,
he performed handsomely, surrounding the visiting star with
Agnes Ethel, Fanny Davenport, Mrs. Jennings, Davidge,
Clarke, Harkins, and Holland. He also handled the finances.

Since no one seems to have either complained or rhapsodized about the settings, they were presumably adequate but not distinguished.

A notable production of *The Merry Wives of Windsor* which ran from November 19 to December 8, 1872, at the Fifth Avenue Theatre, Odell, without elaborating, pronounced "one of the minor celebrities in the Shakespearean field." Winter listed the principal players and indicated that "Daly made the arrangement," but declared it inferior to the 1886 version. He added that the costumes were a mixture of fashions that were "wholly unauthorized" and consequently "produced an injudicious medley."

Love's Labour's Lost, first produced by Daly at the New Fifth Avenue Theatre on February 21, 1874, and running until March 2, was chiefly interesting because it had never before been produced in New York. Judge Daly quotes a number of appreciative letters from Richard Grant White, Joseph N. Ireland, and A. Oakey Hall, commending Daly's ingenuity, which his brother pointed out was "indeed a labor of love.'" This arrangement of the comedy was in five acts and was "scenically admirable." The Frenchwomen were portrayed by Ada Dyas, Fanny Davenport, Sara Jewett, Nina Varian, and Nellie Mortimer; the self-exiled nobles included Harkins, Clarke, Louis James, Hart Conway, and Frank Hardenbergh. Winter cited the "memorable" performances given by the veterans William Davidge as Holofernes and Charles Fisher as Armado.

During the financially disastrous season of 1873–1874, Daly, then managing three theatres, presented *A Midsummer Night's Dream* in the cavernous Grand Opera House August 19–September 8, 1873. Although the production was handsomely mounted—"one of the scenes, a woodland, painted by G. Heister, was, in particular, an admirable work of art"—the play failed, snuffed out in the panic of 1873. Perhaps the most notable aspect of the production was the cast, which included the great clowns, G. L. and C. K. Fox as Bottom and Snug, and a "pretty and intelligent child," Fay Templeton, as Puck.

During the following winter season, Daly was having such financial difficulties at his Fifth Avenue Theatre that he tried importing stars to revive his waning income. E. L. Davenport and Carlotta Leclercq were the two chief attractions. On January 11, 1875, they were featured in a comedy revival of *The Merchant of Venice*, a badly mangled version in "four acts and four scenes," without act five, such as had been performed at the Prince of Wales Theatre, London. The "rich dressing" and "picturesque setting" of this revival made "small amends for the irreverent and often incapable treatment of the text," wrote Towse. *The Merchant of Venice* ran a week and did not succeed in lightening the financial burden of the theater. Affairs continued in a bad way until February 17, 1875, when Daly struck pay dirt with *The Big Bonanza*.

A significant series of Shakespearean productions featuring Edwin Booth, "America's foremost actor" according to the playbills, was scheduled by Daly to begin on October 4, 1875. The original plans had to be postponed when the actor was thrown from his carriage at his home in Connecticut. Finally, with his maimed left arm in a sling, Booth opened in *Hamlet* on October 25. In the course of four weeks under Daly's management, he presented ten plays, six of them by Shakespeare. On November 3, *Othello* followed *Hamlet*. According to his usual custom, Booth played Iago, leaving the title role to D. H. Harkins of Daly's company. The New York *Post* review commended Booth and Daly upon their "bravery" in producing tragedy with Daly's comedy troupe, but the paper admitted that "the experiment was justified by its success." On November 8, Booth gave *Richard II*, in an acting version especially prepared by himself. This performance was the first revival of the play in New York and marked Booth's initial portrayal of the character. After one more tragedy, *King Lear*, on November 16, he concluded his Shakespearean roles with two comedies, *The Merchant of Venice* and *The Taming of the Shrew*. According to Winter, Booth always used a variant of Garrick's *Katherine and Petruchio*, reducing the farce to two acts and presenting it as an after-piece. On this occasion he used *The Stranger* as the other half of the bill.

The main emphasis of Daly's Theatre, following the successful engagement of Booth, was once again placed upon the manager's adaptations. The remainder of the 1875–1876 season after Booth closed on November 20 was devoted to *The New Leah* and the very successful *Pique*. During *Pique*'s seven-and-a-half-month run, Daly introduced a number of single performances of various sorts. In that casual way, he produced *As You Like It* on May 24, 1876, with Lawrence Barrett, E. L. Davenport, and Fanny Davenport in the leading roles.

The next season Daly tried to repeat the success of Booth by starring, successively, E. A. Sothern in *Our American Cousin* and *David Garrick* and Joseph Jefferson as Rip Van Winkle. After these engagements, he fell back upon the classics. In particular, he revived his recent production of *As You Like It*. E. L. Davenport again played Jacques. "Of all the interpretations of Jacques I can recall, his was the best in its philosophical pose and carriage, in reflective or caustic humor and oratorical skill," wrote the critic Towse. A superior cast, headed by Fanny Davenport, Charles Coghlan, and William Davidge, enabled the comedy to hold the boards from November 18 until December 2, 1876. Coghlan, whom Daly had imported from England upon the advice of Clara Morris, enacted *Hamlet* later in the season, presenting the tragedy at his own benefit matinee on March 10, 1877. Fanny Davenport was his Ophelia.

Daly's next excursion into Shakespearean management later

the same year starred the phenomenally beautiful English actress, Adelaide Neilson. All the theatrical histories of the period carry accounts of this charming woman, née Elizabeth Brown, who died in Paris in 1880 at the age of only thirty. Miss Neilson made three trips to the United States—in 1872, again in 1874, and finally in 1877, when she appeared under Daly's management. She was immensely popular in this country; her performances were rewarded with enthusiastic reviews; and she made a great deal of money here. For her last American appearance, she played in *Twelfth Night, Cymbeline,* and *Romeo and Juliet,* her most famous role. For these productions, she provided her own texts of the plays. Daly furnished a supporting cast of distinguished players headed by Eben Plympton (an excellent Romeo), Charles Fisher, Davidge, and Mrs. Gilbert.

Daly's final Shakespearean productions of this early period took place the week of December 22, 1877, at Booth's Theatre, which he managed for a brief time. During that week, Fanny Davenport made her final appearance under his management in *As You Like It, The School for Scandal,* and *Twelfth Night.* In behalf of two of these productions, Daly wrote Winter on December 20, 1877:

Permit me to ask your interest for the performances of Shakespearean comedy which are to be given at Booth's Theatre. . . . Perhaps my request will not pass wholly unheeded when I further state that with these performances will cease my interest in theatrical management for some years at least, and most likely, forever—as far as New York is concerned.

True enough, these performances marked the close of the first, and most varied, period of Daly's career. He had produced all but one (*The Undercurrent*) of his original plays. He had laid the foundations for his many successful French and German adaptations. He had established himself as a man of taste, if not of success, and was one manager who had invariably insisted upon the importance of first-rate acting. He had given New York audiences a liberal amount of Shake-speare and other English classics. Despite these accomplish-ments, he was, financially, a failure. It was to be another seven years before Daly would present Shakespeare again, this time in prosperity and prominence.

In 1879, after an unsuccessful stay in England, Daly opened his jewel box of a theater at Thirtieth Street and Broadway. There he assembled a distinguished company, including Ada Rehan, John Drew, Mrs. Gilbert, and James Lewis. The mood of the company was humor; adapted German farces, so lively and so ephemeral, set a merry pace; gradually the theater came to be known as the home of joyous comedy. By 1886, the theater was established as the foremost in New York. Plays by Bronson Howard, Edgar Fawcett, and A. W. Pinero were produced alongside the latest Parisian successes of Sardou, Dumas *fils*, and Georges Ohnet. German comic opera succeeded as brilliantly as German farce. Next, old English comedies were handsomely revived: Colley Cibber's *She Wou'd and She Wou'd Not* in 1883, *The Country Girl*, based on Garrick and Wycherley, in 1884, and Farquhar's *The Recruiting Officer*, in 1885. At last the time was again ripe for Shakespeare.

Now, however, Daly's approach was to be new. Produc-tions of the greatest English dramatist were to be lavishly, magnificently staged; an attempt was to be made, in other words, to suit the décor to the poetry. And of course the texts had to be rigorously inspected. No taint of bad taste, no coarse word, no indelicate allusion could be endured in a theater whose standard was beauty or by an audience whose manners were dictated by fussy society editors. All the best people went to Daly's. Finally, the version had to be printed from the prompt-book, bound in with a facsimile of the first quarto and a preface by William Winter, the resulting bro-chure to be distributed to first-night auditors. Such were the activities connected with Shakespearean production. Of course, there were also specially chosen musical pieces, choruses and crowds, "authentically" designed costumes, and some of the most elaborate sets ever mounted on an American stage. For *As You Like It*, Daly is reported to have sent a scene painter to France to make an exact copy of the Forêt d'Ardennes, and for the final act of *The Taming of the Shrew*, he used a backdrop based upon a canvas by Paolo Veronese.

The first of these elaborate revivals was *The Merry Wives of Windsor* (January 14 to February 13, 1886). The version which Daly used was in four acts, "altered and emended" by himself and printed in 1886 with a preface by William Winter. The action runs along smoothly enough through the first half of the play. Daly's first act comprises nearly all the first three scenes of Act I of Shakespeare though the speeches near the end are cavalierly juggled so that Falstaff may be allowed to trumpet as the curtain speech, "Sail like my pinnace to these golden shores. Rogues, hence, avaunt!" Act II follows Shakespeare's general order beginning with I, iv and continuing through the first two scenes of Act II. In Daly's last two acts, however, confusion breaks out. In order to compress Shakespeare's last three acts into two, he is forced to omit entirely IV, i, wherein Evans catechizes his student, and V, i, between Falstaff and "Master Brook." Scene iv of Act III, Anne Page's wooing by her three lovers, is wrenched out of its ordinary position and inserted after IV, iv; and the few lines of IV, v (96–103, 111–130) which are retained are similarly pushed back to follow IV, vi. (Line references are all to the Kittredge edition of Shakespeare's plays.) Dame Quickly's speech in III, iv, 105–115, voicing her wishes that all of Anne's suiters might win the girl, is transferred by Daly to the end of IV, vi to give Mrs. Gilbert, playing the part, the curtain speech of Daly's IV, i. Next, to squeeze the comedy into four acts, Daly is forced to pack five scenes into Act III and three into Act IV. Finally, he has added an epilogue for Falstaff constructed from various speeches uttered by the fat knight in *2 Henry IV*. An overall idea of this pandemonium may be gathered from the following chart:

Daly	Shakespeare
Act I	Act I, scenes i, ii, iii
Act II, scene 1	Act I, scene iv
scene 2	Act II, scenes i, ii
Act III, scene 1	Act II, scene iii; Act III, scene i
scene 2	Act III, scene ii
scene 3	Act III, scene iii
scene 4	Act III, scene v
scene 5	Act IV, scene ii
Act IV, scene 1	Act IV, scene iv; Act III, scene iv; Act IV, scene vi
scene 2	Act IV, scene v; Act V, scenes ii, iii
scene 3	Act V, scenes iv, v

In his preface, Winter has indicated that "phrases here and there have been modified, in suitable reference to refined taste." "Here and there" is an understatement. Scene i, Act IV disappeared entirely, presumably banished because of its obscenities. The word "God" is deleted four times and changed to "Heaven" in four other passages. Other verbal changes are numerous: Shakespeare's robust and precise "lecher" becomes "villain"; "belly" either vanishes or collapses into the undistinguished "stomach." (Alas, what is Falstaff without his belly!) To "lie" with a woman, as Shakespeare fearlessly suggests? Never. "Lie" becomes "sup." "Hell" is rendered "torment" or, incomprehensibly, "ocean." A host of other improprieties—"lechery," "priest," "guts," "fornication," "panderly," "cuckold," and "dickens"—apparently left this verbal prettifier at a loss for a decent synonym; so they vanished completely.

In addition to meddling with lines and words, Daly saw no harm in transferring speeches from one character to another, a practice he continued to follow in all of his Shakespearean revivals. The motive for his so doing was to give more, and better, lines to his featured actors; inevitably, Miss Rehan walked off with the major share of such transfers, although James Lewis and Mrs. Gilbert also profited. As Mistress Ford, Ada Rehan was awarded nineteen lines taken from Mistress Page (played by Virginia Dreher), including the significant, "Wives may be merry, and yet honest too." Mrs. Gilbert, playing Dame Quickly, was given four lines from the Host (Frederick Bond), in addition to the previously noted rearrangement to allow her a curtain speech. The thirteen-line epilogue cobbled up for Falstaff (Charles Fisher) from another comedy climaxed these changes.

More serious than these changes, which offended only the informed, were several errors in casting. The two merry wives were enacted by Ada Rehan and Virginia Dreher, two young and beautiful actresses, much too fresh and sparkling in their silks and laces for the noted gossips Mistress Ford and Mistress Page, whom Fat Jack himself admitted were neither young nor beautiful. Indeed, Daly seems to have overlooked completely the fact that Mistress Page had a marriageable daughter, Anne, played by the startlingly lovely Edith Kingdon. Towse, in addition to mentioning these changes in characterization, pointed to the similar defect in the husbands of the two women, falsely played with "exquisite" and "courtier-like behavior" by John Drew and Otis Skinner.

Judge Daly mentions these criticisms, adding that the reviewers also objected to "the sumptuousness of the production and the modernism of the acting." To the latter charge he demurred on the basis of "naturalism" in speech, manner, and action, which he said "came nearer to a reproduction of the play as Shakespeare staged it" than the current "artificial standards." The almost Oriental sumptuousness he justified by pointing out that the text referred to Page and Ford as men of substance.

Faults of this sort resulted in the play's being withdrawn

after a month. Towse's final description of the revival as a "spiritless parody" seems an adequate summary of the production. Not permanently dispirited, however, Daly again revived *The Merry Wives* in 1898 (January 11–24). On this occasion Miss Rehan and Mrs. Gilbert were all that were left of the cast of a dozen years before. But the fact that Miss Rehan was by now of a more appropriate age to play Mistress Ford failed to save the day. Charles Clarke was pronounced a "perfunctory" Falstaff, and even Winter admitted that this was a "stop-gap" presentation.

On January 18, 1887, the unflagging Daly staged another major Shakespearean production, *The Taming of the Shrew*. This revival was unquestionably his most successful venture into the field of Shakespearean drama and, from all accounts, must be reckoned one of the truly great presentations of the play. Inasmuch as Daly restored the two scenes of the Induction, and made the main play four acts in length, the production deserves to be described as the first American attempt to present the play in any reasonable resemblance to its original pattern. As such it superseded the popular short farce, *Katherine and Petruchio*, which had held the stage in America since 1768, when it was first given at the John Street Theatre by Lewis Hallam's company.

The success of Daly's revival was instantaneous. Ada Rehan created a furor as the shrew. The initial run of the piece lasted until April 30, for a consecutive showing of 121 performances, a remarkable record for a Shakespearean revival. Subsequently, of course, the comedy remained constantly in the repertoire of the Daly company. Its first important replaying occurred a year later, at the Lyceum Theatre, London, during the third European tour of the troupe. And on August 3, 1888, a performance was given at Stratford-on-Avon for the benefit of the Library Fund of the Shakespeare Memorial. According to Judge Daly, this was the first performance of the play ever given there. Its success prompted the installation of a gift from Daly, a statue of Ada Rehan as Katherine.

After the English triumph, Daly produced the play in Paris at the Vaudeville Théâtre. There, Constant Coquelin, the great comedian, saw the performance and consequently determined to play Petruchio. The French version, by Paul Delair, called *La Mégère Apprivoisée*, was given by Coquelin in Paris and later (1892) in New York.

Ada Rehan continued to star in the play, and Daly continued to produce it through the years. Theatrical records list an imposing total of revivals. Indeed, Daly frequently came to use the play as a means of reviving his fortunes after a failure and to hold the stage until a new piece could be prepared. The popularity of this production—and of Miss Rehan —never waned. Her interpretation of Katherine has been accepted by critics as one of the finest ever given.

Despite pretensions about the completeness of his text, Daly nevertheless perpetrated many minor and several major excisions, amounting in a few speeches to actual mutilation. True enough, both scenes of the Induction were restored (to allow William Gilbert histrionic success as Christopher Sly) with almost literal fidelity, but the rearrangements of the rest of the comedy rendered this textual scrupulosity ironical. In fact, the Induction seems to have been retained mainly so that Daly could advertise his devotion to "pure" Shakespeare; further, it provided a novelty for audiences; and finally, the second scene allowed for the mounting of a most lavish bedroom set, an example of the opulence which contributed to Daly's sense of fitness in Shakespearean production.

The changes which Daly made were largely confined to the play itself. First of all, he reduced Shakespeare's five acts to four by telescoping Acts III and IV into one act of three scenes. The jumble in the latter is most confusing. For scene 1, he used all of Shakespeare's Act III (both scenes); as scene 2, he combined scenes ii and iv of Act IV, in both of which the subplot of Tranio, Hortensio, Lucentio, and Bianca is featured so that there is no appreciable distortion; but for scene 3, he had, consequently, to telescope scenes i, iii, and v of Act IV. The result is a single scene dealing with the "taming," which may be satisfactory in terms of setting (Petruchio's house in the country), but speeds up the process so rapidly that the illusion of reality is lost and the characters of both Katherine and Petruchio become so exaggerated that the change, particularly in Katherine, seems arbitrary and contrived rather than properly motivated.

A second kind of revision consisted of rearrangement and reassignment of lines to allow Ada Rehan to star. Her entrance was postponed till the second act. She was thus allowed, wrote Towse, to start her performance "at the highest pitch of quivering indignation at her command." She "thereby secured a most picturesque and effective entrance." But the effort of maintaining this concept "left her without any reserve force for climaxes. Consequently, her performance was lacking in light and shade, and grew weaker instead of stronger toward the end." Once on stage, however, she remained the star. To give her a curtain speech in Act II, Daly interpolated twelve lines from Garrick's version. In Act III, her appearance was again delayed until after Bianca's wedding ceremony. Both she and Petruchio were eliminated from Act IV, scene 1 (Shakespeare's V, i). Finally, the lines of the last scene were reordered to give Katherine the final speech of the play. On a somewhat lesser scale, Daly made certain revisions for John Drew as Petruchio. He was allotted Tranio's lines of Act I, scene ii, 274–279, to give him the curtain speech of Act I, and with Katherine, he shared the distinction of being eliminated from Daly's Act IV, scene 1, the scene in which the involvements of the Bianca subplot are settled.

In connection with this reordering of lines, Daly's greatest blunders were committed in his altering of the famous Katherine-Petruchio duet of Act II. The changes here involve a third type of revision, the elimination of words, phrases, and lines for the sake of refinement. As a result, the lines about wasps, arms, and coxcombs went the way of "lechery" and "belly" and this delightful scene frequently shrinks into vapidity. In place of the lines excised, Daly substituted a few meaningless speeches simply to allow Katherine to speak as much as the taunting Petruchio. After his line, "And, will you, nil you, I will marry you," she echoed, insipidly, "Whether I will or no?" Again, after Petruchio's "With gentle conference, soft and affable," she interposed, "This is beyond all patience;—don't provoke me." Lastly, after Petruchio's challenge, "For I am he that's born to tame you," she can only answer, "Indeed! We'll see, my saucy groom." In place of her answer, "Yes, keep you warm," to his question, "Am I not wise?" Daly had her say, "Yes; in your own conceit, keep yourself cool with that or else you'll freeze"; to this Petruchio replied (Daly's version), "Marry, warm me in thy arms, sweet Kate," instead of Shakespeare's "Marry, so I mean, sweet Katherine, in thy bed." To bring out Ada Rehan's best talent—a certain archness—Daly inserted for her, following Petruchio's "That she shall still be curst in company," the lines, "A plague upon such impudence! O, for revenge! I'll marry him—but I will tame him!" And thus for the moment, the whole play was metamorphosed into the taming *by* the shrew.

Other examples of the third kind of revision are numerous. "By Saint Jeronomy!" was omitted. The word, "God," was changed to "Love" or to "Heaven." The word, "whoreson," and the phrase, "lewd and filthy," were deleted. And "bedfellow" appeared as "wedded wife."

There were, of course, dissenting voices amidst the almost universal acclaim tendered *The Taming of the Shrew.* "Interesting and attractive" as he found the Daly version, Percy Fitzgerald thought the Adelphi Theatre production with Oscar Asche and Miss Brayton, directed by Otho Stuart, better. Although Jerome K. Jerome considered Miss Rehan's Katherine "magnificent," he always regarded Drew in Shakespeare as "A Yankee at the Court of King Arthur." A. B. Walkley admired Miss Rehan and Drew but labeled the other performances "feeble . . . crude . . . soporific." These adverse criticisms, it will be noted, are mainly English. American critics, except Towse, found nothing to condemn.

The success of the revival led Daly to provide a sumptuous banquet on the occasion of the hundredth performance. A round table, seating forty-nine, was set up backstage with "an immense circular bed of roses as its centre." Among the distinguished guests were Bronson Howard, Mark Twain, General Sherman (who acted as toastmaster), the Honorable R. O'Gorman (Mayor of New York), Laurence Hutton, Lester Wallack, William Winter, Horace H. Furness, and selected members of the Daly company (the Big Four). After a most elaborate meal, most of the guests made short speeches. Daly's was the most interesting, for he spoke of his intentions in reviving Shakespeare.

I fully believe that where the sole purpose in producing a Shakespearean play is to make money by spectacular profusion, disaster is likely to result. . . . Ever since I began management, now some 18 years, I have devoted a period in every season to the production of a Shakespeare play or an old comedy. None of these productions was ever offered by me to the public with the expectation that it was destined to popular favor by reason of the outlay made upon it.

I freely confess that I did not anticipate the enormous popular success of this revival. My motive has been to give, in return for the very large share of popular support which I have always received, an opportunity to my own generation of seeing the works of our greatest masters in their best shape; and if this purpose has resulted in my accomplishing what might be deemed a great managerial success, then I am willing to be credited rather with a worthy motive than with unparalleled foresight and sagacity.

To vindicate Shakespeare, I set my judgment against that of Garrick, and you have the result. Shakespeare was right.

Daly's production of *The Taming of the Shrew*, whatever reservations one may entertain about it, was an eminently successful revival, mainly because its humor was suited to the tenor and methods of the Daly company. Its farcical elements in particular were cakes and ale to these actors. On the other hand, *A Midsummer Night's Dream*, which was to follow as the next revival, presented an entirely different problem. Neither Daly nor his actors had the talent or the imaginative grasp to convey either the poetry or the spirit of the fairy play. In Daly's hands, *A Midsummer Night's Dream* became a spectacle, not a play at all. Evidently, Daly shared the opinion, first enunciated by Hazlitt, that the piece was incapable of being performed; so he "staged" it. The critics were almost unanimous in their condemnations. Even Winter treated it sparingly.

Daly's revisions were typical. Since the plot of *A Midsummer Night's Dream* is fundamentally meager, he could not afford to eliminate any parts of it; consequently, his excisions were ruthless cuts of many well-known and much loved poetic passages. It was in connection with *A Midsummer Night's Dream* that Archer pointed out the fatal resemblance between *Daly* and *Dele*. For example, he eliminated the description of Robin Goodfellow and Titania's speech on the wind, the rains, and the floods, and cut some of the most charming lines from Lysander and Hermia's wonderful love duet in I, i. Archer estimated that "two-thirds of Mr. Daly's cuts are quite unnecessary, while . . . a full third is positively detrimental." For some blunders there is no accounting; where Shakespeare wrote,

> Were the world mine, Demetrius being bated,
> The rest I'ld give to be to you translated,

Daly had Miss Rehan say

> Were the world mine, it would I give
> To be to you transformed.

The only explanation one can offer is that Daly somehow confused "bated" with "baited," which had disagreeable or
inelegant overtones. Certainly it was such prudery that
prompted him to change "virgin patent" to "maiden heart and
vow," "from her bum" to "from beneath," and "lovers, to
bed" to "lovers, now list."

Again Daly has rearranged lines in order to project Helena,
played by Ada Rehan, into a more important part than Shakespeare envisaged for her. To accomplish this, he eliminated
scene ii from his Act I in order to allow Helena the curtain
speech; in Act III, he rearranged the lines to permit Helena
to enter last and thus assume a more effective position; finally,
in Act IV, he transferred lines from Demetrius to Helena.
His reordering of the concluding lines of the play was simply
arbitrary and pointless. To Oberon he gave Robin Goodfellow's lines, and then ended with Titania reciting parts of
Oberon's concluding speech. In general, however, *A Midsummer Night's Dream* is notable among Daly's Shakespearean adaptations because, except for the complete omission of
IV, ii, he did preserve the ordering of the scenes throughout.

The most distressing elements in the production were connected with the staging. The scenes were much too garish,
especially the panoramic illusion of Act IV, which Archer
says was "justly jeered at by the first night gallery." As a
consequence of their peculiar entrance from a "spasmodically
jerking" barge moving through "an epileptic forest," Theseus
and Hippolyta, according to Shaw, "were made to perform
a sort of egg-dance among the sleeping lovers, pretending not
to see them until the cue came for recovering their eye-
sight. . . The four lions in Trafalgar Square are not more
conspicuous."

But the most outrageous effect was the installation of blink-
ing electric lights in the hair and wands of the fairies. "Surely
these scintillations should be subjected to some rule, however
fantastic or conventional," complained Archer. "As it was,

when Oberon says, 'I am invisible,' he seizes the opportunity to blaze forth like the Eddystone light." The whole effect was one of "chaotic discordance." Isadora Duncan, who was one of the dancing fairies, relates that she objected to the wings Mr. Daly made her wear. "I tried to tell Mr. Daly I could express wings without putting on papier-mâché ones, but he was obdurate," she reports. However, on opening night, her dance was so well executed that "the public broke into spontaneous applause." Instead of pleasing Daly, this put him into a "towering rage." "This isn't a music hall!" he thundered. So the next night Miss Duncan found all the lights "turned out" when she came on to do her dance.

Discussing Daly's approach to Shakespeare on the basis of this production, Shaw has contended that the manager did these fantastic things "partly because he was brought up to do such things, and partly because they seem to him to be a tribute to Shakespeare's greatness, which, being uncommon, ought not to be interpreted according to the dictates of common sense." Such a man as Daly, a man who is not an artist, continued Shaw, "regards art as a quaint and costly ring in the nose of Nature."

The utter incapability of Daly's comedians properly to pronounce Shakespeare's verse was the final charge against the production. Not only the English critics but also the Americans complained of this defect. "The poetry suffered severely in its delivery by unaccustomed lips," wrote Towse; and Montgomery, whose review shilly-shallied between praise and condemnation, had to admit that "the blank verse of this play was mangled out of its music."

Despite the complaints of the critics, *A Midsummer Night's Dream* had a run of 79 performances, from January 31 to April 17, 1888. Indeed, Daly's Theatre and the Star Theatre (featuring the visiting Irving and Ellen Terry in *Faust*) were the only ones open on the night of the memorable blizzard of March 12. The play was revived on March 5, 1890, in New

York, and was presented in London at Daly's during the summer of 1895. A special company, organized by Daly and Arthur Rehan, a relative of Ada's, presented Daly's version in the smaller cities of the United States.

After the lapse of a season, Daly returned to Shakespeare on December 17, 1889, when he presented *As You Like It.* His text, which was privately printed in 1890, is not cut quite as much (in actual lines, 417) as some of his other versions of Shakespeare, but the ordering of the scenes has been much tampered with. These rearrangements, said Winter, were made principally "in the interest of scenic symmetry," but one suspects that this symmetry was not so much designed for scenic effectiveness as it was to provide Ada Rehan with the curtain speeches in four of the five acts (Act II ends with a song). The final arrangement of scenes was as follows:

Daly	*Shakespeare*
Act I, scene 1	Act I, scene i
scene 2	scenes ii and iii
Act II, scene 1	Act II, scene iii
scene 2	scenes v, i, iv
scene 3	scene vi
scene 4	scene vii
Act III	Act III, scene ii
Act IV, scene 1	Act III, scene iii
scene 2	scene iv
scene 3	scene v
scene 4	Act IV, scenes ii, i
scene 5	scene iii
Act V	Act V, scenes i, iii, ii, iv

The many cuts "in the interest of good taste" involved the typical deletion of lines of Elizabethan smut together with the accustomed changes of words: "God" to "Heaven," "spit" to "cough," and "bastard" to "little child." On the subject of these verbal revisions, Daly stirred up some bitter comment by his change of Rosalind's "my child's father" to "my father's child," thereby making Rosalind refer to herself in answer to Celia's query, "But is all this for your father?" rather than to Orlando, and her intentions regarding him.

The basis of the difficulty not only lay in Daly's prudish interpretation or distortion, but also involved a comparison between Ada Rehan and Julia Arthur. Miss Arthur preferred the reading of the first Folio, "my child's father." Her usage called down the wrath of William Winter, who labeled the "bad reading not only indelicate but senseless." Even though Furness "declined to discuss the passage" and quoted Moberly's statement that "Shakespeare would have smiled at Rowe's emendation," yet Winter persisted. Such a statement as Winter's "to make Rosalind . . . refer to Orlando as the father of a child she is yet to bear is instantly to vitiate a lovely ideal of womanhood and to evince entire ignorance of human nature" indicates his limitations as a critic, but shows him at the front of popular taste and reaction.

Winter's adversary in this question of textual reading was Norman Hapgood. Hapgood's rebuttal, in his book *The Stage in America*, included a letter from Kittredge, who was "surprised" that an actor [Miss Arthur] should have been "blamed for *restoring* the text of Shakespeare." Winter's reply to Kittredge was that "Princess" Rosalind would never have been so "vulgar and flippant" for, said Winter, "even if you think it right to make Rosalind talk like a prurient wanton, you have no warrant to make her talk like a fool."

Mr. Hapgood's final statement has gained interest with time.

I put this little tiff on record [he wrote] merely because Daly-ism has played a large role in American stage history. It was the *Ladies' Home Journal* standards in regard to Shakespeare. It is a tiresome task to prepare Shakespeare for drawing-room tables. This needs less a scholar than a prude. Respect for facts and scholarship cannot be forced on a man. If Mr. Winter differs from a most imposing list of authorities, the explanation is simple. You cannot prove that Velasquez paints better than Bougereau, or that the great Elizabethan's taste was deeper than Mr. Daly's. You can prefer a pink and blue tea room to a cathedral if you choose. No law will ever make Dalyism over. Its adherents will rewrite Shakespeare to suit their own tastes to the end of time, while certain coarse men will persist in relishing the Elizabethan genius.

The actual production of *As You Like It* elicited even more controversy than did the textual emendations. Of course Winter and Judge Daly were lavish in their praise of the production and the acting, especially Miss Rehan's Rosalind. Odell remembered Miss Rehan's performance as "an outstanding triumph," but also recalled two other "notable" Rosalinds, Mary Anderson and Helena Modjeska. Brander Matthews called John Drew's Orlando "one of the most satisfactory it has ever been my privilege to admire." When the revival was produced in London at the Lyceum Theatre, July 15, 1890, it received a rave review from Cecil Howard in *The Theatre* according with the "enthusiastic reception" of the audience.

But there were adverse criticisms. Towse was not as opposed as usual, for he concluded that "the piece made no extraordinary demand upon the histrionic faculties of the company." The *Herald* review was more stringent; the reviewer found Daly's comedians too "modern" and unpoetical. The critic was especially displeased with Ada Rehan's "effort to be arch." With this judgment the critic, Ayres, agreed in finding her Rosalind "in the domain of the soubrette." To this he added one of the very few uncomplimentary remarks ever made of her voice. "Her delivery is unnatural, drawling, noncommittal, pointless" was his condemnation. He also found John Drew's Orlando "trooperlike rather than loverlike." W. Graham Robertson has reported that Irving was disgusted at the whole production of *As You Like It*, labeling it in Daly's hands "a comic opera." But the most considered review was an anonymous one in *Blackwood's*. There, the critic judged the production for its beauties of costume and scenic arrangement as well as for the "admirable presentation" of the songs. But the final opinion was that the presentation failed to do "adequate justice" to the play. Daly's actors, "whose strength lies in the delineation of eccentricities," were simply lacking in "dignity of style" and "knowledge of the art of speaking blank verse." Merely "good fun," he concluded, was not enough. And yet the rollicking fun of the production achieved for it an initial run of sixty-two performances in New York, as well as popular success in London a year later. The version remained in Daly's repertoire until 1898.

For his next Shakespearean revival, Daly returned to *Love's Labour's Lost*, the text of which he had reworked in 1874. He now changed the spelling from Labour to Labor and reduced the play from five to four acts. In spite of these and other "judicious" changes he could not overcome the "laborious artifice" inherent in the piece; as a consequence it lasted a bare two weeks, from March 29 until April 11, 1891. As for earlier productions, he was praised by his brother, by Winter, and by Odell for the devotion and sense of artistry which prompted him to revive *Love's Labour's Lost*. Odell commended him as "the only New York manager who could conceivably have brought out the present offering."

Daly's 1874 offering had been a fairly straightforward job of cutting. In it he had preserved the ordering of the scenes, rearranging the act divisions to accord more easily with the length of the scenes. Consequently, his Acts I and II coincided with Shakespeare's. Act III included Shakespeare's very short Act III (207 lines) and all three scenes of Act IV. Act IV was divided by Daly into two scenes, the first using Shakespeare's V, i, the second using V, ii, 1–156. Then for Act V, he used the remainder of V, ii, including the Pageant of the Nine Worthies and the final songs of Spring and Winter.

By 1891, Daly had become a more experienced revisionist. He had the authority and daring with which success had endowed him; he had Winter's word that "so far as he could go without much experience Shakspere went in *Love's Labor's Lost*." As a consequence, Daly's changes in Shakespeare were more involved. Act I remained essentially the same, except that part of the deleted section of Armado and Moth was restored including the song, "If she be made of white and red." The restoration necessitated a change from "God" to "Heaven."

In Act II, he retained the unaccountable reassignment of lines whereby Biron (Daly's spelling) was given the speeches of Dumain (lines 195, 196) and Dumain those of Biron (lines 209, 211, 213). In 1891, he cut the scene short to give the Princess of France, played by Ada Rehan, the curtain speech, an interpolated "Oh!" and a laugh, following the lines

> I'll give you Aquitaine and all that is his,
> An you give him for my sake but one loving kiss.

The major change in Act III was in staging. During the development of the action, simply for the purposes of scenic effectiveness, Daly had it gradually grow dark, so that the scene of the lovers in the woods, Shakespeare's IV, iii, was played in moonlight. Certainly this was a romantic notion, but it meant that Ferdinand, Longaville, and Dumain all had to read poetry and Biron a letter by the light of the moon.

The reduction of *Love's Labour's Lost* to four acts meant simply that Daly combined Acts IV and V of the 1874 version, or, in terms of Shakespeare, that Act IV comprised Shakespeare's V, i and V, ii. Here Daly allowed himself the most frivolous sort of rearrangement. First, he followed V, ii (with cuts of course) from line 1 to line 479; then he skipped to lines 756–881, then back to lines 485–745, and finally, line 888 to conclusion. His obvious plan was to have the Pageant of the Nine Worthies follow the wedding arrangements, although one wonders why such a revision should have been preferred to Shakespeare's order. Further, Daly eliminated the statement referring to the death of the King of France in Act V, scene ii, "Dead, for my life!" As a consequence, the Princess' determination to postpone the marriages for twelve months seems based on mere whimsy, though attributed by Winter to good sense, rather than upon the necessity imposed by mourning. In the 1874 version, when Marcade said, "The king, your father—" the Princess replied, "Ailetto—for my life!—and calleth for us?" In the 1891 edition, she simply answered, "For my life! He calleth for us?" A note in William Winter's hand beside Maria's speech

> At the twelve month's end,
> I'll change my *black gown* for a faithful friend

indicates, "This sh'd be changed—as the death of the King of France is not mentioned, & no one except Marcade wears black." Perhaps it was Winter who suggested the eccentric ending.

Finally, in accordance with his ideas of appropriateness, Daly, in both versions, changed the order of the two songs with which the play concludes. Instead of keeping Shakespeare's sequence—Spring, then Winter—he reversed them, and, still not content, cut both songs in half. Both songs were presented as parts of tableaux. The failure of these and other innovations to attract audiences in 1891—in 1874, the production had likewise lasted but two weeks—prompted Daly to withdraw *Love's Labour's Lost* on April 11. It was never again revived by him.

Daly opened his 1891–1892 season on November 25 with a series of five successful revivals: *The Taming of the Shrew*, *The School for Scandal*, *The Last Word*, *As You Like It*, and *Nancy and Company*. These productions carried him through until January 22, 1892. The remainder of the theatrical year he devoted to Pinero's *The Cabinet Minister;* a French adaptation, *Love in Tandem;* and Tennyson's *The Foresters*. The season closed on April 23, Shakespeare's birthday, with an appropriate performance of *As You Like It*. The company then went on tour to Chicago and the west coast, and it was consequently not until February 21, 1893, that Daly ventured upon his next Shakespearean revival, *Twelfth Night*. The piece had a short run until April 8, when the company temporarily disbanded, to reassemble in June for a year's stay at Daly's Theatre, London. There, beginning on January 8, 1894, *Twelfth Night* achieved the phenomenal record of 119 performances, being withdrawn on May 4 to allow the company to conclude its European stay with *As You Like It*. From then on, the comedy remained in the Daly repertoire until its final performance on February 10, 1898.

In making *Twelfth Night* over into a four-act starring vehicle for Ada Rehan, Daly perpetrated some of his most heinous offenses against Shakespeare. Although he had referred to the play, on the programs, as "Shakespeare's Very Favorite Comedy," he had no qualms about cutting a total of 618 lines from the text. The defense of such ruthlessness was offered by Winter, who complained that "*Twelfth Night* would be tedious unless it were cut."

The greatest violence, however, was done not to the text but to the order of the scenes. Daly spoiled the opening by beginning not with Orsino and "the food of love," which strikes the keynote of the play, but with the seacoast, Shakespeare's II, i; to this scene he added, as background music, "a distant chorus" singing Ariel's song "Come unto these yellow sands" from *The Tempest;* then, to avoid a change of setting, he followed this scene of Antonio and Sebastian with the prior seacoast episode, Shakespeare's I, ii, of "Viola, a Captain, and Sailors." These two seacoast incidents made up Daly's Act I, scene 1.

Evidently the manager had some qualms about these variations and must have written Furness. The editor of the New Variorum replied in a letter dated January 27, 1893:

In the name of sanctity why do you think I'll be shocked at any changes which a modern playwright thinks best to make in the omission or transposition of scenes in Shakespeare? His stage is not our stage, his audiences are not our audiences. 'Tis only additions like Dryden's, Tate's, and Garrick's that are lese majeste.

Your partial combination of the two seacoast scenes strikes me as excellent. . . . You are one in whom I put absolute trust.

Others were not so kind. Archer referred to the opening scene as a "barbarism," and for once Odell was objective. Writing in *Shakespeare from Betterton to Irving,* he indicated that in Daly's version "It was all for scenery and the play well lost. In running together scenes . . . or in transposing scenes far out of their natural sequence . . . Augustin Daly was the most flagrant offender. . . . Whatever Irving's sins in this respect, Daly's were as scarlet in comparison." And *Twelfth Night* was "the worst that Daly attempted."

For his scene 2 in Act I, Daly combined Shakespeare's first and fourth scenes. And for scene 3, concluding Act I, he telescoped Shakespeare's third and fifth scenes along with the second scene from Act II. This last device brought Viola back to Olivia's hall, a handsome set, in such a manner that she arrived at the place she had just left. But for Daly this inconsistency was completely obliterated by the fact that his arrangement allowed Viola the curtain speech to conclude his Act I; the audience retired to the foyer to chat and relax with Ada Rehan's voice reciting the lines from Shakespeare's Act II, scene ii, beginning

> I left no ring with her. What means this lady?
> Fortune forbid my outside have not charm'd her!

ringing in their ears.

Daly's Act II was equally jumbled out of all order. For his first scene he used Shakespeare's fourth and for his second scene, Shakespeare's third. The purpose of this reversal is a mystery; it merely attests to the magnificent fluidity of Shakespeare's play. Further, he moved the song, "O mistress mine," from Act II, scene iii, using only eight of the original eleven lines of it, forward into the place of "Come away death" and then completed the shift by inserting "Come away death" into the place Shakespeare had put "O mistress mine." Also to his own scene 2 he added snatches of other old English songs, so that the act concluded with Sir Toby, Sir Andrew, and the Clown singing

> Sunday, Monday, Tuesday
> Which is the properest day to drink?
> This is the properest day to drink!

Having made such a beginning, Daly had to gather up some of the pieces in Act III, which he presented in two scenes. Scene 1 corresponded to Shakespeare's III, iii; but scene 2 was again a strange mixture—II, v; III, i; III, ii; III, iv, in that order—evidently dictated by the staging: all the scenes occurred in Olivia's garden. By closing Act III with Shakespeare's scene iv, Daly gave Ada Rehan her second long curtain speech. As she spoke the lines, she "sank on a seat in thought." The actual physical conclusion of the act then followed, "a serenade . . . by several of the Duke's musicians . . . the Duke in disguise in their midst. The moon rising over the distant waters." One reviewer indicated that the song used was "Who is Silvia?" from *The Two Gentlemen of Verona* rewritten as "Fair Olivia, who is she?"

Act IV concluded the mélange by combining Shakespeare's Act IV, scenes i, ii, iii, and V, i, into a single scene. Instead of having the Clown render solus the final song, "When that I was and a little tiny boy," Daly had it "sung in part by the Clown and Maria and the Chorus by all assembled, who dance." However, for Viola he reserved the next-to-the-last line, "But that's all one, our play is done," after which the Chorus sang, "And we'll strive to please you every day," and danced.

On the subject of Daly's promiscuous use of song, Shaw was particularly outspoken.

The musical side of Mr. Daly's revival [he wrote] is a curious example of the theatrical tradition that any song written by Shakespeare is appropriate to any play written by him. . . . "Come unto these Yellow Sands" is no doubt very pretty; but so is the speech made by Ferdinand when he escapes, like Viola, from shipwreck. Yet if Mr. Daly had interpolated that speech in the first act of *Twelfth Night*, the leading dramatic critics would have denounced the proceeding as a literary outrage; whereas the exactly parallel case of the interpolation of the song is regarded as a happy thought, wholly unobjectionable.

Twelfth Night presents an intriguing contradiction. Obviously, Daly and Winter made a mess of the text. Archer said that he seems to "cut and rearrange as much as he possibly can, without absolutely going the length of Dryden, Tate and Cibber, and rewriting his author." But, at the same time the revival was delightful; "whatever his lapses of taste, he has truly *revived* the play," Archer was forced to conclude. To this he added praise of Robert Bosworth as the sea captain, John Craig's Orsino, James Lewis' Sir Toby, Herbert Gresham as Sir Andrew, Violet Vanbrugh as Olivia, and especially of Ada Rehan's Viola—"a creation of indescribable beauty and charm." Certainly the success of the revival justifies Archer's praise. Daly's revivals had many faults, but they were errors of judgment common to his age. One must not fail to appreciate the opulence and care of the productions, their service to the Shakespearean tradition and to the stage, and their well-intended effort to provide entertainment.

Although *Twelfth Night* had been a sprightly revival, Daly's subsequent production, *The Two Gentlemen of Verona*, was a dismal failure. Viola and Rosalind provided material worthy of stars but to mold Julia into the central figure of *The Two Gentlemen of Verona* Daly not only had an insufficiently drawn personality to work with, but he was also inextricably involved in a minor play which could not stand up under his rough handling. Such worth as there is in the play he distorted so ridiculously that Shaw labeled the revival "a vaudeville . . . founded by Augustin Daly on Shake-speare." To this Shaw added a general condemnation of that "school" of managers which considered Shakespeare "a wretch-edly unskillful dramatic author."

The distortions in this play not only resulted in rearranged scenes and lines but also frequently succeeded in making the plot and the characterizations even less distinct than Shake-speare had left them. For example, in Daly's Act II, scene 1 (Shakespeare's I, iii and II, ii), by the curious omission of the first 44 lines of I, iii, the surrendering of Proteus' lines to Julia, and the strange ordering of the two scenes, Julia enters to bid Proteus goodbye immediately after his father finishes telling him he is to go to Milan. How she could have found out the news other than by sheer intuition is a mystery. However illogical her entrance at that point may be, the rearrangement gives her the first scene curtain speech of Daly's Act II.

As a matter of fact, Miss Rehan speaks the curtain lines in all four acts as well as in the above-mentioned scene. Daly's Act I ends with Julia's soliloquy from Shakespeare's Act I, scene ii. To close Act II, she speaks lines 34–38, transposed to follow lines 80–90. By ending Act III with Shakespeare's IV, ii, Daly manages a third act curtain speech for Julia. Final-ly, at the conclusion of the play she not only recites Valen-tine's lines from Act V, scene iv, but also speaks an epilogue transferred from *The Famous History of the Life of King Henry the Eighth*.

A complete picture of Daly's reordering of the scenes of *The Two Gentlemen of Verona* shows the following redistri-bution:

Daly	*Shakespeare*
Act I, scene 1	Act I, scene 1, scene iii, lines 1–44
scene 2	scene ii
Act II, scene 1	Act I, scene iii, lines 45 to end;
	Act II, scene ii

scene 2	scene iii
scene 3	scenes i and iv
scene 4	scene vii
Act III, scene 1	Act II, scene v
scene 2	Act II, scene vi; Act III, scene i; Act IV, scenes iii and ii
Act IV, scene 1	Act IV, scene i
scene 2	Act IV, scene iv, lines 1–42
scene 3	Act IV, scene iv, lines 43 to end; Act V, scene ii
scene 4	Act V, scenes iii and iv

When Kittredge asserted that the final scene of the play "sacrifices everything to crude sensationalism," he was referring to Shakespeare's treatment. To increase the "sensationalism," Daly added a storm, merely for purposes of scenic effect since there is no indication in the text of any change of climate. In a bitter mood as a result of the many excesses of this revival, Archer ventured the ironical suggestion that Mr. Daly be appointed "Honorary President of the Elizabethan Stage Society" since his revivals were "object lessons in support of the Society's tenets"—that Shakespeare should be recited word for word on a bare platform.

Public disapproval was more effective than Archer's irony. In New York, *The Two Gentlemen of Verona* was presented only twenty-six times, from February 21 through March 19, 1895. In London, it lasted the week of July 2–7, 1895. It was never revived again by Daly.

Since Winter worked over the text, it is only fair to allow him the final word. His one sentence in defense of the changes is almost incoherent:

The preparations for actions which intrinsically are slight, should not be more elaborate and important than the actions themselves, and, therefore, at several points, the progress of the movement has been assumed rather than shown—an arrangement whereby, in this case, the action is much accelerated.

No wonder he considered Shakespeare's language unrefined.
For his 1895–1896 season, Daly had announced a revival of
Henry IV. But the playbills for *The Countess Gucki* (Jan-
uary 28–February 29, 1896) notified the patrons that "Mr.
Daly's production of Shakespeare's *Henry the Fourth* is de-
ferred until next season." Later that year, Daly's arrangement
of *Henry IV*, "A Blending of the First and Second Parts of
Shakespere's Play," was privately printed, "As first played at
Daly's Theatre, New York, November ——, 1896." In the
preface, Winter explained that "with Ada Rehan as Prince
Henry and James Lewis as Falstaff, a competent cast of about
forty characters, and scenes and dresses correct and beautiful,
it should make its opulence felt, and should prove in the highest degree a public benefit and delight." But this "delight"
never materialized. In November, instead of *Henry IV*, Daly
offered *As You Like It* followed by Boucicault's *London
Assurance*, and on December 21, he staged his production of
Much Ado about Nothing. *Henry IV* remained, nevertheless,
an ambition of Mr. Daly's. A pamphlet announcing his twentieth season carried the notice that "The final production of
the season will be Mr. Daly's new arrangement into one play
of the two parts of Shakespeare's comedy of *Henry the
Fourth*." The only distinctive change was in casting, for this
announcement listed the following proposed cast:

Falstaff will be undertaken	by William Owen
Henry the Fourth	by George Clarke
Hotspur	by Charles Richman
Prince Hal	by Cyril Scott
Poins	by Herbert Gresham
Dame Quickly	by Mrs. Gilbert
and	
Lady Percy	by Miss Rehan

A number of reasons for Daly's failure ever to produce
Henry IV can be adduced. First of all, the production had
originally been designed as a sort of theatrical trick. Although

Miss Rehan had played a number of "breeches" parts, among them Shakespeare's Rosalind, Julia and Viola as well as Hypolita in *She Wou'd and She Wou'd Not*, and Sylvia in *The Recruiting Officer*, this would have been (except for her role of Pierrot in pantomime) her first assumption of a purely masculine role. By 1896 she was too well established in public favor to have to curry fame in such a fashion. Also, it is more than likely that a great part of the original incentive for Miss Rehan to play Prince Hal was to compete with Julia Marlowe's rendition of the role during the same season. The Marlowe-Taber company actually produced the piece in Milwaukee in September 1895, and the Tabers then played it in Philadelphia, and New York at Wallack's Theatre, March 19–20, 1896. But the production attracted only for its novelty as Miss Marlowe was completely miscast as Prince Hal, and the Hotspur of her husband, Robert Taber, was "overdone and noisy." Their failure in this venture probably gave Daly pause.

Daly's immediate reason for not doing the play in November, as announced in the printed version, was probably twofold. The death of James Lewis in September 1896 had left him temporarily without an actor capable of handling the role of Falstaff. Then, too, there was the continuing competition with Miss Marlowe, for when she and Taber presented *For Bonnie Prince Charlie* at Wallack's, February 8, 1897, Daly countered with *Meg Merrilies* on March 12th.

The final, and perhaps most cogent, argument against a production of *Henry IV* as Daly envisaged it was its sheer difficulty. As it stands in the printed version, the play is both too long ever to have been presented in the course of three or even three and a half hours and also too involved. For once, the scenes do appear to have been somewhat judiciously cut and arranged. In general, they are divided among three groups of characters: Hal, Falstaff, and their associates at the Boar's Head Tavern; King Henry IV and the Nobles; and Hotspur

and the Plotters. The first three acts are largely devoted to
1 Henry IV with the insertion of *2 Henry IV*, Act III, scene
ii, a comedy scene centering about Falstaff and the Justices,
into *1 Henry IV*, Act IV, scene ii, the scene in which Falstaff
discusses his "press'd" recruits. The composition of Daly's first
three acts was as follows:

Daly	Shakespeare
Act I, scene 1	Act I, scenes i and iii
scene 2	scene ii
scene 3	Act II, scenes ii and iv
Act II, scene 1	Act III, scene ii
scene 2	scene iii
scene 3	Act II, scene iii, Act III, scene i
Act III, scene 1	Act IV, scene i
scene 2	scene ii (with insertion from *2 Henry IV* of III, ii)
scene 3	Act V, scene i
scene 4	scene ii
scene 5	scenes iii, iv, and v.

It will be seen from this summary that Daly had omitted
three scenes: II, i; IV, iii, and IV, iv of *1 Henry IV* and compressed practically all the rest into his first three acts. The
fitting together was fairly competent, but when he added a
fourth act from *2 Henry IV* the play became unwieldy. Daly's
Act IV, which he based entirely on *2 Henry IV*, was arranged as follows:

Daly	Shakespeare
Scene 1	I, ii
	II, ii and iv (lines 383–395)
Scene 2	III, i
	IV, iv and v
Scene 3	V, iii
Scene 4	V, v, concluding with Hal's speech from V, ii, 129–133, 143–145.

The task of telescoping the major action of *2 Henry IV* into one concluding act was simply too great. The production, even Daly must have realized, would have been preposterous. The final plans for *Henry IV*, as projected for 1898–1899, seem almost absurd. To have starred Ada Rehan as Lady Percy would have necessitated not a revision of Daly's already printed text of *Henry IV*, but a new play altogether. The part of Lady Percy is, at best, a minor one.

In addition to the abandonment of *Henry IV* and the rival Scotch production in 1897, Daly's feud with Julia Marlowe took other turns. When Miss Marlowe announced a revival of *Romeo and Juliet* for the spring of 1896, Daly likewise gave notice of a production of the tragedy. Since Miss Rehan was then engaged in *The Countess Gucki*, following which the company was to embark for a summer season in London, he went entirely afield and secured the socially prominent Mrs. James Brown Potter (of whom Shaw said, "she seems . . . congenitally incapable of genuine impersonation") and her handsome leading man, Kyrle Bellew, to play the star-crossed lovers. Because of booking difficulties encountered by Miss Marlowe, Daly's production of *Romeo and Juliet* was the first to reach the boards, on March 3, 1896. The Marlowe-Taber presentation opened a week later, on March 9, at Wallack's Theatre.

Daly's stroke, as Miss Marlowe's biographer, Charles E. Russell, has admitted, was masterful. Mrs. Potter and Mr. Bellew were not only two of the handsomest of New York's theatrical idols, but they were also two of the most talked about actors on the stage. To present them as the immortal Romeo and Juliet was "an animation in the pulse" of the city.

It is difficult to judge the relative merits of the two productions. Julia Marlowe's Juliet became one of her best known and most admired roles, but all the criticisms refer to the finished impersonation, the result of many years of study and performance, both with Taber and with her second husband, E. H. Sothern, rather than to the specific enactment of the part in 1896. Her production lasted only a week, but the whole engagement of the Tabers at Wallack's was scheduled for only two weeks and included *She Stoops to Conquer, The Hunchback, As You Like It,* and *Henry IV,* in addition to *Romeo and Juliet.*

The Daly production is also an unknown. One reviewer called it "a popular as well as artistic success," but pooh-poohed Daly's pretensions about the text. On the playbills, Daly had asserted that "*The Furness Variorum Edition* is the basis of the acting arrangement of Romeo and Juliet as here presented." The reviewer thought the "six act—seven tableaus" version used by Mrs. Potter and Bellew bore "a close resemblance to the Lyceum version" of Henry Irving. Russell has added that even the "magnificence" of the production could not "atone for the obvious defects in acting and reading." Winter's comments were vague and damned with faint praise. The revival, for all its fascinations, was withdrawn at the end of three weeks.

Daly's next Shakespearean revival, *Much Ado about Nothing* (December 21, 1896 to February 7, 1897), was hardly more successful than *Romeo and Juliet.* Towse has suggested that Daly should not have ventured the production since "his company had been sorely weakened by death and desertion, and he had little left but his scene painters." As for Ada Rehan, "she never really got into the skin of Beatrice." Significantly, Daly did not present his *Much Ado about Nothing* in England, where since 1882 it had been one of the triumphs of Irving and Miss Terry.

Daly made the play into a five-act spectacle, each act having but a single scene. As he had done in *The Taming of the Shrew,* he postponed the entrance of the heroine; this delay evoked the wrath of the critic Henry Austin Clapp of the Boston *Advertiser* who called it "a shocking piece of audacity and a cheap concession to . . . the 'star' theory." *In toto,* Daly's revision appeared as follows:

Daly *Shakespeare*

Act I I, i, 1–29, 95–111, 147–162
Enter Beatrice
I, i, 30–94, 163–330, 119–146
I, iii
II, i

The act ends with serenaders singing "The God of Love he sits above, etc." transposed from V, ii.

Act II II, ii
II, iii (omits lines 134–155, 190–212)
III, i
III, ii

Act III III, iii (omits lines 123–136, 139–152)
IV, ii

Act IV IV, i
This act concludes with an interpolated conversation between Beatrice and Benedict during the course of which she incites him to kill Claudio.

Act V V, i
V, ii
V, iv

In the words of Mr. Clapp, the representation of *Much Ado about Nothing* exhibited the "characteristic marks of Mr. Daly's revivals." He complimented the manager for his "usual care in dressing and setting," but indicated that "the arrangement of the scenes and the management of the dialogue" showed "the usual mélange of shrewdness and unwisdom, a nice concern for the integrity of the text in one passage being followed by a reckless or deliberate defiance of the poet's thought in another."

Daly was essentially a man of the nineteenth century; his theater represented the tastes of his times; and it was declining with the closing years of the century. So, too, his Shakespearean revivals had reached the peak of achievement with *The Taming of the Shrew, As You Like It,* and *Twelfth*

Night. His last three efforts, *Much Ado about Nothing, The Tempest,* and *The Merchant of Venice,* were pale imitations of his past grandeur. True, they kept up his standard of opulence, and they offered some interesting impersonations—notably Sidney Herbert's Shylock and Ada Rehan's Portia—but they were derivative rather than new productions.

There is no question that by 1896 Daly's Theatre was beginning to decline. It had social prestige, it is true, which it retained until the end. But Daly had found no actors to replace the departed members of his company: John Drew, Otis Skinner, Virginia Dreher, Edith Kingdon, James Lewis. Ada Rehan and Mrs. Gilbert were not enough to carry the entire burden. Sidney Herbert was talented, but was best in limited character parts. Just as important, too, was Daly's failure to keep abreast of the times. Conditions, methods, plays were changing. The theater world was consciously standing on the threshold of the twentieth century with mechanical developments, business syndicates, and new playwrights (Wilde, Shaw, Fitch) already knocking at the door.

Growing public interest in musical comedy, and the consequent increased financial returns from his musical productions, had been altering the repertoire of Daly's company since 1880, but with the phenomenal success of *The Geisha* in 1896, the mode was completely established. *The Circus Girl* the following year and *The Runaway Girl* in 1898 carried on the vogue. Perhaps because of this tendency, perhaps because of its peculiar stage history as a musical piece, perhaps simply because he imagined it musically—for all or one of these reasons, Daly's production of *The Tempest* was largely conceived as a musical play. For the roles of Miranda and Ariel, he cast Nancy McIntosh and Virginia Earle, both more noted for vocal than histrionic achievement, and in his rearrangement of the text he featured songs and dances. Thus all four acts of his version concluded with spectacles featuring music and dancing by Ariel and the "attendant spirits." For music he used both Arne and Purcell, arranged by F. Ecke, and an additional score by K. Raubert. Music and scenery together apparently seemed to Daly the quintessence of the poetic drama. Even Towse found *The Tempest* "delightful" as "entertainment."

Daly opened the curtains of the stage upon the shipwreck scene, without the dialogue of I, i, but accompanied by music. The stage directions indicated "The action begins with the storm, culminating in the wreck and sinking of the ship. After which the elements become subdued, the clouds clear away and sunrise on the island covers the scene with rose tints and reveal the beauty of the shore." The dialogue of Daly's first act was, then, all derived from scene two. Several theatrical and musical effects were introduced. When Prospero laid aside his robe, the stage directions were: "Waving his wand, a young tree springs up nearby, upon which he hangs his robe and rests his wand." After Ariel's line, "And hither come in't. Go! Hence with diligence!" in Act I, scene ii, Daly introduced a song, "O bid thy faithful Ariel fly." After "And make a vassal of him" in Act I, scene ii, he used "Full fathom five," in place of "Come unto these yellow sands," which was transferred to the conclusion of the act with an accompanying dance of the spirits around Ferdinand. His Act II combined Shakespeare's first two scenes with the opening scene of Act III so that it concluded with Miranda and Ferdinand's charming love scene, Ariel's song "Where the bee sucks," lifted from Act V, and the inevitable dance by the spirits. For Act III, Daly confected his customary mélange. The act consisted of the following.

Shakespeare's III, iii
　　　　　IV, i, 164–192
　　　　　III, ii, 48–73
　　　　　IV, i, 194–195, 221–235
　　　　　III, ii, 76–132
　　　　　IV, i, 1–59, 118–124, 146–157, 125–127, 60–117.

The rearrangement was motivated in part by the manager's desire to end the scene with the Masque of Iris, Ceres, Juno, and the Nymphs in a "graceful dance." Some of these changes seem simply arbitrary and silly. In particular, he spoiled Prospero's great speech telling of the "melting" of the spirits "into the air," including "We are such stuff as dreams are made on" by having it spoken *before* the spirits *melt*. Daly's fourth and final act coincided with Shakespeare's Act V but omitted 156 out of 318 lines. The conclusion was again a picture: "The walls of the cave dissolve; the sea appears beyond, and a ship approaches the shore. Prospero's Spirits guiding the Ship and singing 'Merrily, merrily, shall I live now' "—Ariel's song transferred from Act V.

The production ran for three weeks, from April 6 to 23, 1897. Tyrone Power excelled as Caliban, Ada Rehan played Miranda, and Percy Haswell took over the role of Ariel in the final week to release the Misses McIntosh and Earle for the strenuous rehearsals of *The Circus Girl*. Miss Rehan's Miranda was praised for its "simplicity," although Winter chided her with "just a little touch of involuntary playfulness."

Daly's final Shakespearean revival was an elaborate production of *The Merchant of Venice*, which opened on November 19, 1898 and lasted until January 2, 1899. The stage history of *The Merchant of Venice* has always been involved in a controversy about the portrayal of Shylock. Macklin and Kean enacted the role sympathetically and restored "the Jew that Shakespeare drew." Irving, J. W. Wallack, and Booth followed this custom. Daly entrusted the role to a relatively unknown actor, Sidney Herbert, for he had rearranged the play as a starring vehicle for Ada Rehan. Actually, his version did not so much distort the play as it focused the attention away from Shylock to Portia. The sets, which were the most ornate he had ever used, also contributed to this change in emphasis. Portia thus became a kind of jewel set among the treasures of her father's house; she was the richest casket after all.

As usual, Daly rearranged the scenes of the play about certain stage settings. Whereas Shakespeare's varied scenes— of merchants, of the pleasant life at Belmont, of low comedy— combined to lend the comedy a sense of the fluidity and bustle of life, Daly's version had only a feeling for picturesque tableaux. This resulted in a curiously static quality, for Daly's text gives no impression of movement, but rather of an impressive stateliness in which Portia reigned as a rare and exotic, but hardly human, figure.

The censorship of certain passages also contributed to the static quality of the play. There is a surprising amount of lewdness in *The Merchant of Venice,* much of it spoken by Portia and Nerissa. The cutting of many of Portia's remarks (e.g., Act I, scene ii, "I am much afeard my lady his mother play'd false with a smith") dignified her character, but in so doing made her less real.

Daly presented Portia as the commanding figure in the opening of two acts, II and III, in addition to giving Portia the curtain speeches in three of the five acts, III, IV and V. And by eliminating Gratiano's final speech, which is somewhat lewd, he gave Portia the concluding lines of the play. The completely revised text compares as follows with Shakespeare:

Daly	*Shakespeare*
Act I	I, i
	II, ii to line 120
	I, iii
Act II, scene 1	I, ii
scene 2	II, ii beginning with line 121,
	II, iii, iv, v to line 59
Act III, scene 1	II, i to line 24
	II, vii, ix

scene 2	II, viii to line 7
	III, i to line 17
	II, iii, lines 12–25
	III, i beginning with line 22
scene 3	III, ii, iv
Act IV	IV, i
Act V	III, v
	V

In the last act Daly introduced the song, "Tell me, where is fancy bred," from III, ii.

As a rejoinder to Winter's high-flown praise of Ada Rehan's Portia, it is almost a relief to read Alfred Ayres's criticism in *Theatre Magazine* that "she frequently mispronounced, continually misread and often betrayed a misconception of the author's intent."

Daly's admiration and love for Shakespeare were not invariably accompanied by taste and intelligence. The irony is that his efforts are frequently remembered as much for their excesses as for their excellences; Shaw, who saw many of these productions, labeled them "fricassees," though he was equally appalled by the productions of Irving and Tree. J. R. Towse, drama critic of *The Evening Post* and author of *Sixty Years of the Theatre*, judged that Daly "had artistic instincts and ambitions, but not the knowledge, the persistence, or the material to bring his more serious endeavors to full fruition."

Daly's productions of Old English comedies followed the same general pattern as his Shakespearean revivals: the plays presented before 1880 were staged without much preparation or elaboration and featured a large number of actors, members of his company and outside "stars" brought in to do favorite roles; after 1880, all the revivals were lavishly staged productions centering about the personality of Ada Rehan. Many of the texts of these later versions were privately printed.

In general, Daly selected the tried and true classics, works

by Sheridan, Goldsmith, Farquhar; but he also produced a
number of pieces infrequently seen on the American stage,
plays by Cibber, George Colman the Younger, and Mrs. Inchbald. Even though other nineteenth-century managers leaned
heavily upon the works of the past, Daly's productions of the
classics had particular significance because his was the foremost theater in America and consequently set the style.

Brander Matthews has defined the phrase, "Old Comedies,"
as "a selected group of successful plays which had been produced in the eighteenth century . . . and which had survived
on the stage, being acted at irregular intervals at the Haymarket Theatre in London, at Wallack's and later at Daly's
in New York, and at the Boston Museum." Daly was function-
ing in accordance with a stage tradition. The significance of
his revivals has, however, another historical aspect: often they
marked the final showing of these pieces by the commercial
theater of the United States.

While stipulating that "no two students of stage history
would agree" on the plays to be included in any list of old
comedies, Matthews catalogued some eighteen pieces as truly
representative. In the list, plays with asterisks were produced
by Daly:

*Cibber's *She Wou'd and She Wou'd Not* (1702)
*Mrs. Centlivre's *The Busybody* (1709)
*Mrs. Centlivre's *The Wonder* (1714)
 Garrick's *High Life Below Stairs* (1759)
 Colman's *Jealous Wife* (1761)
 Foote's *Liar* (1762)
 Garrick and Colman's *Clandestine Marriage* (1766)
*Goldsmith's *She Stoops to Conquer* (1773)
 Sheridan's *The Rivals* (1775)
*Sheridan's *The School for Scandal* (1777)
*Sheridan's *The Critic* (1779)
*Mrs. Cowley's *The Belle's Stratagem* (1780)
*Holcroft's *The Road to Ruin* (1792)
 O'Keeffe's *Wild Oats* (1794)
*Colman the Younger's *The Heir at Law* (1797)

To the plays on this distinguished list one should add the following, produced by Daly, which also qualify as "Old Comedies" according to Matthews' own definition:

Vanbrugh and Cibber's *The Provoked Husband* (1728)
Garrick's *The Country Girl* (1766), a revision of Wycherley's *The Country Wife*
Goldsmith's *The Good-Natured Man* (1768)
Sheridan's *A Trip to Scarborough* (1777), an adaptation of Vanbrugh's *The Relapse*, presented by Daly as *Miss Hoyden's Husband*
Mrs. Cowley's *A Bold Stroke for a Husband* (1783)
Mrs. Inchbald's *Wives as They Were, Maids as They Are* (1796)

All of the pieces on both lists fall distinctly within the limits of the eighteenth century. Matthews has commented upon the "curious" exclusion from the category of "Old Comedies" of plays by Shakespeare and his contemporaries as well as comedies of the Restoration. Wycherley appears on Daly's list by virtue of Garrick's revision, and Vanbrugh is admitted only as collaborator and revisionist. Daly did produce two plays by Farquhar, *The Inconstant* (1702) and *The Recruiting Officer* (1706), and one by Massinger, *A New Way to Pay Old Debts* (1633), which properly speaking do not belong in this discussion but which are included nevertheless mainly because, in his treatment of them, Daly managed to inculcate the same spirit of fun and sense of historical quaintness as he did in his revivals of the true "Old Comedies."

All the plays thus far mentioned have some common characteristics. First, they were part of the current treasure of dramas drawn upon for production during the nineteenth century. Archaic and silly as many of them now seem, both in method and plot, and caricature-like as their characters may appear today, they were actually no more outmoded on the nineteenth-century stage than were the plays of such contemporaries as Sheridan Knowles, Bulwer-Lytton, Boucicault, Charles Reade, and Tom Taylor (indeed, Matthews added these playwrights to his list). Secondly, since they were part and parcel of the repertories of most stock companies during the century, a manager could be almost certain that the members of his company would be familiar with the "business" and perhaps even the lines of those plays. Finally, of course, most of these comedies had already been somewhat diluted and revised to accord them with the tastes of the times. As Winter has indicated, "In producing these Old English Comedies, Daly found it essential to alter each of them, in some particulars. Adverting to the lax times when they were written, the spectator is not surprised at the precautionary exercise of prudence and taste."

In his first season as a full-fledged manager, Daly produced twenty-one plays in six months, including pieces of every type: Shakespeare, French and German adaptations, current English and American plays, and a group of "Old Comedies." The first of these was Cibber's *She Wou'd and She Wou'd Not*, in which the charming Mrs. Scott-Siddons appeared as Hypolita. The revival ran for two weeks, from October 25 through November 6, 1869. The cast included George Clark, James Lewis, William Davidge, and Agnes Ethel. On the basis of her known success as Viola and Rosalind one may guess that Mrs. Scott-Siddons must have made a fascinating Hypolita, for this romantic "breeches" role represents Cibber's oversentimentalized treatment of the same love chase which, in part, prompted Shakespeare's heroines to assume male disguise. Certainly, the success of this early production must be accounted part of the reason for Daly's later revivals of the play with Ada Rehan in the leading role.

Massinger's *A New Way to Pay Old Debts* was presented three times during this first season, on November 23 and 27, 1869, and again on January 5, 1870. Such performances for a single night or two or three indicate clearly the familiarity of these plays. Members of a stock company presenting twenty-one plays in a six-month interval could hardly be expected to learn twenty-one new parts, some of which would be called for only a few times, and the fact is that certain plays, including this one by Massinger and Mrs. Inchbald's *Wives as They Were, Maids as They Are* (which ran three nights, December 6 through 8, 1869), were well known and required only a brushing-up on the part of the actors in order to be produced.

For these performances of *A New Way to Pay Old Debts*, Daly obtained the services of E. L. Davenport whose impersonation of Sir Giles Overreach was generally admitted to be the best upon the stage. After a series of disputes with this versatile and great actor, Daly again called upon him during a period of financial difficulties in December 1874. Davenport returned to the Fifth Avenue Theatre to do Shylock and Sir Giles. But the actor was, as Dithmar states, "too large a figure for Mr. Daly's pretty little stage." The performer himself wrote that "to act at D's place much has to be sacrificed to upholstery and furniture." Davenport's second withdrawal from the company meant not only the loss of a distinguished actor, but also the permanent removal of Massinger's play from Daly's production schedule.

Also during the 1869–1870 season, Daly revived Mrs. Centlivre's *The Busybody*, from January 3 through 11. The play involves some rather ridiculous situations, but it is lively and amusing. What Mrs. Centlivre lacked in literary ability, she made up with her knowledge of the stage and dramatic technique. *The Busybody* had been performed over 450 times from the date of its first performance at Drury Lane, May 12, 1709, until 1800, and had gone through 39 editions including translation into German.

The last of Daly's Old Comedy revivals for 1869–1870 was Goldsmith's *The Good-Natured Man*, which opened on May 24, 1870, and ran until June 6. On this production, the first in New York for 52 years, Daly used up all the profits of his great success of the season, *Frou-Frou*. His explanation was indicative of his intentions in reviving the classics: "Oh, I did it because my brother, the Judge, said he would like to see it acted. Of course, I knew there was no money in it."

During his next season Daly had two big hits, his dramatization of Collins' *Man and Wife,* and Bronson Howard's *Saratoga.* He put on only one Old Comedy as part of a series of plays produced between the two successes. George Colman the Younger's *The Heir at Law* was given for one night—November 22, 1870. The production is unimportant except as it demonstrates the play's longevity and illustrates again the extensive repertoire of the stock actors of the nineteenth century. Mrs. William Winter was a member of the cast, playing Caroline Dormer.

Again in 1871–1872 after a six-month run of his opening play, Daly returned to a series of revivals. The first of these was *Wives as They Were, Maids as They Are* on March 21, 1872; the next night came *The Provoked Husband.* Originally an unfinished piece left by Vanbrugh, this comedy had been completed by Colley Cibber and produced at Drury Lane on January 10, 1728. At the Fifth Avenue it was interpreted by a cast headed by Harkins, Davidge, LeMoyne, Fanny Davenport, Mrs. Gilbert, and Linda Dietz. Daly's ability to produce such plays on successive nights with almost entirely distinct casts (except for D. H. Harkins) shows the strength of the company he had so carefully selected. His company was, indeed, a most satisfying mixture of established and experienced players—Crisp, Davidge, LeMoyne, Mrs. Gilbert, Fanny Morant—and new popular favorites—Harkins, James Lewis, Fanny Davenport, Clara Morris, Linda Dietz, most of whom went on to become stars. Only a company of great versatility could have encompassed the plays he produced.

Holcroft's *The Road to Ruin* was the first Old Comedy revival in 1872–1873, October 28 and 29. It was followed on October 30 by Mrs. Cowley's *The Belle's Stratagem.* Since nothing but the playbill now remains of this production, it is difficult to evaluate its effectiveness. One interesting thing about it is, however, immediately apparent. The cast of characters included Lord and Lady Touchwood and Kitty Willis; hence, Daly must have used a standard version, for when he made his own revision of the piece in 1893, he entirely eliminated these characters and the subplot in which they figured. Fanny Davenport, Louis James, and William Davidge, who had played the main parts in 1872, were again featured in Daly's revival of the comedy the week of November 4, 1874, but Fanny Morant, who had played Mrs. Rachett, was replaced by Mrs. Gilbert.

Farquhar's *The Inconstant* was also presented by Daly in 1872 (November 6–18). Again it is impossible to judge the production accurately since the playbills list only the names of the artists: Clara Morris and George Clarke played the lovers; they were supported by G. H. Griffiths, B. T. Ringgold, and Fanny Davenport.

December 9, 1872 is a significant date in the chronology of Daly's career since it marks the occasion of his first presentation of Sheridan's *The School for Scandal*. This production was unique not only because it lasted but a single night, but also because it was the only time Daly presented the play in anything like its original form. Fanny Davenport was a dazzling Lady Teazle. Other roles were played by Fisher, Davidge, Griffiths, L. James, G. Clarke, Ringgold, J. Lewis, Owen Fawcett, Fanny Morant, Nellie Mortimer, and Linda Dietz. When Daly next revived the piece on September 12, 1874, he had set the impress of his taste and style upon the text and the sets.

A second comedy by Mrs. Cowley, *A Bold Stroke for a Husband*, was presented from December 12 to 22, 1872. This play used frequently to be distorted in production, but from the strong cast which Daly provided it is clear that he gave prominence to both the moral and the humorous elements of the plot.

The 1874–1875 season was full of vicissitudes for Daly.
Unable to find an enduring success, he was forced back upon
many revivals. Included were the already mentioned presen-
tations of *The School for Scandal* and *A New Way to Pay
Old Debts*. Two new productions of Old Comedies were also
staged: Sheridan's *The Critic* on October 10 and Goldsmith's
She Stoops to Conquer on December 14. This production of
The Critic was the first of many revivals of the piece by Daly.
The interest on this occasion was that it was presented in a
condensed version and played by Fanny Davenport, James
Lewis, and William Davidge; further, it ran a week on a triple
bill with *The Two Widows*, a comedy in one act adapted
from the French, and *The Hanging of the Crane*, a poem by
Longfellow, read by D. H. Harkins and illustrated—so ran the
playbill—by a series of "tableaux vivants." Goldsmith's play
had only one performance. It was never again produced by
Daly although the preliminary announcement for the 1898–
1899 season forecast a major revival of *She Stoops to Conquer*
featuring Miss Rehan.

After the reopening of his theater in 1879, Daly stuck closely to German farces and comic operas and to French melodramas in order to establish himself on a sound financial basis,
and it was only after three successful seasons that he ventured
a revival, of Cibber's *She Wou'd and She Wou'd Not*. The
production was in the nature of a trial, both for his theater
and his company. It opened on Saturday, January 13, 1883,
and ran for two weeks until January 31.

Opinion was divided. Dithmar and Odell, both writing
from the vantage point of history and in the mellowness of
memory, looked back and found Miss Rehan's Hypolita full
of promise. It revealed, said Dithmar, "the breadth of her
talent," and started her on a "great career"—the words are
now Odell's—"as the most captivating comedienne of her
time." Towse also wrote of the production in retrospect, but

he remembered the Daly company as "ill-adapted to the interpretation of artificial literary comedy or imaginative poetic
plays."

Towse further found fault with the way in which the comedy was cut. He charged that Daly revised the play "remorse-
lessly," partly in "the interests of propriety" and partly "to
bring it within the capacity of his company, but chiefly for
Ada Rehan," who was not then the actress she afterwards became. In the light of his mangling of Shakespeare's texts,
Daly's revisions of Cibber, himself a revisionist, seem hardly
disturbing. True, he postponed Hypolita's entrance in Act I
to allow her a more effective spot following instead of preced-
ing the scene between Octavio and Philip. This reversal had
the added attraction of permitting Miss Rehan to come on
stage late enough for all the audience to be seated. Further, in
order to reduce Cibber's play to four acts, Daly combined
Acts III and IV, but that was a practice for which he had
established precedents—both French and Lacy's editions carried suggestions to this effect. Finally, Daly gave Hypolita the
curtain speech of the last act by combining Cibber's lines
intended for Don Philip with some new and coy poetry of
his own.

She Wou'd and She Wou'd Not, although not a great play,
was distinctly a novelty. As such, it became fairly popular
with Daly. His next successful revival of the piece occurred
in London at the Crystal Palace Theatre during the summer
of 1884, on the occasion of the company's first visit abroad.
As a result of the success there, Augustin wrote jubilantly to
Joseph on August 30 that "The press is most unanimous. There
is not one that is not enthusiastic over the performance. They
call it a revelation. . . . You have no idea what a surprise my
company has been here." Later revivals took place in New
York in 1885 and 1886 and in Germany, both in Hamburg
and Berlin, during the company's visit there in the summer
of 1886.

The success of *She Wou'd and She Wou'd Not* encouraged Daly to revive *The Country Girl*, adapted from Garrick's reworking of Wycherley's *The Country Wife*. Inasmuch as Garrick had already deleted the most outrageous aspects of the comedy, Daly had only minor excisions to effect. Odell called this process "fumigating" and indicated that it resulted in "a very funny and wholly inoffensive bit of mirth." The piece enjoyed a month's run, from February 16 to March 12, 1884. Its success, said Judge Daly, "showed that coarseness does not add to the humor of a comedy." Winter's explanation of the purification process unconsciously suggests a note of immorality far deeper than even Wycherley intended. Referring to Ada Rehan's personification of Peggy Thrift as "a comical image of demurely mischievous girlhood," Winter elaborated upon the purpose of the portrayal. "The ideal is that of an apparently simple girl, who, in practice of the wiles of love and courtship, comically develops a sudden and astonishing dexterity." Perhaps Mr. Winter simply chose his words badly, but the phrase "a sudden and astonishing dexterity" could hardly have described the Peggy Thrift of Daly's text. Towse, of course, found the piece "valueless as an example of dramatic construction, style, manners, or anything else. It was not even a reflection of the original work, which in some respects was fortunate. Ada Rehan did not in the least resemble the true Peggy Thrift, for whom she substituted, with amusing effect, her own attractive self."

Miss Rehan's "attractive self" kept *The Country Girl* in the Daly repertoire. It was played again in 1886 and in 1898 enjoyed a successful replaying from February 11 to March 15. In Europe it served the company in Hamburg, Berlin, and Paris during the summer of 1886.

After *The Country Girl* Daly was committed to one Old Comedy or Shakespeare revival every season. The remaining Old Comedy revivals occurred in groups: first, two plays by Farquhar; secondly, three comedies by Sheridan; and finally, plays by Mrs. Cowley and Mrs. Centlivre. The two comedies of Farquhar which Daly now revived were *The Recruiting Officer*, February 7–23, 1885, and *The Inconstant*, January 8–February 4, 1889. The whole emphasis of *The Recruiting Officer* was changed by Daly. Instead of a rollicking, frequently lewd, but always brisk comedy on the military profession and its methods, as the title indicated, Daly made the play over into a comedy of love by shifting the spotlight of interest to Sylvia and her romance. The preface makes clear his intentions. "The transposition of some of the scenes was thought necessary to make the story intelligible, or to put the audience into the secret of the plot: a wise measure in comedy, which was not so well understood in Farquhar's times, when the art of dramatic construction was not yet fully developed, as it is today." When one compares Farquhar's bright original with Mr. Daly's watered version or with the German farces he was currently producing, one is at a loss to understand how a manager of Daly's prominence and capability could have written so fatuously about "the art of dramatic construction."

The omissions in Daly's *The Recruiting Officer* were mainly centered about "the elimination of a few of the grosser touches of the original." The famous incident of Molly of the Castle, which gives an insight into the characters of Plume, Kite, and Sylvia was, of course, left out. The extremely funny and revealing fortune-telling scene was bereft of its two best episodes—those with Pluck the Butcher and Thomas. Finally, a completely new epilogue was added for Sylvia, replacing Farquhar's original one designed to be spoken by Captain Plume. In all, Daly reduced Farquhar's five acts to three, chiefly by combining Acts I and II and Acts IV and V.

Charles P. Daly, writing for The Dunlap Society, has asserted that "*The Recruiting Officer* is the earliest play known to have been acted in North America," but on the basis of more detailed scholarship Quinn has warned that "he would indeed be rash, in view of the many occasions on which 'the first theatre in America' has been discovered, who would attempt to fix finally a date for that event." Nevertheless, *The Recruiting Officer* had been a great favorite on the eighteenth-century stage in America. Daly's prudery, it is interesting to note, was evidently not traditional. It was condemned by one reviewer who wrote that "if the piece hung fire at times, if it seemed a trifle heavy and monotonous, it was because the spectators had been credited with a prudery which they did not seem to possess."

Even more caution was evidenced by Daly when he produced *The Inconstant*. By eliminating the coarseness as well as several of the scenes, he managed to reduce Farquhar's five acts to four. He compressed the two scenes of Farquhar's Act I into the first scene of his own Act I; then for his second scene he used Farquhar's II, i. This device enabled him to close his first act with Mirabel and Oriana's Kate-and-Petruchio-like duet. With John Drew and Ada Rehan's success as Shakespeare's saucy lovers still in the memories of playgoers, Daly's sense of theater served him well.

Daly's Act II, the usual jumble, consisted of

> the second half of III, i
> II, ii
> the first half of III, i
> III, ii
> III, iii

all run together into one scene. From III, iii, however, he omitted Dugard's efforts to redeem his sister's honor as well as the plot to have Oriana enter a convent. The act concluded with Oriana's fainting, a device which of course fixed attention upon Miss Rehan. As a consequence of the elimination of the convent episode, Daly's Act III, scene 1 jumped to Farquhar's IV, iii; Daly's III, 2 then reverted to III, iv, and his final scene (3) in Act III consisted of IV, iv. Again, in order to have Oriana the central figure at the fall of the curtain, he had her speak the interpolated line, "Oh! Oh! Oh! Now I shall run into a real madness," whereupon she also rushed about the stage distractedly. Daly's final act (IV) embraced Farquhar's Act V with the omission of scene iii. This rushed the action so that there was no period of suspense while the page, Oriana in disguise, went to get help for Mirabel, trapped by the adventuress, Lamorce. The consequent telescoping of the action was silly: Oriana left and returned almost immediately with the necessary assistance. Besides, Daly changed the character of Lamorce. In his version, there was no indication of her real nature, or her real intentions; she was distinctly not a loose woman, so the whole episode became a sort of charade and its dramatic effectiveness, including the moral lesson, was replaced by sheer vapidity. A further consequence of the changed status of Lamorce was that it rendered Mirabel's speech contrasting Lamorce and Oriana completely extraneous; it was omitted. In its place, a simpering epilogue, written by William Winter, was recited by Oriana.

The greatest injustice which Daly did to the play was the transfer of interest from "the inconstant" Mirabel to "the way to win him" (the subtitle) as it was effected by Oriana. Whereas the original Mirabel had been designed as the central character and was so played by Farquhar's friend, Wilks, who originated the role at Drury Lane in 1702, in Daly's version Oriana became the main figure, speaking the closing lines of all four acts and being generally the personage about whom the action was all designed.

It was in 1874 that Daly again presented *The School for Scandal*, this time in his own revision. The date is interesting, for on July 19, 1873 Stephen Fiske had written him, "if you want a big cast to open the new theatre why not do my adaptation of *The School for Scandal?* I *Made* it a magnificent play—one scene to an act." Towse says that Daly followed the Bancroft model and indicated that "the representation—distinctly inferior to that at Wallack's—was, nevertheless, excellent." In particular, he praised Charles Fisher's Sir Peter and Louis James's Joseph Surface. Fanny Davenport's Lady Teazle he found "remarkable only for her loveliness."

By 1891, Daly had consolidated his version of the Sheridan play; this version now starred Ada Rehan. The scenes were reordered as follows:

Daly	Sheridan
Act I	I, i; II, ii
Act II	II, i followed by I, ii; II, iii, III, i
Act III	III, ii and iii; IV, i
Act IV	IV, iii (the "screen" scene)
Act V	V, ii and iii

He omitted entirely Act IV, scene ii, a short scene in which Rowley brings money from Charles Surface to "Mr. Stanley" and Act V, scene i, Joseph's interview with "Mr. Stanley"; and he eliminated much of the "coarseness of the scandal-mongering colloquies," especially in the first act.

This rearrangement of *The School for Scandal* called forth some of Norman Hapgood's bitterest rebukes. "Sheridan wrote his comedy for a company of players," pointed out the author of *The Stage in America*, "and Lady Teazle is a part no more 'fat' than others in the play." But Mr. Daly had remedied Sheridan's "oversight." The orchestra played when Miss Rehan entered or left the stage. She took a speech belonging to Charles Surface in order to have the last chance at the audience. "In dialogues where six or eight persons are of equal importance, she sat at the side while the others talked, and when it was her turn for a word she walked out into the center, all the others faded off, and the word was spoken. Again and again in several scenes was every bit of art sacrificed to the desire to force this actress into the middle of the stage." Despite Miss Rehan's unusual gifts, Mr. Hapgood considered it poor taste and "worse than futile" to make the whole play over into nothing but a background for Lady Teazle.

The grossest instances of this tendency were in the scenes between Sir Peter and Lady Teazle. When Miss Rehan spoke, Sir

Peter obediently pretended he was dead. When he spoke, Miss Rehan went over to an interpolated musical instrument and pounded for the attention of the audience. She gave the imitation of a trotting horse in one place, and went through a variety turn in another.

Towse found the "gem" of this production to be the Sir Oliver Surface of Harry Edwards; he also admired John Drew's Charles Surface, but felt that Ada Rehan's Lady Teazle "could not be counted among her conspicuous successes."

The production nevertheless achieved a measure of popular success, running for fifty performances from January 20 to March 2, 1891. Subsequently, *The School for Scandal* remained a standby in Daly's repertoire, being revived again and again. At the time of its presentation in January 1893, Joseph Daly acknowledged a royalty check for the week the piece was played, an indication that he had probably assisted his brother in the revision.

Daly did two other Sheridan plays. His first presentation of *The Critic* was on October 10, 1874. For this performance, he condensed the piece into a one-act version, which, said Towse, "would only with difficulty have been recognized by its author." Since no copy of Daly's rearrangement is in print, it is difficult to evaluate his adaptation. Considering Towse's statement and the praise of Winter, who indicated that the piece featured Ada Rehan as Tilburina, one may conclude, however, that Daly distorted Sheridan's burlesque.

When he again revived the play from December 26, 1888 through January 14, 1889 on a bill with *The Lottery of Love*, Daly called his version *A Tragedy Rehearsed*. From this title and from Winter's remarks, it appears that his one-act version was based on the second and third acts of Sheridan's play. Later revivals occurred January 31—February 14, 1895 (with *The Orient Express*) and March 20–25 and April 1, 1895 (with *Nancy and Company*).

Daly's other condensation of Sheridan was called *Miss*

Hoyden's Husband, a one-act version of *A Trip to Scarborough.* The piece was played on a double bill with *Haroun Al
Raschid and his Mother-in-Law* from March 26 to April 12,
1890. Odell has left the only comment upon the comedy, a
complaint that Daly's "actors could not approximate the style
of 1780—*A Trip to Scarborough* was first performed at Drury
Lane on February 24, 1777—far less of 1695, the date of *The
Relapse,* upon which Sheridan had based his play."

Daly's next revival was the previously produced *The Belle's
Stratagem,* now redone for Ada Rehan. As distinct from the
earlier (1872, 1874) renditions, the comedy was now greatly
revised. On this occasion Daly chose to omit the whole subplot, including the characters of Lord and Lady Touchwood
and Kitty Willis; by so doing, he eliminated the moral of the
play, retaining only the silly love-chase picturing Letitia
Hardy's wiles being successfully exercised upon the unwilling
Doricourt.

The role of Letitia was perfectly suited to Ada Rehan.
Daly's version cut Mrs. Cowley's comedy from five to three
acts, and the new first act revealed Miss Rehan deliberately
trying to irritate Doricourt by a pretense of stupidity, which
included the singing of a foolish interpolated song, "Where
are you going to, my pretty maid?" At the conclusion of the
act, old Hardy, played by James Lewis, concerned about a
costume for the impending masquerade, was made to recite
these distressing lines: "Hang me if I don't send to my favorite
little Lewis, at the theatre, and borrow his Mendoza dress—I
know the dog likes a glass of wine; so I'll give him a bottle of
my '48, and he shall teach me how to play the part."

Daly used the masquerade party as his second act. Here the
only significant change was in Flutter's remarks; mistaking
Letitia for a woman of the town, he originally declared her
definitely to be Lord Jennett's mistress. In Daly's version,
Flutter said of her, "She's jilted and been jilted by half a
hundred men about town," making her an altogether different

kind of person. Finally, Daly rearranged the Epilogue to have Doricourt recite, first, the last four lines, after which Letitia spoke lines 1–2 and 9–12 and ended the performance. The 1893 production of *The Belle's Stratagem* ran for two weeks, from January 3 to 15.

Daly's final Old Comedy revival was Mrs. Centlivre's *The Wonder: A Woman Keeps a Secret* given from March 23 through April 4, 1897. The plot of this comedy, which Mrs. Centlivre based on Edward Ravenscroft's *The Wrangling Lovers*, is basically rather silly inasmuch as it depends upon suspicion which could easily be cleared up at any time; the prolonging of the confusion, however, allows the characters to enjoy themselves and to entertain the audience.

The importance of all of Mrs. Centlivre's plays has always been largely in terms of their stage careers; they provided great acting parts for many decades. *The Wonder* is no exception. From Wilks to Wallack it offered, in the character of Don Felix, a role to challenge the talents of actors. Garrick, Kemble, and Kean all essayed the part; indeed, for the final performance of his theatrical career, Garrick chose to impersonate Don Felix in *The Wonder*. In this tradition, Charles Richman upheld the standards. The *Times* called his Don Felix "the best hit of his life" and commended the "vivacity, variety and force of his acting."

Despite Richman's success, the play was nonetheless Ada Rehan's. For the last time in the field of Old Comedy Daly made a play over. It was distinctly the heroine's play. As Violante, Miss Rehan spoke the last few lines (adapted from the Prologue), which illustrate the tenor of the Old Comedies at Daly's:

> A few mistakes our sex may well excuse—
> And this our plea no woman should refuse.
> Your approbation, ladies, can't but move
> The hearts of men which first you taught to love.
> And they must applaud if you but favor
> And to success but give the savor.

CHAPTER 7

American Impresario

A most unholy trade.
                    Henry James
To haul the culture-wagon.
                    Mark Twain

Among the many significant achievements
of Augustin Daly, probably none stands more firmly in the
annals of the American theater than his successful invasions
of England, France, and Germany. In taking his company
to Europe, he was reversing the customary flow of theater
events with a daring which earned him Lester Wallack's
praise, "the pluckiest thing ever done."

Daly's actors were not, of course, the first Americans to
perform on continental stages. From the time of Hackett's
first visit in 1827, a steady flow of American performers had
courted the London public. Forrest, Charlotte Cushman,
E. L. Davenport and Mrs. Mowatt, Booth, Jefferson, and
Mary Anderson, to mention only the outstanding, had
established the practice. But Daly's was the first complete
company to invade Europe from America. The significance of his visits, then, is bound up with the recognition of
his company as representing the best in ensemble acting. For
example, Robert Buchanan, while complaining bitterly about
current acting, plays, and production methods in England,
remarked, in *A Look Round Literature*, that "at Daly's there

is a combination so admirable in ensemble, so full of natural talent and acquired fitness, so excellently guided and directed, that it became last summer the talk of London." And William Archer, commenting upon the inanity of *The Countess Gucki*, nevertheless was forced to add, "Though the characters have not even the make-believe reality of marionettes, and though we do not care two pins about them, yet somehow we are entertained, amused. . . . Mr. Daly has scored a success with the emptiest play on record."

Daly's own first visit to London occurred in 1878–1879. In his letters home, Augustin complained of the reception he received in England, as compared with the welcome a British author and producer would enjoy in New York. Yet he brought back from the trip renewed enthusiasm and determination and ideas about theatrical policy upon which he established a most successful theater.

The first foreign trip made by the Daly company was in the summer of 1884. The opening piece, at Toole's Theatre, London, on July 19, was *Seven-Twenty-Eight*. The press notices, as Judge Daly admits, were conservative. But recognition came with the revival of *She Wou'd and She Wou'd Not*, presented at the Crystal Palace Theatre later in the summer. On this occasion, Augustin write Joseph, "The press is most unanimous. There is not one that is not enthusiastic over the performance. They call it a revelation. . . . You have no idea what a surprise my company has been here." Looking back (1916) over "the past twenty years' commerce between the English and American stages," H. G. Hibbert indicated that the commerce "may be said to have begun in earnest with Augustin Daly's visits." Justin H. McCarthy was much more enthusiastic. "It may fairly be stated by the student of the contemporary stage," he asserted, "that a fresh epoch in the history of the English drama began on the day Miss Ada Rehan and the Daly Company made their first appearance before a London audience!"

On this first trip, Daly was associated from the business end with the English actor, William Terriss. Jessie Millward, an English actress, who accompanied Henry Irving and Terriss to America in 1883, says in *Myself and Others* that it was on that trip that "Terriss first saw the wonderful Augustin Daly Company and arranged to bring them over to London. . . . It was a hobby with Terriss to buy plays and dabble in theatrical speculation." Judge Daly indicates that it was Augustin who "admitted" Terriss "to a share in the enterprise," for which he acted as the business manager.

For Daly's succeeding trips to England he had no business associates. The second visit was accomplished in the summer of 1886—"in response to the hearty invitation given in 1884 to return and gratify the newly aroused interest of the English people." The company opened at the Strand Theatre on May 27 with *A Night Off*. The performance of *Nancy and Company*, which followed soon after, elicited from *The Saturday Review* the praise that, "There is not now in London an English company as well chosen, as well trained, as brilliant in the abilities of its individual members, or as well harmonized as a whole, as the admirable company which Mr. Daly directs. They suggest the Comédie Française at its best."

This successful second visit to London was followed by a bolder venture yet, a two-weeks' trip to Germany, during which the company played Daly's English adaptations of several currently popular German farces. Judge Daly reported that this was "the first English-speaking company in nearly three hundred years" to be seen on a German stage. It was, according to John Drew, "the first and only time that an entire American company visited Germany." The company spent a week, beginning August 19, 1886, at the Thalia Theater, Hamburg, followed by six nights at the Wallner Theater, Berlin.

To complete his tour in 1886, Daly next took his company to the Théâtre des Vaudevilles, Paris, where again his visit was the first of an American theatrical company in France. The reception of the Daly players in Paris was only luke-warm. Their "propensity for naturalism in acting" as contrasted with the "conventionality in the movement" of the French actors was, according to La Pommeraye, "shocking" both to critics and audiences. Daly, however, decided before he left to return again to Paris and "storm its prejudices." The European jaunt of 1886 was brought to a close by a week each in Liverpool (September 6, Royal Alexandra Theatre) and Dublin (September 13, Gaiety Theatre).

The Daly Company's third European excursion in 1888 was distinguished by the production of *The Taming of the Shrew*. This magnificent performance thrilled audiences in London, where it was hailed as "the first performance of a Shakespearean comedy by an American company in Europe." In Paris Daly thus made good his claim to return and conquer, and in Stratford on August 3, the company presented the first performance of *The Taming of the Shrew* ever given there.

After the customary two-year interval, the Daly Company next appeared in London in 1890. By now the repertory was established: the players opened on June 10 at the Lyceum Theatre with *Seven-Twenty-Eight*, followed by *Nancy and Company*, of which one anonymous reviewer commented that "even apart from the acting, there is more talent than in such current London favorites as *Miss Decima, Husband and Wife, The Late Lamented*." The 1890 London season, which lasted two months, was brought to a close with *The Taming of the Shrew* and *As You Like It*, both of which received the by now favorable reviews.

Instead of the accustomed trip to California which had become the established practice for alternate summers, Daly returned to Europe again in 1891. London audiences were more receptive than those in San Francisco, and travel to Europe was decidedly more comfortable than the tedious week-by-week cross-country stands which a California engagement necessitated. The European season began August 31 with a week at the Vaudeville Théâtre, Paris, a feature of which was the production of Daly's *The Lottery of Love,* already familiar to Parisians as *Les Surprises du Divorce.* The success of this adaptation gave proof of the change in attitude of French audiences toward Daly and vindicated his earlier ambitions. A month in London, beginning September 9, concluded the European season of 1891. In the summer of 1892, Daly again took his troupe to California.

When he next returned to Europe, it was to open his own theater, Daly's, on Cranbourn Street, Leicester Square, London, on June 27, 1893. The opening address was "A Song of Union," written specially by Clement Scott. Augustin himself made a short speech from notes prepared by Joseph for the occasion. Despite the popularity of the company, Daly found it difficult to establish his theater on a sound financial basis. He had previously, as Judge Daly points out, largely depended upon the audiences of established theaters, especially the Lyceum, but Daly's new theater had no public. Furthermore—a fact which neither of the brothers seems to have realized—Daly gave offense to Londoners by naming his theater after himself and by hoisting the Stars and Stripes over the building. "Playgoers who had tendered him profuse hospitality as a visitor resented his assumption, as a resident, of the 'boss' attitude," explained the author of *Fifty Years of a Londoner's Life.* After a short summer season of revivals of *The Taming of the Shrew* and *The Hunchback,* and a week of *Love in Tandem,* the company went on vacation. The autumn season opened with *Dollars and Sense,* and the company prepared to spend the complete winter season of 1893 and 1894 in London, the only time Daly spent a whole season away from New York.

The difficulties he encountered in London are best illustrated by a letter, dated January 25, 1894, which he wrote to William Winter:

I have had a very hard fight of it over here, opposed as I have been by *every* London manager from Irving and Tree down. They have all shown a most unworthy spirit of jealousy, especially for people who have already (or expect yet to) received such generous and friendly receptions from my countrymen. . . . They tried to influence certain writers on the press against me and my work. . . . The public I have always had. My distresses or diasppointments have only been those naturally the outcome of all new theatres. I expected some, and was prepared. I have been through this "mill" in pioneer-ing the way for new theatres *three* times before.

But by the time he wrote, the "pioneer-ing" was practically over. With *The School for Scandal* reaching fifty performances and *Twelfth Night* over a hundred, the theater finally came into its own. The triumph was fittingly concluded with a production of *As You Like It* in May.

In the summer of 1895, Daly returned with his comedians to his Leicester Square Theatre. But, under the management of George Edwardes, the policy of that playhouse was gradually being so well established in favor of musical comedies that, on their succeeding trips in 1896 and 1897, the Daly Company was forced to find other quarters in order not to upset the phenomenal runs of *The Geisha* and *An Artist's Model*. Consequently, in 1896, the company went to the Comedy Theatre, Haymarket, for its six weeks' stay.

The final European excursion of the Daly Company began auspiciously in the summer of 1897 with an open-air performance of *As You Like It* at Stratford. From there the troupe went on to perform in Newcastle, Birmingham, Nottingham, Edinburgh, Glasgow, London, Liverpool, and Manchester. The London performances were given at the Grand Theatre, Islington. The success of this last ambitious tour was a satisfactory climax to a total of nine visits by the Daly Company to Europe, a company which, according to D. Forbes-Winslow, "achieved such fame that it rivalled the Comédie Française." The company did indeed have "an established

place in the heart of the British public." In his history of
Daly's, the Biography of a Theatre, Forbes-Winslow concludes that the company "left a mark on [English] theatrical
enterprise," for truly "Daly's productions set London talking
and thinking."

Daly's trips to England were not solely for the business of
presenting his plays and opening a theater there. He made
worth-while connections with British playwrights. Daly's
was the first theater to present in the United States some of
the major works of T. W. Robertson, Frank Marshall, W. S.
Gilbert, James Albery, H. J. Byron, Jerome K. Jerome,
A. W. Pinero, and Alfred Tennyson.

Tennyson himself selected the Daly company, particularly
Miss Rehan, to interpret his pastoral comedy, *The Foresters*.
At the aging poet laureate's request, the première occurred in
New York on March 17, 1892. In undertaking the production,
Daly accepted a task of no common difficulty; but the results,
to judge from the critics' reception, were highly successful.
The final production, with music by Sir Arthur Sullivan and
costumes by Graham Robertson, was in its opulence and general method very similar to Daly's Shakespearean and Old
English Comedy revivals. This similarity extended even to the
fact that Joseph Daly received royalty checks for the weeks
the piece was being produced, thereby indicating that whatever revisions were introduced in production had been made
by Joseph.

Daly's relations with contemporary English playwrights
extended also to Oscar Wilde. (Daly and Shaw, however, met
only as producer and drama critic.) Wilde sent Daly *A Good
Woman* with an accompanying note, saying "I should sooner
see her [Miss Rehan] play the part of Mrs. Erlynne than any
English-speaking actress we have, or French for that matter."
For some unknown reason, Daly rejected the play, but in 1897
he wrote Wilde asking for a comedy. Wilde replied on September 22 that he was "very much flattered . . . and I would

like extremely to write a play some day for that brilliant and fascinating genius, Ada Rehan," but he declined because of other commitments. Later on in the year, Wilde was in Naples and "much in need of money" and reconsidered Daly's offer. He let Daly know through his publisher, Leonard Smithers, that he was ready to do a play for £100 down, £100 on delivery of each act, and the "usual royalties . . . from which the payments on account will be deducted." But again there were no tangible results.

In view of his many French and German adaptations and of his numerous revivals of Shakespeare and the Old English comedies, one can perhaps understand why Daly acquired a reputation for managing an exclusively "foreign" theater. In his study, *A History of the American Theatre*, Arthur Hornblow has condemned Daly together with Wallack and Palmer, the three leading producers of the period, for their "Anglicism and classicism." "American drama," he asserted, "virtually did not exist. Our boards were crowded with French and English plays in which the characters expressed foreign ideas and behaved like foreigners." Montrose J. Moses, in *The American Dramatist*, has been equally outspoken: "Wallack with his English proclivities and Palmer with his numerous D'Ennery and Sardou adaptations . . . and Daly with his German dependence, might hardly be deemed influences on the American dramatist." Moses was merely parroting contemporary opinion. In *The Nation* in 1875, Henry James had complained that "the mirror [held up to nature], as the theatres show it, has the image already stamped upon it—an Irish image, a French image, an English image." Howells' review of the 1879 season in *The Atlantic* has already been mentioned; it pointed to the same objections. Finally, Mary Crawford in a book called *The Romance of the American Theatre*, has added that "what is pretentiously called the leading American theatre [Daly's] is not an American theatre at all . . . but a cheap copy of an English theatre, from the stage of which American writers and plays are rigorously excluded."

These accusations, however, hardly tell the whole truth. Many of Daly's adaptations really deserve to be called American pieces; they were "localized" and "naturalized" both in terms of incident and character. *The Big Bonanza* and *Uncle Sam*, one German, the other French, were both made over into American plays; dramatizations such as *Pique* and *Divorce* were also intrinsically American, whereas *Under the Gaslight*, *The Red Scarf*, and *Horizon* could hardly be labeled anything but American studies. Even in the midst of his condemnation, Howells praised Daly's adaptations, commenting "I have always especially admired his art in nationalizing foreign plays. He gave them to us with much of local color and atmosphere. . . ."

Secondly, in two published articles on the American drama, Daly made eloquent pleas for American writers to turn their attention to the stage and write for it. He insisted that "it does not matter whether an American dramatist chooses American material or not. His work, so long as it is added to the volume of work done in America and in the American spirit, belongs to the American drama." Such a statement, of course, incorporates and justifies Daly's many adaptations of French and German plays. His concern for creating an American drama was in fact so strong that it led him to express the most jingoistic kind of statement. In a letter to the *Herald* in 1874, Daly condemned the journalists for the "absence" of an American drama, claiming that their harsh criticisms "pulled up by the roots" the "young shoots" put out by native playwrights. He felt that the newspapers were being inconsistent in lamenting the lack of American plays and yet in allowing their drama critics to be so harsh on indigenous efforts.

But Daly did more than express opinions; in seeking to implement his theories, he not only produced many American pieces, but also attempted to entice American writers to compose for his company. Daly's role in searching out new American plays and playwrights was justly acknowledged by Brander Matthews, who wrote in *These Many Years* that Daly "was anxious to develop American dramatists, and here he stood in most complete opposition to Lester Wallack."

Bronson Howard is generally regarded as one of the first significant American playwrights. Of him, *The Literary History of the United States* comments, "he left playwriting a profession, and the American social comedy an art." Despite this accolade, H. P. Mawson, in "A Brief Biography" of Howard, complains that his early efforts in the dramatic field were unappreciated; Mawson relates that "for four years Mr. Howard wrote plays for managers' wastebaskets." Moses and Hornblow have similarly descanted upon Howard's difficulties in establishing himself. Yet, of the dramatist's first four plays, three were produced by Daly. *Fantine* was performed in Detroit in 1864, but *Saratoga* in 1870, *Diamonds* in 1872, and *Moorcroft* in 1874 were all first presented by Daly. In addition, as W. W. Austin points out in an article in *Munsey's Magazine* in 1899, "Daly made a fine allowance to Mr. Howard in the shape of royalties, and from that time began the practice of paying American dramatists for their labor." And in 1906, Howard himself stated that, "except for Daly, I was practically alone; but he offered me the same opportunity and promise for the future that he gave to himself. From him developed a school of managers willing and eager to produce American plays on American subjects. . . ."

Even in 1906, however, Howard was not telling the whole truth about the extent of Daly's encouragement. Perhaps he had forgotten. Yet his early letters remain as witnesses. On April 7, 1871, Howard wrote to Daly:

I have a half-formed idea that if I can make tolerably definite arrangements for the production of two or three pieces next season, I may give up editorial work entirely. In case I do that, I can drive ahead rapidly with the comedy for your theatre, and besides can give you all the time you want for general work on translations, adaptations, etc.

Several weeks later, he inquired, "Do you care to arrange for two and one half hours' work a day at $25 per week? . . . I think such an arrangement would cover all the literary work you need." Apparently, no engagement was made at that time, but a definite working agreement was made in 1874. Several years later, in 1879, Howard referred to this "short service" at Daly's theater, during which time—the engagement lasted three weeks at $50 a week—"I was at work on an adaptation from the French of the 'Officer of Fortune,' afterwards [1877] produced by you as 'The Princess Royal.' " It was also during this period of collaboration that Daly suggested to Howard the adapting of two of Molière's comedies, *L'École des Femmes* and *L'École des Maris*. Consequently, for awhile after he ceased to be employed by Daly, Howard continued to occupy space at the theater to complete his adaptation, produced by Daly on October 18, 1879, as *Wives*.

The actual nature of the agreement between Daly and Howard is clear from a letter from the playwright, dated July 17, 1878, and written from his home in Ypsilanti, Michigan.

Personally, I shall be very glad indeed to be with you. Can we not make arrangements for what may be called partial-time services? I, for instance, to occupy a desk in your office, or another office in the theatre, for four hours every day—say from 12 to 4 P.M.—to read plays & do all other kindred work you may care for —this to be independent of, & without reference to, the adaptations of plays. . . . Say $25 a week. . . . Then, for the adaptations, etc., let *them* rest *entirely* on the "small percentage of the gross."

Although this letter did not result in the re-employment of Howard, their earlier collaboration must not have been displeasing to either party, for Howard continued to allow Daly the first option on his new plays and, in 1885, in response to a query from Daly, he wrote from England that he would be "glad" to return to his former position, "working up your plots and subjects."

These letters thrown a revealing light upon Daly's significance in assisting the development of an American drama. His business correspondence shows that he was just as eagerly pursuing other American writers.

A contract, drawn up on June 12, 1872, indicates that Bret Harte "agrees to write a play in five acts suitable for the Fifth Avenue Theatre and suited to the individual artistic peculiarities of the Company." The agreement also stipulated that the play would be "completely finished" by September 1, and that Harte's payment was to have been a royalty of $50 per night.

For the next twenty years Daly continued to dicker with Harte. During 1873 and 1874 the writer was laboring on a western piece without success. At Daly's insistence, Boucicault, back from a long visit to Europe, agreed to help. The drama was to be called *Kentuck*, a name which would have anticipated Augustus Thomas' successful use of states as titles for plays. Daly had agreed to a royalty payment of $100 a night, but Boucicault felt that the original sum was insufficient for both himself and Harte, so Daly upped the fee to 12 per cent of the gross receipts nightly, 6 per cent for each author. Although Boucicault actually prepared "a cast *raisonnée*" and succeeded in making the "dilatory and erratic" Harte conform to a daily schedule, the play never materialized. Harte eventually finished the play by himself. It was produced by Shook and Palmer at the Union Square Theatre on August 28, 1876, under the title, *The Two Men of Sandy Bar*, and it was a failure.

Harte's next project for Daly actually reached fruition. Although *The Two Men of Sandy Bar* had failed, it had, however, introduced to the American stage one popular character, the Chinese laundryman, Hop Sing, played by C. T. Parsloe. Harte, who had earlier discovered that character

types were the basis of successful writing, now persuaded
Mark Twain to collaborate with him upon a new piece featuring a similar Chinese character.

Twain has described the incident with typical gusto in one
of his letters to Howells:

> This is a secret . . . that Bret Harte came up here [Hartford]
> the other day & asked me to help him write a play & divide the
> swag & I agreed. I am to put in Scotty Briggs (see Buck Fanshaw's
> Funeral, in "Roughing It") & he is to put in a Chinaman (a won-
> derfully funny creature, as Bret presents him—for five minutes—in
> his Sandy Bar play). This Chinaman is to be the character of the
> play, & both of us will work on him & develop him. Bret is to draw
> a plot, & I am to do the same; we shall use the best of the two, or
> gouge from both & build a third. My plot is built—finished it yes-
> terday—six days' work, 8 or 9 hours a day, & has nearly killed me.

The result was *Ah Sin*. After a try-out in Washington, the
piece opened on July 31, 1877, as the final production of the
season, at the Fifth Avenue Theatre.

Judge Daly relates how Twain attended the "distinguished"
first night and made a speech. "Some of the papers next day
thought the speech better than the play." In his remarks,
Twain admitted that *Ah Sin* was "a very remarkable play . . .
the result of great research, and erudition, and genius, and
invention—and plagiarism." From synopses, it is apparent that
Ah Sin "attempted to present frontier life, and included a
supposed murder, a vigilante plot, and general entertainment
by the diverting Ah Sin."

The receipts from the play, according to Joseph Daly,
"gradually dwindled week by week for five weeks, with considerable loss to Daly." For the costly presentation of *Ah Sin*,
one must certainly credit Daly with a very practical demon-
stration of his devotion to the American drama.

In 1882, Harte turned up again with another idea for a play.
Judge Daly quotes a letter from him about "the play—wh.
Shakespeare ought to have written but wh., as he did not,

I may possibly undertake." These communications from Harte terminate in the eighties when Harte was writing Daly from Glasgow. From that city, Harte sent his dramatization of *The Luck of Roaring Camp*, but it found no favor with the manager. Harte had changed the "Luck" to a girl; in the last two acts, she was "a grown young lady placed at school in Paris by her rough but devoted fathers."

The "never suppressed desire" on the part of Harte, Twain, Howells, and James to write successful plays is an interesting, but infrequently noted, tendency on the part of these late-nineteenth-century writers of fiction. Despite the keen interest and even practice on the part of the foremost literary figures of the period, most of the historians of American literature have ignored the drama, leaving it to the specialists. "There is no word about it in the substantial volumes by Richardson and Wendell, none in the ordinary run of text-books, not a mention of a playwright, producer, actor, or stage even in the 400 odd pages of Pattee's *A History of American Literature Since 1870*," states Percy Boynton. Indeed, Pattee discusses both Harte and Joaquin Miller at length without mentioning either their plays or their interest in the drama; he mentions Blanche Willis Howard, but not Bronson Howard; he discusses Mary E. Wilkins Freeman and Eugene Field, and even refers to Flaubert, but has no reference at all to Clyde Fitch. To the list—Richardson, Wendell, Pattee—one must add Van Wyck Brooks. *New England: Indian Summer*, for instance, ignores the drama; he devotes space to an account of the growing interest in art and music in Boston, but never indicates that there was also a decided love of the drama at the same time; he enumerates other "cultural" institutions: the museums and the schools, but does not list a single theater; he dismisses the plays of Howells in a single footnote. Boynton has attempted to explain this "silence" on the part of the historians by insisting that "the period had almost no dramatic significance. . . . The basic reason for this is that literary conditions did not induce or encourage playwriting in the English-speaking world. . . . The greatest genius in story-telling was loose in the channel of fiction. . . ."

Yet one can point out that the tremendous influence of *Uncle Tom's Cabin* was in no small measure the result of its presentation by numerous touring companies which, indeed, came to be known as "Tom Shows." Likewise, the enormously successful burlesque version of *Evangeline* certainly played a part in popularizing that work. Finally, one has only to consult the letters which Harte, Twain, Howells, James, and others wrote to Daly (and in all probability to other producers as well) to understand that these writers sought, earnestly and sincerely, to be playwrights. And certainly the original work of Bronson Howard, Clyde Fitch, Augustus Thomas, James Herne, to mention only a few, cannot be dismissed with a shrug and with Boynton's label, "no significance." The influence of the drama can be no better illustrated than in this short note from Twain to Daly:

A fine and beautiful thing is a child's worship. . . . I have written wonderful books which have revolutionized politics & religion in the world; & you might think that is why my children hold my person sacred; but it isn't so; it is because I know Miss Rehan and Mr. Drew personally.

And at a dinner to Henry Irving in London in June 1900, while making one of his famous speeches, Twain was more serious than usual when he declared that "The greatest of all arts is to write a drama. It is a most difficult thing. It requires the highest talents possible and the rarest gifts."

Daly tried patiently and persistently to get Twain to write for the stage. Acknowledging that "there is more money in books than in plays," Twain nevertheless expressed himself as being "cheerfully willing to intrude . . . upon the dramatic field." Actually, he made several attempts to intrude. As early as 1867, he had projected *The Quaker City Holy Land Excursion*, but he never finished the play. He worked diligently at the dramatic version of *The Gilded Age* and, according to Howells, literally reveled in its financial success. Although Dixon Wecter referred to it as a "modest" success, Twain wrote Howells in 1881 that he had made $70,000 out of the dramatization. The character of Sellers, as portrayed by John Raymond, did indeed enjoy a satisfying stage life; on the strength of it, Twain resolved to do a sequel. In this venture he persuaded Howells to be his collaborator. His ambition was great. As he wrote Howells in 1884, he wanted to repeat the success of Sellers "once or twice more" and thereby establish him "permanently as *the* American character, to be used by future generations of authors and actors."

But the play did not match the grandiose aims of its authors. Raymond declined the comedy because he felt the "character," as Dixon Wecter has pointed out, "had been exaggerated to the brink of lunacy." As a consequence, Twain turned upon Raymond bitterly. Both he and Howells, however, continued to dicker with actors and producers for the play's production. Their letters for the four years 1884–1887 contain references to their difficulties. Finally, the authors themselves presented the piece at a "trial matinee" at the Lyceum Theatre on September 23, 1887. It was called *The American Claimant, or Mulberry Sellers Ten Years Later,* and the piece was a miserable failure. The plot, as "embalmed" in Twain's novel, *The American Claimant,* published in 1892, more than justified Raymond's verdict and that of the public. It is, said Mr. Wecter, "one of the humorist's most strained and least successful efforts."

Curiously enough, when the novel appeared Daly considered it good material for dramatization and wrote Twain making the suggestion that it be adapted for the stage. The author, then in Bad Nauheim for the cure, wrote back, "You bang away and dramatize the book *your* way & that will be *my* way. . . . These are mighty good baths, & if you want to try them come here & I will treat to bath tickets."

Judge Daly reports that even after the failure of *Ah Sin*, Twain sent a play called *Bob Sawyer's Adventures* to Daly in 1884. In all probability, this was the play which Daly rejected in a letter to Twain dated February 27, 1884:

My dear Mr. Clemens:

I fear that *Tom Sawyer* would not make a success at my theatre. After a very close reading, I must disagree with you on the point that grown-up people may successfully represent the boys & girls of your piece. Tom might be played by a clever comedian as a boy, but the other parts would seem ridiculous in grown peoples' hands.

I would really like to have a comedy from you for my company & I regret that I cannot find this one suitable.

Very truly,
A. Daly

Certainly this failure, though disappointing, did not prevent Twain's projecting other dramatic pieces, both comic and tragic. His concern for the theater was enduring. In an "illuminating" article, "About Play-Acting," referred to by Brander Matthews, he lamented the absence of tragedy from the New York stage:

America devotes more time, labor, money and attention to distributing literary and musical culture among the general public than does any other nation, perhaps; yet here you find her neglecting what is possibly the most effective of all the breeders and nurses and disseminators of high literary taste and lofty emotion—the tragic stage. To leave that powerful agency out is to haul the culture-wagon with a crippled team.

It was Twain who first suggested to Daly that he should "provoke" Howells into writing a play. Negotiations between writer and manager began in 1874 when Howells wrote, "I have long had the notion of a play." The "notion" did not, however, materialize, probably because, as Howells indicated, "it's rather tragical . . . and I can't deal exclusively in tragedy." Farce comedy did prove to be his dramatic forte. In the spring of 1876, Howells, recalling Daly's "very kind invitation" to "send anything I might write in the way of a play," dispatched *The Parlor Car*, a farce which Daly announced would be staged during the 1876–1877 season. Other requirements interfered, and Howells finally published it in *The Atlantic Monthly* instead, "preferring to have the piece criticised in advance." Indeed, periodical publication provided the only audiences for most of Howells' thirty-odd plays.

Daly's failure to produce *The Parlor Car* did not by any means discourage Howells. On September 15, 1876, he sent another comedy, *Out of the Question*, and on February 10, 1884, he forwarded *A Counterfeit Presentment*, as Barrett "played it with marked success here [Boston]." As usual, Daly took advantage of an author's eagerness to write for the theater and asked Howells to "naturalize" a German piece for him. In addition, Daly's adaptation of Estabanez' *Un Drama Nuevo* in 1874 may well have prompted Howells' better version of 1877.

Throughout the years, Howells continued both to write plays and to interest himself in the theater. He wrote numerous articles on the stage and on playwrights for various periodicals; he was instrumental in securing American recognition of certain foreign plays and dramatists; and he constantly corresponded with actors and producers in an effort to have his own pieces staged. He sent his plays to Mrs. Fiske, to Joe Jefferson, to Rosina Vokes, to Henry Irving, and to William Gillette. He even engaged in a kind of genteel blackmail, for after the actress Sara Jewett had submitted some of her poetry to *The Atlantic*, Howells sent her a play in which he hoped she might star. He wrote R. W. Gilder, editor of *The Century*, about the publication of his plays in that magazine and, in 1894, his publishers, Harper and Brothers, informed him that, in response to his suggestion, they were endeavoring to insert an advertisement of his farces into the programs distributed at Frohman's theater.

During the years, Howells kept in touch with Daly and

continued to offer his pieces to the manager. Finally, in January 1893, the producer wrote to ask Howells, "Why don't you try to do a full evening's play for my theatre & for Miss Rehan? Henry James has just finished a very charming work. One-act pieces bring no profit & give very little lasting reputation to author, actor or manager." This appeal attracted Howells. Five days later, he sent Daly a volume of his farces with an accompanying note in which he stated, "There is a sort of filmy sequence between three of the farces: Afternoon Tea, The Mouse Trap, and A Likely Story. I suppose it would be quite impossible to give an evening of them together, even if they were each one good enough." This last statement, with its note of hesitant pleading, hardly seems to justify the lapses of those critics who have ignored Howells' interest in the drama.

Perhaps the most interesting practitioner of the "most unholy trade," as he called it, was Henry James, who in the 1890's deliberately interrupted his career as a novelist to undertake the hauling of the culture-wagon. His case is not only interesting for the light it throws on James, but also for the fact that James's interest in the theater represents so well the typical enthusiasm of contemporary writers. James's dedication was prompted by several reasons. Though probably not the most important, there was the need for money. His novels and stories had brought him only scanty returns. He saw the wealth being accumulated by Pinero, Jones, and "the unspeakable" Oscar, writers whom he considered his inferiors. Ever of an ambivalent nature, he was constantly lured by the world which he saw in conflict with art. The theater offered the opportunity to reconcile his divergent interests, to suit his inclinations to his great talents. Finally, there was James's deep and sincere interest in the drama as an intellectual and artistic challenge. As he wrote his brother,

I feel at last as if I had found my *real* form, which I am capable of carrying far, and for which the pale little art of fiction, as I have practiced it, has been, for me, but a limited and restricted substitute. The strange thing is that I always, universally, knew *this* was my more characteristic form—but was kept away from it by a half-modest, half-exaggerated sense of the difficulty (that is, I mean the practical odiousness) of the conditions. But now that I have accepted them and met them, I see that one isn't at all, needfully, their victim, but is, from the moment one *is* anything, one's self, worth speaking of, their *master*, and may use them, squeeze them, lift them up and better them. As for the form *itself*, its honor and inspiration are in its difficulty. If it were easy to write a good play, I couldn't and wouldn't think of it; but it is in fact damnably hard (to this truth the paucity of the article— in the English-speaking world—testifies) and that constitutes a solid respectability—guarantees one's *intellectual* self-respect.

This concern for the theater was with James a lifelong interest. His extensive list of articles on the drama (many have recently been collected by Alan Wade in *The Scenic Art*) indicates his constant enthusiasm. As in the case of Howells, it is pathetic that he never achieved success in this field, for one of the desires of his life was to write for, not about, the theater. "To be read 200 years after your death," he confessed, "is something, but to be acted is better."

According to the account in Judge Daly's *The Life of Augustin Daly*, the relationship between Daly and James was, for Daly, unfruitful. The Judge states that Daly suggested to James the writing of a comedy, *Mrs. Jasper*. As Leon Edel, in *The Complete Plays of Henry James*, points out, James described the piece as his first attempt at a "*comedy*, pure and simple." The plot was based on James's story, "The Solution," which in turn had been constructed from an anecdote related to James by Fanny Kemble.

According to James's chronology, he began the play late in 1891, having met Ada Rehan that fall; it was she who issued to him Daly's invitation to do a play for the company. In August 1892, James delivered the play. Daly wanted certain revisions to which James agreed, for he conceded that there was a lack of action, "vainly dissimulated by a superabundance (especially in the last act) of movement." Further changes and revisions caused the postponement of the production for an entire season, until Daly eventually decided to introduce the piece during 1893–1894, when the company was spending an entire year in London, inaugurating a new theater. As a consequence, after another round of revisions, the piece was finally scheduled to go into rehearsal late in 1893. Models were constructed and scenery was built; costumes were discussed and designed. Then, after a final reading on December 6, the play was abandoned. Neither Daly nor the actors had much confidence in the piece, now called *Mrs. Jasper's Way*. Daly was experiencing unexpected difficulties in launching a new theater. The truth was that the venture was considered too precarious. To Daly, as Mr. Edel suggests, the production meant little, though in James's life it loomed large. Yet it was only one of several disappointments he was to suffer in the theater.

Even while James was impatiently waiting for Daly to produce *Disengaged* (James' final title for the play), he had, in the spring of 1893, sketched out another comedy with Ada Rehan in mind. In his notes for *The Chaperon*, he speaks of "having something in my hand ready for Daly in the event of there arising between us a question of a second play." No such question arose, of course, but the idea he had outlined for Miss Rehan was used by him in 1895 as the basis of a one-act piece, called *Summersoft*, prepared for Ellen Terry.

As with Twain and Howells, the plays of Henry James have yet to find their audiences; it is doubtful if they ever will. In supervising their publication, James admitted their weakness, yet by issuing them at all, he demonstrated, as had Howells, his desire for an audience, even if only that of the library. "Of a published play," he wrote, "it cannot exactly be said that it has not been performed at all; for the disconcerted author, at least the printed book grows mildly theatrical, the frustrated effort approximately positive." Perhaps the great novelists of the late nineteenth century could have been somewhat relieved of their frustrations had they been able to foresee the success many of their novels, in dramatized form, have had on the twentieth-century stage.

There were other literary figures of the time who also had connections with the Daly Theatre. Oliver Wendell Holmes, it will be remembered, prepared the poem which served as the opening address for the new theater on December 3, 1873. Daly's presentation of Longfellow's poem, *The Hanging of the Crane*, as part of a triple bill which also featured *The Two Widows* and *The Critic*, was more elaborate. The poem was recited by D. H. Harkins; special music was arranged by Dodworth; the seven "pictures" were painted by Witham; the actors who depicted the "living tableaux" were Mr. Davidge and Mrs. Gilbert, Mr. Ringgold and Miss Varian, and Mr. Fawcett and Miss Grey. This odd bill, particularly strange for a commercial theater, ran for a week.

It must be remembered, too, that Daly produced *original* plays by contemporary dramatists. Here is the list:

Olive Logan's *Surf* (January 12, 1870)
Edgar Fawcett's *Our First Families* (September 21, 1880) and *Americans Abroad* (October 5, 1881)
W. D. Eaton's *All the Rage* (April 30, 1881)
James Herne's *Shore Acres* (December 25, 1893)

The brevity of the list is deceptive. Daly's own original plays should certainly be added; and the works of older playwrights, John Brougham and Dion Boucicault, as well as revivals of the work of Richard Penn Smith should be mentioned. In addition to the original pieces, Daly produced dramatizations and adaptations by still other American writers, Fred Williams, Olive Logan, M. F. Egan, John Brougham, T. B. de Walden, Henry Paulton, Joseph Hatton, and Sidney Rosenfeld. Daly was also interested in the work of Clyde

Fitch, who in 1894 was revising a piece for him entitled *Gossip*, which he "altered . . . in accordance with the manager's suggestions." But neither *Gossip* nor *Nathan Hale*, offered by Fitch in 1897, met the needs of the company, so they were not produced by Daly.

From 1892 to 1896, Daly corresponded with Thomas Nelson Page about a play, *In Old Virginia*. Frank R. Stockton, like many another novelist, tried his hand at playwriting; along with his manuscript play, *All in the Family*, he sent a note acknowledging Daly's help and indicating that he had accomplished "the improvements you suggested." Charles Gayler, Blanche Willis Howard, H. C. Bunner—all sent plays. On November 2, 1896, R. W. Chambers finished the dramatization of his novel, *A King and a Few Dukes*, a task which he undertook at Daly's suggestion. Harold Frederic and Paul Leicester Ford likewise prepared dramatizations of their own novels for Daly. Brander Matthews sent Daly at least five of his plays. Joaquin Miller was another who attempted to write a play. "Here is the little Comedy-Drama," he wrote Daly. ". . . if you think it can be made to fit, let me have a line by Monday, please. If not, let me have MS. One is always a bit anxious about the youngest born, and Jacob yearns for his Benjamin down in Egypt." F. Marion Crawford, too, was haunted by the desire to write plays. Letters to Daly indicate that he worked on plays and dramatizations for several years, revising them to suit Daly's suggestions. The list could, of course, be extended to include the dozens of lesser known and unknown writers who submitted their work to Daly. Certainly their faith, and his interest and suggestions, indicate an extensive concern for the creation of an American drama, no less true for being largely overlooked by the literary historians.

Daly's relations with these contemporary English and American writers provide a fitting close to this "account of the late-nineteenth-century American stage." For his efforts show him as an aggressive producer, a man of catholic interests in the drama and, above all, a person who saw himself in the main stream of theatrical tradition, a continuing tradition which looked backward, forward, and around.

Index

320

INDEX